Interpreting Globalization

Value Inquiry Book Series

Founding Editor
Robert Ginsberg

Managing Editor
J.D. Mininger

VOLUME 361

Central European Value Studies

Edited by

Vasil Gluchman, *University of Prešov, Slovakia*

Affiliate Editors

Jaap van Brakel, *University of Louvain*
Eckhard Herych, *University of Mainz*

Assistant Editors

Arnold Burms (*Belgium*) – Herman Parret (*Belgium*) – B.A.C. Saunders (*Belgium*) – Frans De Wachter (*Belgium*) – Anindita Balslev (*Denmark*) – Lars-Henrik Schmidt (*Denmark*) – Dieter Birnbacher (*Germany*) – Stephan Grätzel (*Germany*) – Thomas Seebohm (*Germany*) – Olaf Wiegand (*Germany*) – Alex Burri (*Switzerland*) – Henri Lauener (*Switzerland*)

The titles published in this series are listed at *brill.com/vibs* and *brill.com/cevs*

Interpreting Globalization

Polish Perspectives on Culture in the Globalized World

Edited by

Leszek Koczanowicz, Piotr Jakub Fereński
and Joanna Panciuchin

BRILL

RODOPI

LEIDEN | BOSTON

Cover illustration: image taken by Piotr Jakub Fereński, used with permission.

Library of Congress Cataloging-in-Publication Data

Names: Koczanowicz, Leszek, editor. | Fereński, Piotr Jakub, editor. | Panciuchin, Joanna, editor.
Title: Interpreting globalization : Polish perspectives on culture in the globalized world / edited by Leszek Koczanowicz, Piotr Jakub Fereński, and Joanna Panciuchin.
Description: Boston : BRILL, 2021. | Series: Value inquiry book series, 0929-8436 ; 361 | Includes bibliographical references and index. | Summary: "The main hypothesis of the volume is that globalization is a cultural phenomenon. Therefore, the book offers an explanation of how globalization emerged from cultural exchange between groups, nations, and religions. The contributions in this volume register the thematically multi-dimensional and theoretically complex contribution of Polish research on globalization. Polish debates on globalization, as presented in this book, on the one hand reflect international disputes and controversies, and on the other address local issues. As their crucial feature, the articles compiled in this volume exhibit a special sensitivity to historical and contemporary cultural contexts. They do not approach globalization as an abstract process, instead exploring it through the lens of clearly defined factors"– Provided by publisher.
Identifiers: LCCN 2020046617 (print) | LCCN 2020046618 (ebook) | ISBN 9789004443785 (hardback) | ISBN 9789004443792 (ebook)
Subjects: LCSH: Globalization–Social aspects–History. | International cooperation–Social aspects. | Globalization–Poland. | Social change–Poland.
Classification: LCC HM841 .I68 2021 (print) | LCC HM841 (ebook) | DDC 327.1/709–dc23
LC record available at https://lccn.loc.gov/2020046617
LC ebook record available at https://lccn.loc.gov/2020046618

Typeface for the Latin, Greek, and Cyrillic scripts: "Brill". See and download: brill.com/brill-typeface.

ISSN 0929-8436
ISBN 978-90-04-44378-5 (hardback)
ISBN 978-90-04-44379-2 (e-book)

Copyright 2021 by Leszek Koczanowicz, Piotr Jakub Fereński and Joanna Panciuchin. Published by Koninklijke Brill NV, Leiden, The Netherlands.
Koninklijke Brill NV incorporates the imprints Brill, Brill Hes & De Graaf, Brill Nijhoff, Brill Rodopi, Brill Sense, Hotei Publishing, mentis Verlag, Verlag Ferdinand Schöningh and Wilhelm Fink Verlag.
Koninklijke Brill NV reserves the right to protect this publication against unauthorized use. Requests for re-use and/or translations must be addressed to Koninklijke Brill NV via brill.com or copyright.com.

This book is printed on acid-free paper and produced in a sustainable manner.

Contents

Acknowledgments VII
List of Figures and Tables VIII
Notes on Contributors IX

Introduction: Thinking Globally 1
  Piotr Jakub Fereński, Leszek Koczanowicz and Joanna Panciuchin

PART 1
Cultural Theory of Globalization

1 Generality and Universality in Globalization 13
  Leszek Kopciuch

2 The Status of Global Studies and Transformations in the Social Sciences 21
  Franciszek Czech

3 Musicology and Globalization 38
  Bożena Muszkalska

PART 2
Cultural History of Globalization

4 Towards Historical Performatics?
  Gesture as the Origin of Speech. A Case Study 47
  Mirosław Kocur

5 "There Is Neither Barbarian Nor Greek…"
  On the Tools of the Globalist Interpretation of History in Medieval Thought. An Example of the Reception of New-Testamental Ideas in the Historiography of the 11th and 12th Centuries 72
  Stanisław Rosik

6 Were the Natural Sciences Global in the 19th Century? The Case of
   Charles Darwin   80
     Piotr Badyna

7 The Spanish "Crisis of the 17th Century"   91
     Magdalena Barbaruk

8 Nation-Forming Processes in Latin America
   A New Integration Model?   105
     Tadeusz Paleczny

PART 3
Contemporary Culture and Globalization

9 From Córdoba to Tora Bora
   *Globalization in the World of Islam, the World of Islam vis-à-vis
   Globalization*   127
     Daniel Boćkowski

10 Locality and Globality: Various Dimensions of Money   134
     Adam Nobis

11 Global Paths of Cultural Institutions
   Attendance, Participation, or Education   150
     Karolina Golinowska

12 The Political Role of Cities: A Global Perspective   161
     Piotr Jakub Fereński

13 One Wrong Turn: Doug Rickard in the World of Google Street View   175
     Rafał Nahirny

   Index   189

Acknowledgments

We are very grateful to all persons who made possible the creation of the book. First of all, we are appreciative to the authors of the texts included in the book who have cooperated with the journal Culture-History-Globalization for years contributing to the development of global studies in Poland and East Central Europe. As the editors we feel indebted to Prof. Adam Nobis the chair of the Department of Globalization and Communication at the Institute of Cultural Studies at Wrocław University and the organizer of the seminar on globalization who initiated and was a driving force of the journal Culture-History-Globalization. Prof. Mirosław Kocur the head of the Institute of Cultural Studies at Wrocław University and Prof. Przemysław Wiszewski the Dean of the Faculty of History and Paedagogy at Wrocław University supported the work on the book.

Dr Patrycja Poniatowska has contributed to this volume as a translator, additionally providing preliminary editorial interventions and offering some helpful comments on my argument.

Figures and Tables

Figures

2.1 Growth of selected globalization indices (%), 1985 = 100%   22
2.2 The number of articles addressing globalization in the selected twenty-five journals in 1985–2009   25

Tables

2.1 Selected ways of defining globalization as identified by Jan Aart Scholte   27
8.1 Analytical model of nation-making processes in Latin America   107

Notes on Contributors

Piotr Badyna
is a historian. He works in Department of Economic History, Demography and Statistics, Institute of History, University of Wroclaw in Poland. His scientific interests include: culture, mentality, economy, ethics, ethos, axiology and spiritual culture of the Old Polish period, as well as the perception of nature and methods of its conceptualization, the state of knowledge of natural science and farming from the 16th to the 18th century. Co-creator and technical editor of the scientific journal *Culture-History-Globalization*. Author of over fifty scientific articles, editor and co-editor of collective works, author of two scientific books: *Model człowieka w polskim piśmiennictwie parenetycznym XVIII w. (do 1773 r.)* (*The Human Model in Polish Parenetic Literature of the 18th Century Until 1773*) and *Obraz rodzimej przyrody dzikiej w kulturze staropolskiej. Wybrane zwierzęta łowne w dziełach ks. Krzysztofa Kluka i Jakuba K. Haura* (*The Image of Native Wild Nature in Old Polish Culture. Selected Game Animals in the Works of Priest Krzysztof Kluk and Jakub K. Haur*). One of his latest works is the co-author article "Testing the Trivers-Willard Hypothesis on Polish Kings and Dukes" published in the *Anthropological Review* in 2019.

Magdalena Barbaruk
is an Assistant Professor of Institute of Cultural Studies at Faculty of Historical and Pedagogical Sciences at University of Wroclaw. Barbaruk specializes in a cultural potential of literature, the literary "mapping" of space in Spain and Latin America. Barbaruk is the author of three books and numerous articles in Polish, also in Spanish and English, including the monograph *The Long Shadow of Don Quixote* (Peter Lang Publishing, 2015) and *Sensy błądzenia. La Mancha i jej peryferie* (*Meanings of Wandering. La Mancha and Its Peripheries*, 2018). In 2012–2014 at Jagiellonian University (Poland), she carried out the project "La Mancha as a land of literature. The cultural status of literary routes" (National Science Center, Poland). One of the result was a documentary "Błędne mapy" ("The Errant Maps"). From 2018 Magdalena Barbaruk is conducting the scientific project "Trajectory of the word. The cultural impact of Amereida" (National Science Center, Poland). The research are carried out in Chile, Bolivia and Argentina in cooperation with the School of Architecture and Design at Pontifical Catholic University of Valparaíso.

Daniel Boćowski
is a Professor at the Institute of Sociology at the University in Bialystok; Head of Department of Sociology Politics and Security. He also works at the Institute of History of the Polish Academy of Sciences. Daniel Boćkowski specializes in the terrorism, religious fundamentalism, international security issues, social cyber security, as well as the political situation in the MENA region. Boćkowski is the author and editor of a few books and numerous articles in Polish and English, including: *Na zawsze razem. Białostocczyzna i Łomżyńskie w polityce radzieckiej w czasie II wojny światowej (IX 1939–VIII 1944)* (Neriton 2005), "Between the East and the West: The Penetration of Contemporary Islam into Poland," *Limes*, vol. 2, no. 1, "Big Shopping Centers as an Objects of a Potential Terrorist Attacks," *Securitologia*, no. 2, 2017. He is the deputy editor of *Studia z Dziejów Rosji i Europy Środkowo-Wchodniej*.

Franciszek Czech
is a sociologist and political scientist at the Department of Intercultural Studies of Jagiellonian University in Cracow. Franciszek Czech specializes in research on political culture (globalization discourses, popular understanding of politics, conspiracy theories) and area studies of South-East Asia (the Philippines). He is the author of two books: *Koszmarne scenariusze. Socjologiczne stadium konstruowania lęku w dyskursie globalizacyjnym* (*Nightmare Scenarios. Sociological Study of Construction of Anxiety In a Globalization Discourse*, 2010) and *Spiskowe narracje i metanarracje* (*Conspiracy Narratives and Metanarratives*, 2015).

Piotr Jakub Fereński
is a cultural researcher and historian of ideas. He works at the University of Wroclaw. He also teaches at the Academy of Fine Arts in Wroclaw. He is an art critic and exhibition curator. Author of nearly 115 publications, including books like: *O pochodzeniu idei. Relatywizm w amerykańskiej antropologii kulturowej* (*The Origins of Ideas. Relativism in the American Cultural Anthropology*, 2011), *Kierunek eksperymentalny. Początki pierwszych w Polsce studiów kulturoznawczych* (*The Experimental Studies. The Beginnings of the First Cultural Studies in Poland*, 2012), *Materie kultury. Heteronomie życia mieszkańców współczesnych miast* (*The Matter of the Culture. Heteronomies of the Life of Inhabitants of Modern Cities*, 2018). Piotr J. Fereński is the co-editor of *ΠΡΑΞΗΜΑ. Journal of Visual Semiotics, Culture-History-Globalization* and *Format*. He has completed many scientific, social and artistic projects. He conducts research in Poland, Russia, Ukraine, as well as in South and North America. He is interested in the relationship between aesthetics, ethics and classicism in the aspect of economic

disputes about the shape of modern cities. He also analyzes utopian urban and architectural concepts. Currently he is conducting a research on strategies for dealing with the memory of the 20th century regimes in Chile, Spain, Poland and Ukraine.

Karolina Golinowska

is an Assistant Professor at the Institute of Culture Studies at Kazimierz Wielki University. Karolina Golinowska specializes in the cultural theory that refers to the problems of the cultural memory, heritage and practices of its institutionalization, as well as cultural politics with an emphasis on art and cultural institutions' practices. She is the author of two books – *Narracje sztuki w kulturze płynności* (*Art Narratives in the Culture of Liquidity*, 2014), *Polityki kultury* (*Politics of culture*, 2017) and co-author of two another ones: *Feminizm po polsku* (*Feminism in Polish*, 2018) and *Przeobrażenia pamięci. Przeobrażenia kanonu* (*Transformation of memory. Transformation of canon*, 2019). She is the author of numerous articles in Polish and English language such as "Nostalgia for the PRL in contemporary Poland," in: *Twentieth Century Communism*, 2016; "Between the Global, National, and Peripheral. The Case of Art Museums in Poland," in: *Stedelijk Studies*, 2014; "New Lanark: idee, utopie, dziedzictwo," ("New Lanark: Ideas, Utopias, Heritage"), *Culture-History-Globalization*, 2018.

Mirosław Kocur

is Professor of Performing Arts and Theatre Anthropology at the University of Wrocław (UWr) and Professor of Acting and Directing at the Stanisław Wyspiański National Academy of Theatre Arts (NATA). He holds the Chair of Cultural Studies at UWr. During the 70-ties, he participated in Jerzy Grotowski's paratheatrical projects and his Theatre of Sources. In 1984, he graduated from the Faculty of Theatre Directing at NATA, where he took classes with Tadeusz Kantor and Andrzej Wajda. Later he served as Artistic Director of the Second Studio of Wroclaw, a company established in place of the Laboratory Theatre, after Grotowski left Poland. Kocur has made significant contributions to performing studies and the advancement of theatre education. His research, based on his rich theatrical experience and inspired by Grotowski's anthropology, focuses on reconstructing the origins of performing practices and on performance-as-research. He also studies the modern acting techniques and travels extensively to research cultural performances in Asia and Africa. His main theatre productions include: "Elijah by Buber" (Switzerland 1989), "Bacchae by Euripides" (Italy 1990), "Second Coming" (UK 1991), "Waiting for Godot by Beckett" (USA 1992), "The Metamorphosis by Kafka" (USA 1994), "Asinaria by Plautus" (Greece 2003), "Women at the Thesmophoria" (USA 2005), "Hamlet,

First Quarto by Shakespeare" (Poland 2010). His main scholar publications in English include: (*Polish*) *Theatre as a Rhizome of Echoes: The Case of Acropolis* (2015), *On the Origins of Theater* (2016), *The Second Birth of Theatre: Performances of Anglo-Saxon Monks* (2017) and *The Power of Theater: Actors and Spectators in Ancient Rome* (2018). He is also the chief editor of the series „Interdisciplinary Studies in Performance" at Peter Lang Publishing House.

Leszek Koczanowicz
is a Professor of Philosophy and Political Science at Faculty of Psychology at the SWPS University of Social Sciences and Humanities. Leszek Koczanowicz specializes in theory of culture, social theory, and cultural aspects of politics. His previous appointments include inter alia Wroclaw University, SUNY/Buffalo (1998–1999 and 2000–2001), Columbia University (2004–2005), and SUNY/Geneseo (2013), Helsinki Collegium for Advanced Studies (2015–2016). Leszek Koczanowicz is the author and editor of twelve books and numerous articles in Polish and English, including *Politics of Time: Dynamics of Identity in Post-Communist Poland* (Berghahn Books, 2008), *Lęk nowoczesny. Eseje o demokracji i jej adwersarzach* (*Modern Fear: Essays on Democracy and its Adversaries*, 2011), and *Politics of Dialogue. Non-Consensual Democracy and Critical Community* (Edinburgh University Press, 2015). Recently his was an editor (with Idit Alaphandry) *Democracy, Dialogue, Memory: Expression and Affect Beyond Consensus* (Routledge, 2018). His recent publication is *Anxiety and Lucidity: Reflections on Culture in Times of Unrest* (Routledge, 2020).

Leszek Kopciuch
is a Professor of Philosophy at Faculty of Philosophy and Sociology at the Maria Curie Skłodowska, University in Lublin. Leszek Kopciuch specializes in a history of philosophy, ethics, theory of values, philosophy of culture, and philosophy of human creativity. He is the author and editor of ten books and numerous articles, including *Wolność a wartości. Max Scheler, Nicolai Hartmann, Dietrich von Hildebrand, Hans Reiner* (*Freedom and Values. Max Scheler, Nicolai Hartmann, Dietrich von Hildebrand, Hans Reiner*, 2010), *Studia nad filozofią Nicolaia Hartmanna z bibliografią polskich przekładów i opracowań po roku 1945* (*Studies on Philosophy of Nicolai Hartmann with Bibliography of Polish Translations and Research after 1945*, 2013), *Szkice systematyczne z filozofii dziejów* (*Systematic Essays in Philosophy of History*, 2014), and *Kryzysy, kreatywność i wartości* (*Crisis, Creativity, and Values*, 2015). His recent publication is *Kreatywność a wartości* (*Creativity and Values*, 2020).

Bożena Muszkalska

is a Professor of Musicology at the University of Wroclaw and at the Adam Mickiewicz University in Poznań. She is also a head of the postgraduate studies "Sound and Soundscape". She gave guest lectures in Germany, Austria and Russia. Muszkalska is the author and editor of 8 books and numerous articles in Polish, English and German, i.a. *Traditionelle mehrstimmige Gesänge der Sarden* (1985), *Tradycyjna wielogłosowość wokalna w kulturach basenu Morza Śródziemnego* (*Traditional Polyvocality in Cultures of the Mediterranean Basin*, 1999), „*A jednak po całej ziemi słychać ich dźwięk". Muzyka w życiu religijnym Żydów aszkenazyjskich* ("*And yet, their sound is heard all over the earth." Music in the religious life of Ashkenazi Jews*, 2013), (coed. with Regine Allgayer Kaufmann) *BodyMusicEvent* (2010), (ed.) *The Kolbergs of Eastern Europe* (2018). She has carried out numerous project associated with field research in Poland, Sardinia, Portugal, Belarus, Lithuania, Romania, Ukraine, Siberia, Brasilia, Turkey, Australia and Guatemala. Her research interests include: Jewish music, soundscape of Jewish Wroclaw, musical cultures of Polish diaspora, traditional multi-voice singing and methodological issues.

Rafał Nahirny

is an Assistant Professor at the Institute of Cultural Studies at the University of Wroclaw. He wrote a book about Jeremy Bentham's machinery of power. Interested in new technologies, with particular emphasis on surveillance and control, as well as the ethics and aesthetics of privacy. He conducts research on the world of Google Street View, drones and non-places of digital capitalism.

Adam Nobis

is a Professor at the Institute of Cultural Studies at the University of Wroclaw. He heads up the Global Studies Laboratory and is the editor-in-chief of *Culture-History-Globalization*. His research deals with various global phenomena and interactions between them. He focuses on the relationship between contemporary global phenomena and the past. He is the author of over 200 scientific papers published in Polish, English, German and Russian, including nine books. Among them: *Zmiana kulturowa: między historią a ewolucją* (*Cultural Change: Between History and Evolution*, 2006), *Globalne procesy, globalne historie, globalny pieniądz* (*Global Processes, Global Histories, Global Money*, 2014), *Studia globalne* (*Global Studies*, 2014), *A Short Guide to the New Silk Road* (2018, published also in Polish and Russian).

Tadeusz Paleczny
is a Professor of Sociology and Cultural Sciences at the Faculty of Political and International Studies at the Jagiellonian University in Cracow. He is a head of the Chair of Theory and Researches of Intercultural Relation in the Institute of Intercultural Studies. His main field of academic studies and investigations are: multiculturalism, ethnic and international relations, intercultural relations. Visiting Professor at Minnesota State University (1986–1987), Free University (Berlin 1989), John Hopkin's University (1990), researches in Brazil (2000, 2003, 2006, 2008, 2009). Tadeusz Paleczny is the author of eighteen books and numerous articles in Polish, English and Portuguese, among them: *Mit i ideologia powrotu wśród emigrantów polskich w Brazylii i Argentynie (Myth and Ideology of Return-migration among Polish Immigrants in Brazil and Argentina*, 1992), *Rasa, etniczność i religia w brazylijskim procesie narodowotwórczym. Wprowadzenie do badań latynoamerykańskich przemian społecznych (Race, Ethnicity and Religion in the Brazilian Process of Nationalism Creation. Introduction to Research on Latin-American Social Transitions*, 2004), *Stosunki międzykulturowe. Zarys problematyki (International Affairs. Outline of Issues*, 2005), co-author: *Sobre el estado de los estados latinoamericanos. En el umbral del Bicentenario (On the State of Latin American States. Approaching the Bicentenary*, 2009), *Socjologia tożsamości (Sociology of Identity*, 2008), *Nowe ruchy społeczne (The New Social Movements*, 2010).

Joanna Panciuchin
is a PhD Candidate of Cultural Studies at the University of Wroclaw and a PhD Candidate of Pedagogy at the University of Lower Silesia. Currently, she is working on two doctoral dissertations: the first one concerns performances of resistance in Poland after 1989 (UWr), and the second one deals with the issues connected with the education, emancipation, democracy and Wroclaw's community of Romanian Roma (ULS). Panciuchin is a co-editor in scientific journal *Culture-History-Globalization*. She has published in *Cultural Studies, Culture-History-Globalization, ΠΡΑΞΗΜΑ. Journal of Visual Semiotics, Lower Silesia, Le Monde Diplomatique. Polish Edition*.

Stanisław Rosik
is a Professor, dr habil., historian, medievalist at the Institute of History at the University of Wroclaw, head of the Laboratory of Research on Early History of Central Europe. Stanisław Rosik since 2017 is the president of the Standing Committee of Polish Medievalists. His fields of research are: early Slavs and their religion, beginnings of Central Europe, esp. Poland, Silesia and Pomerania,

German and Polish historiography and hagiography of 10–13th c. He is the author of over 250 publications, including several books, e.g.: *Conversio gentis Pomeranorum. Studium świadectwa o wydarzeniu (XII wiek)* (Chronicon 2010), *Bolesław Krzywousty* (Chronicon 2013), *The Slavic Religion in the Light of 11th- and 12th-Century German Chronicles (Thietmar of Merseburg, Adam of Bremen, Helmold of Bosau)* (Brill, in print). Stanisław Rosik is the project manager in the International Research Project "Poland and Pomerania in shaping European civilization (from the Slavic tribes to the turn of 12th c.)" (2014–2020).

Introduction: Thinking Globally

Piotr Jakub Fereński, Leszek Koczanowicz and Joanna Panciuchin

An avid interest in processes of global compass has been growing steadily at least since the early 1990s. This preoccupation is exemplified in the work of multiple researchers, such as Janet L. Abu-Lughod, Arjun Appadurai, Zygmunt Bauman, Benjamin R. Barber, Ulrich Beck, Manuel Castells, Anthony Giddens, Ulf Hannerz, Mary Louise Pratt, George Ritzer, Roland Robertson, Saskia Sassen, Immanuel Wallerstein, and Wolfgang Welsch. The study of globalization and related global phenomena has also been developing in Poland, wherein a notable role has been played by sociologists, such as Marian Kempny., though global issues have been explored within other research disciplines as well. Nonetheless, an inclusive platform for discussion, sharing research experiences, and fostering new, interdisciplinary cognitive perspectives was lacking for a long time. The foundation of *Kultura – Historia – Globalizacja* (*Culture – History – Globalization*) was a response to this deficit. The idea to establish KHG and launch an accompanying conference series entitled *Historia-Kultura-Globalizacja* (*History – Culture – Globalization*) was hatched by the Wroclaw-based anthropologist and philosopher of culture Adam Nobis. He began to develop the project in close collaboration with the historian Piotr Badyna and the culturologist Piotr J. Fereński. Since the very onset of the journal, its mission has been to assemble varied voices on the historically and currently fundamental relations and factors which determine the nature of both globality and locality. In their calls for papers, inviting scholars to share their research findings and encouraging confrontations of divergent concepts and outlooks, the KHG editors have repeatedly stressed that their object is to delve into processes and phenomena which are "conceptualized in terms of globalization, hybridization, and Creolization as well as those which still look for their theoretical articulation" (www.khg.uni.wroc.pl). While such invitations were primarily addressed to culturologists and historians, as well as to archeologists, (physical) anthropologists, educators, psychologists, social scientists, such as philosophers and sociologists, political theorists, and economists, researchers from other disciplines, e.g., linguists, literary scholars, art historians, and musicologists, have also responded to them.

The concern with global themes displayed by the journal editors was stirred on the one hand by their own research paths and on the other by the political transition of 1989, as a result of which the Eastern-Bloc countries opened up to the world, as international mobility, information flow, and access to research resources and studies produced all over the world radically increased. For example, Adam Nobis's fascination with global processes was equally affected by his long study of emergence and cultural change and by his experience of and reflections triggered by his first trips to Western research hubs (UK), by the development and availability of media technologies (access to content through satellite television and video), by expanding contacts with other scholars, and by proliferating opportunities of finding about their concepts on the Internet. The experience of reality involving the abolition of some spatial, temporal, political, and economic barriers fueled the popularity of investigations focused on "the global ecumene," "the global village," "the world system," "one world," "global society," and their likes. For Polish scholars, all this did not entail obliviousness to the heterogeneous, the different, the local. Researchers became receptive to new ontological dimensions, explored homogeneity and diversity, delved into the domination or the hegemony of Western models of economy and statehood, and pondered emancipation possibilities of information society and relations between economy and culture. Culture proved of particular relevance to the editors of *KHG*.

A long-ranging temporal perspective has been intrinsic to the debates hosted by the journal since its very launching. The first issues (2007–2009) were largely dedicated to discussing whether, in thinking of global processes, we should focus on the very moment we inhabited or perhaps look into the past. At conferences, we deliberated how far back in time we should move to discover the beginnings of globality, considering an array of developments such as migrations, conquests, the dissemination of religious cults and ideas, trade, and the invention of media (starting from script). Side by side with the contemporary facets of cultural differences and the semantics of "otherness," we addressed the global dimension of the formation of human communities, therein pre-historic settlement processes, advancements in agriculture, and the evolution of territorial organization. At the same time, scholars showed how universal phenomena, such as dance, had contributed to the development of culture, e.g., the birth of histrionic and literary practices. They also tried to establish what globalization could have meant to the Huns and the Vikings, and what image of the world was produced in Marco Polo's narratives. At the same time, the journal aspired to directly respond to the most urgent problems of the present. In 2010, when the economic crisis and related social unrests were sweeping across the world, the editors symptomatically encouraged discussions on globality and crises. By far not restricted to the economy, those discussions tackled political and cultural issues, both synchronically and diachronically. The editors emphasized that, historically speaking, preoccupations with the crisis of the idea of the human, culture, or civilization, with the crisis of values, the moral crisis, the crisis of spirituality, etc., were anything but a novelty. On this particular occasion, however, the examination was supposed to focus on the sources, symptoms, and ramifications of crises on the global scale. Hence, the debates concerned not only the security of the state but also the idea of crisis in the philosophy of history, on art in the times of crisis, and on the role and relevance of media in the world marked with transformations. In 2014, when the climate crisis was becoming a universal worry, the editors of *KHG* encouraged researchers to explore relations among nature, the urban environment, and processes of a global character, such as the past and present role of nature in shaping global cultural, social, political, economic, and other developments. The relevant questions were to what extent nature was itself a result of those processes, what risks it faced, and whether urban areas, so often contrasted with "natural landscapes," were indeed the major catalysts of global phenomena. Relations between nature and the city were discussed alongside the culturally entrenched conceptualizations of nature as embodying the natural order and the city as representing the social order.

The community of scholars associated with the journal repeatedly engaged in reflection on self-identification and scholarly self-awareness, therein on the cognitive positions adopted by Central-European scholars from various disciplines (including experimental ones, such as culturology) in their scrutiny of global processes. Important issues included the ways in which globalization is conceptualized, the language (i.e., notions and terms) which is used for this purpose, and the modes of making sense (defining) of particular words when describing and explaining globalization-related phenomena. Researchers analyzed how globality as such was understood, how science and scholarship, themselves factors in contemporary social processes, affected their environment and impacted global processes, and how the role attributed to scientific knowledge and scholars was defined and changing historically and in the contemporary world. They also pondered whether European scholarship was capable of understanding the world as a whole in which Europe is but a small part. As far as the global "lexicon" or "vocabulary" is concerned, interrelations among the applied terms, categories, and concepts on the one hand and the researched things, phenomena, and processes on the other were thoroughly scrutinized and discussed, with special attention devoted to expressions such as the world, universality, locality, humanity, cosmopolitanism, interculturality, global metropolises, migrations, flows, capital, the global market and corporations, international relations, and intercultural interactions. On this occasion, scholars repeatedly underscored that, never innocuous, words were inherently entangled in particular political and economic contexts or, in other words, in power relations. Essentially, the *KHG*-affiliated scholars tended neither to regard globalization as a historical necessity nor to think of it in terms of the end of history. They questioned the idea that globalization represented the direction in which the entire world inexorably headed. Rather, they observed that global processes and phenomena were subject to transformations, with their forms and components mutating and fluctuating as well. One of the central queries was whether globalization should be viewed as permanent and durable in the first place, with the major conclusion being that globalization involved complex and challenging interrelationships among multiple phenomena, which all added up to a fragile and infinitely subtle construction. Consequently, the scholars insisted that producing an adequate account of those complicated interactions required not only meticulous explorations but also original and daring ideas at the intersection of research, artistic practices, social activism, and political and economic pursuits.

It was no coincidence that researchers based in Central Europe, a region with specific historical experiences, repeatedly debated the links between globality on the one hand and ideologies and utopias on the other. They delved into how various ideas of revolution, progress, and modernization and visions of ideal communities, social orders, legal systems, and spatial arrangements were reflected in global processes and phenomena. Thereby, the fundamental question was whether globality was perhaps uniquely driven by ensembles of beliefs geared to achieving particular religious, artistic, and political agendas and by dreams of ideal, non-existent places. At the same time, the opposite was proposed to be the case, i.e., that the formation and spread of those convictions and visions were responses to global processes. Discussing multiple ideologies and utopias manifesting in architecture, visual arts, theater, literature, and social, economic, and political projects, the researchers identified an array of meanings, norms, and values underpinning them. Contributions to *KHG* also addressed more mundane matters, such as dietary habits (though their focus was still on the relations between consumption and political-economic practices), aesthetic values, identity, fashion, tourism, and the media industry.

The first part of this volume is entitled *The Cultural Theory of Globalization*. Its three chapters were authored, respectively, by a philosopher, a sociologist, and a musicologist, who analyze various theoretical concepts informing cultural research on globality. In Leszek Kopciuch's text, globalization, generality, and universality are the most important notions. Building on his background in philosophy, Kopciuch seeks to explain the paradox of global phenomena losing their "general nature." In his "The Status of Global Studies and Transformations in the Social Sciences," Franciszek Czech examines the term "global studies" itself by tracing its evolution, identifying its central research problem, and trying to define its position within the social sciences. He proposes that the institutionalization of globalization studies is a mirror reflection of changes unfolding across the social sciences. The last chapter in this part of the volume, Bożena Muszkalska's "Musicology and Globalization," outlines globalization processes in musical cultures as framed by the specialist musicological literature. Music scholars predominantly concentrate on world music, whereby they derive their theoretical and methodological inspirations from anthropology and sociology. This vividly conveys the impact of globalization on transformations within scholarly disciplines.

The authors of chapters in the second part of the volume, entitled *The Cultural History of Globalization*, scrutinize cultural phenomena which are analyzed by means of tools used in global studies. Interestingly, they do not focus exclusively on contemporary developments. Mirosław Kocur expands performance studies by adding a globally and historically oriented perspective. He avails himself of a methodology combining culturology, theater studies, performative studies, anthropology, archeology, history, anatomy, neuroscience, and child psychology in order to retrace the origins of contemporary performance. He looks for connections between gesture and speech, a thoroughly universal phenomenon as it were. Stanisław Rosik uses the global-studies perspective to analyze a medieval chronicle authored by Adam of Bremen and a hagiography of St. Otto of Bamberg. He analyzes the Christianization of pagan peoples to highlight some of its underlying concepts which envisioned a global unity of individuals and communities. Piotr Badyna looks for manifestations of globality in the work of Charles Darwin, a classic epitome of 19th-century English natural sciences. As his starting point, Badyna questions Arjun Appadurai's chronology of globalization. While Appadurai insists that global phenomena only started to develop in the 20th century, Badyna argues that Darwin's research and publications – and by extension the natural sciences of his day – meet Appadurai's criteria of globality. Magdalena Barbaruk's chapter concerns the "The Spanish Crisis of the 17th Century" and depicts two dominant approaches to this development, both of them associated with globalization in their separate ways. In one of these perspectives, the origin of the crisis, which involved a drastic impoverishment of the country, is attributed to its imperial wealth. The other perspective emphasizes that the disintegration of Spain's political and economic system coincided with an impressive flourishing of arts, literature, and philosophy. In her explorations, Barbaruk relies not only on global studies but also on culturology and axiology. Tadeusz Paleczny's chapter, which caps this part of the volume, is devoted to examining nation-building processes in Latin American countries against the background of their history and culture. According to Paleczny, the fundamental factors that bolster national integration include language, religion, cultural legacy, and the state. He shows that nation-making processes in Latin America fuel syncretism and hybridization.

Entitled *Contemporary Culture and Globalization*, the last part of the volume is comprised of texts devoted to our contemporary global phenomena. Daniela Boćkowski's chapter addresses the response of the world of Islam and the entire Arab world to ubiquitous globalization. Boćkowski describes various attitudes to the transformations which unfold as we speak of them. While some Muslims want assimilation with Western culture, others wish to retain their clear distinctiveness and advocate devising local equivalents of global cultural patterns. Adam Nobis in his text entitled "Locality and Globality: Various Dimensions of Money" looks into the meanings of concepts such as the local, the regional, the inter-regional, the continental, and the global. He explores the emergence of new kinds and models of money to conclude that locality should not be identified with a concrete place. Rather, the existence and understanding of "place" have multiple dimensions to them, as do various iterations of locality and globality. The chapter contributed by Karolina Golinowska analyzes the relevance of contemporary global processes to cultural policies and to the activities in which cultural institutions engage on the daily basis. One of the key questions asked by Golinowska is how relations between institutionalized culture and social life are transforming today, wherein she focuses on participation and the shift away from conceiving culture in elitist terms. The demand to promote participation and agency appears to be globally articulated, though the question remains whether it indeed translates into real practice. In his chapter, Piotr J. Fereński discusses the political role of cities in the context of globalization. Local economic and social problems intersect with global mechanisms whose effective operations often determine the success of urban hubs. This complex picture is even further complicated by ideologies and strategies of local political parties. Aware that metropolises are mirror images of globalization, Fereński draws on Benjamin Barber to inquire whether the rule of mayors could possibly be the future and hope of urban democracies. Authored by Rafał Nahirny, the closing chapter of this part looks into Doug Rickard's artistic project *A New American Picture*. Nahirny follows Rickard, as the artist traverses the world of Google Street View and uses the found-photography convention to document the life of American suburbs. In doing this, Nahirny critically scrutinizes both the unique aesthetics of Google Street Views photographs and Rickard's own artistic interventions in them.

The contributions in this volume register the thematically multi-dimensional and theoretically complex investment of Polish research on globalization. Polish debates on globalization, as presented in this book, on the one hand reflect international disputes and controversies, and on the other address local issues.

As their crucial feature, the articles compiled in this volume exhibit a special sensitivity to historical and cultural contexts. They do not approach globalization as an abstract process, instead exploring it through the lens of clearly defined factors. The opportunities globalization affords and the risks it entails flesh out in very particular temporal and spatial conjunctures. Owing to this research strategy, the two perspectives – the local and the global – overlap and complement each other.

Culture is axial to the contributors' arguments. They regard globalization first and foremost as a cultural phenomenon. This does not mean that they avoid addressing political and economic developments. On the contrary, such issues are often tackled, but they are placed within the context of culture. After all, politics to a large extent depends on cultural developments and can itself be regarded as part of culture (not least because values and symbols play a significant role in politics). In globalization processes, cultural expansions and hybridizations frequently precede strictly political decisions. Moreover, if the grounding in common or shared cultural values is lacking, supra-national integrations which are based merely on mutual economic or political connections tend to fall apart as soon as the community of interests comes to an end. This theoretical inflection obviously results from the disciplinary profile of the journal, but it is also the trademark of the scholars affiliated with it. Culture is not only a mirror which reflects economic and social processes; rather, it is a force independent of them. Because cultural transformation processes are crucial formative factors of globalization, which shape its dimensions and forms, without understanding them, debates on globalization will always be fragmentary and reductive.

As explained at the beginning of this Introduction, the development of Polish research on globalization in the 1990s and later was linked to Poland's new opening to the world and particularly to Western societies. The flow of goods and information, the importation of cultural production, the freedom of traveling, and first and foremost access to new media technologies essentially contributed to social and mental transformations. When at the turn of the 1970s Alvin Toffler was envisioning an electronic village as an embodiment of the so-called third wave (in human history), whose origin he discerned in the transition of the U.S., the U.K. and the Netherlands to a computerized model of work organization, and when he was describing the launch of experimental interactive TV systems (with video cameras and microphones) in Japan's Osaka, in Poland having an analogue telephone with a round dial (an almost century old invention) at home was a rare and coveted luxury. Given this, the perspectives presented in this volume cannot be fully grasped without recognizing how seminally significant it was to break away from this isolation by dismantling political and economic barriers. Nevertheless, their soaring interest in concepts such as transnational ecumenes, world systems, global villages, etc. does not mean that Central-European scholars did not study the transmission of values, norms and cultural patterns before. On the contrary, they were profoundly committed to exploring the ontological dimension of phenomena unfolding across local, ethnic, state, linguistic, religious, and civilizational boundaries. The processes buttressing interconnections among various cultural and social actors and phenomena on the one hand and enduring differences among axiological and symbolic systems on the other were discussed in such varied contexts as the defining core of modernity, historical stages in the development of humanity, and transformations within power relations, ownership structures, production models and the distribution of goods. Heated polemics ensued over the unity of the human species and the homogeneity of cultures, with scholars seeking to identify the factors that determined the form and content of life, and to develop conceptualizations of cultures, ethnic groups, and nations that went beyond their image as monads, islands, or isolated spheres. Side by side with historiosophical studies, the researchers critically examined the concept of mutually untranslatable conceptual schemes, which, as the philosophy of science, analytical philosophy, and also anthropology insisted, could imply radical, uncrossable cultural differences. Philosophers and humanities scholars born in Poland time and again revisited the ideas conveyed in Dante Alighieri's civitas humana, which could be construed as envisaging a supranational human community, and particularly focused on the writings of Vico and Johann G. von Herder. They engaged in disputes on Kant's anthropology, on Hegel's and Marx's philosophy of history, on evolutionists, and on diffusionists. They inquired into biological, geographical, and historical determinism, into historical necessities, and into what accelerated the transmission and adaptation of models, behavior, and phenomena, what fostered and what thwarted interdependences among cultures, societies, and political, social and economic systems. The Polish scholars were preoccupied with the scrutiny of changes in governance modes and geopolitical systems which affected demographic processes and propelled thorough transformations of social structures. They perfectly realized that the history of humanity was woven of ever denser and ever more complex webs of interconnections and interrelationships, while at the same time they lived behind the Iron Curtain, and until 1990-1991, when Germany reunited and the Soviet Union fell apart, had looked at and into the wall-divided world with pessimism. At the threshold of the 21st century they could again explore and speculate on the globe replete with historical and current flows.

This volume is meant as an invitation to discussion on one of the crucial, if not the most important, phenomena of (post)modernity. We believe that all readers will find the contributors interesting conversation partners, all the more engaging for espousing perspectives and approaches which tend to be overshadowed or obliterated in contemporary scholarly discourse.

PART 1

Cultural Theory of Globalization

∴

The first part of the volume consists of three articles authored, respectively, by a philosopher, a sociologist, and a musicologist, who analyze various theoretical concepts informing cultural research on globality. In Leszek Kopciuch's text, globalization, generality, and universality are the most important notions. Franciszek Czech examines the term "global studies" itself by tracing its evolution, identifying its central research problem, and trying to define its position within the social sciences. The last article, Bożena Muszkalska's "Musicology and Globalization," outlines globalization processes in musical cultures as framed by the specialist musicological literature.

CHAPTER 1

Generality and Universality in Globalization

Leszek Kopciuch

The world we inhabit is diverse. This concerns both the natural world and the world of cultures and civilizations. Perhaps the latter, i.e., the cultural world – our world, for it is produced by us and (as a realm of intentional objects) exists only because of us – is characterized by an even greater diversity; and insofar (yet only in this sense and to this extent) we can agree with Hegel's celebrated and controversial assertion that nature is dull ... because it does not vary in time (Hegel 1998, 60–61). It takes an appropriate set of concepts, complete with a pertinent terminological lexicon to veraciously describe the diversity of the cultural world. Most methodologists of the humanities, and of the social sciences too, are likely to squint with suspicion at the terms I have just used. A veracious description, an apt description, and their likes are among the terms which seem to have vanished from the lexicon of postmodern *narratives*. I cannot engage in discussion on such narratives here. The diversity which is meant here might be *non-narratively* acknowledged by advocates of different narratives as well. After all, it forms the ontic basis of the very possibility of such narratives.

This diversity also appears within what we have become accustomed to calling globalization. Its groundings are multiple.

Firstly, globalization processes affect various spheres of culture, such as economics, the economy, the labor market, the diffusion and exchange of political tendencies and solutions, mores and moral ethoses, customs, festivities, leisure pastimes, artistic practices, the art market, etc. Though but a random selection, these examples suffice as the basis of *an a priori thesis* that the multiplicity of various spheres of social life must translate into the diversity of forms that globalization processes unfolding within them take. Consequently, globalization processes in the economy will differ from those in customs and habits, as well as from those in ethoses and morality. In this sense, there is no single, universal, and common globalization; instead, there are various globalizations, which are neither universal across disciplines nor universal within any respective discipline; that is, while restricted to given disciplines, they are not common within their limits, as everywhere enclaves can be found which defy globalization, even if they do not resist the modern. All the more so, there is no single theory of globalization (Nobis 2009, 77–84).

Secondly, contemporary globalization processes follow at least two different trajectories. On the one hand, they are deliberately and purposively inspired and produced; on the other, they occur spontaneously, unintentionally, and unpredictably. At the onset of the IT revolution, hardly anyone was able to anticipate how incisively it would change the shape of human culture and even the form of human relationships. Future stages of this process would in all probability be equally surprising to us, if we were to live to observe them in the first place. It was also illuminating to see the lesson that Internet users taught to those who sought to control the free flow of data and information on the web by introducing ACTA.

Thirdly, contemporary globalization processes are an upshot of universalist ideas and theories developed by philosophers and social thinkers in the more or less remote past. As I wrote on the occasion of a conference held by the University of Wroclaw last year: "It is difficult to resist the impression that within philosophy itself – and more precisely, within the philosophy of history – these questions have long been asked. They had been asked even before the very phenomenon and problem of globalization appeared, even if it is true that, strictly speaking, it was only the 20th century that brought the phenomenon of globalization so emphatically into relief and prompted its intense theoretical examination. However, to legitimize such a hypothesis, we need on the one hand to explore the essential core of globalization processes and on the other to scrutinize the conceptual aims and the conceptual structures of the philosophy of history" (Kopciuch 2012b, 91).

Fourthly, within life situations which humans encounter and with which they grapple, there are certain typologies identifiable on the basis of both recurring ontogenetic developmental stages and recurring types of circumstances. The former include, for example, adolescence, adulthood, and old age; the latter encompass, for example, war, peace, security, threat, crisis, advancement, stagnation, etc. This concerns both the fates of individual people and the dynamics of entire communities and cultures. Such typologies are independent of globalization, which is confirmed by the fact that they existed when globalization was not around yet, at least not in the sense of increasing interconnectedness and interdependence on the global scale. Nevertheless, such typologies, associated with similarity and homogeneity as they are, facilitate globalization processes, and that in a variety of their meanings to boot (two of them will be discussed below).

Thus the whole picture of the problem situation is as follows. We use terms such as, for example, generality and universality to describe globalization-related processes. Without a doubt, these terms are connected with each other in one way or another. It is also obvious that global phenomena are usually universal. It is equally clear that earlier universalist theories of culture have anticipated contemporary theories of globalization. Another evident thing is that what is general and the same in various cultures is a factor conducive to globalization. However, there is an aspect in which universality differs from generality, and consequently global phenomena lose their general character. What does this peculiar paradox consist in? To answer this question, we must explain the terms which appear in the context of globalization. Actually, it is possible to show that, against the – largely sound – theoretical associations which pit particularity, singularity, and locality against universality, generality, and supra-locality (Majbroda 2011, 43), relations between these notions are complex and sometimes not oppositional at all. This is principally important, mainly in the case of universality and generality vis-à-vis singularity and particularity. The point is that singularity and particularity are the defining element underlying diversity, which was our starting point.

I will show this by referring to two theories and the justifications they offer. One of them is the framework of the plurality of civilizations proposed by Feliks Koneczny, and the other is the notion of universal prescriptivism as developed by Richard M. Hare. As a matter of fact, only the former concept directly pertains to socio-cultural relations, while the latter is basically an ethical concept. However, reliance on values, self-assessment, and appraisal of others in moral terms are components of cultural life, and as such they are also comprised in a field that is subject to globalization. Additionally, it should not be overlooked that Hare's understanding of universality and singularity is directly relevant to explaining moral diversity and moral "relativism," both of which persistently surface as globalization progresses (Kopciuch 2012a, 83–98).

As far as Koneczny's hypothetical attitude to globalization processes is concerned, his position is one of the extreme versions of the plurality of civilizations. I call Koneczny's attitude hypothetical, because Koneczny himself did not explicitly ask such questions, which is understandable, given the times in which he lived (1862–1949). The questions that he did ask concerned universality in history and a possibility of inter-civilizational synthesis, with a complete synthesis of civilizations imaginarily representing an extreme enactment of globalization processes. Koneczny answered the former question in the positive, which requires accurate wording. There is no universal history in the sense of a process in which a universal subject (e.g., humanity) participates. There is, however, a universality "in" history, meaning that individual civilizations, which are the subject proper of history, are based on formally universal systems of five values, which Koneczny labeled as the *human quincunx* (1997, 12–14; 1962, 16–19, 100–112). This universality is of formal nature because, while the schemes of values as such (truth, good, beauty, well-being, and health) recur across civilizations, they are fleshed out differently as regards their substance. Furthermore, Koneczny emphasized that these axiological configurations were mutually contradictory, i.e., incommensurate, from civilization to civilization (commensurability is "difference without contradiction"). This obviously suggests how Koneczny answered the other question, that is, one about the possibility of a synthesis of civilizations: "All attempts at synthesizing civilizations have ended dismally. We cannot but conclude that there are and can be no such syntheses. Historical induction teaches us that synthesis is only possible between cultures of the same civilization, because such cultures are commensurate. For their part, civilizations are incommensurate" (1997, 48). Therefore, Koneczny insisted:

> There are no syntheses, but only poisonous mixtures. [...] For how is it possible to look in two ways, in three ways (and in Poland even in four ways) on good and evil, on beauty and ugliness, on loss and gain, on the relation of society and State, of State and Church; how is it possible to have at the same time a four-fold ethic, four-fold pedagogy? Down this road the only possibility is decline into an a-civilisational state, which holds within itself incapacity for a culture of action. (1962, 209)

His answer is negative and justified by the ineffectiveness of synthetic connections between contradictory systems of values: "It is not possible to be civilised in two ways" (Koneczny, 1962, 210).

Let us now recapitulate Koneczny's theses in terms of categories which are used to describe globalization. Firstly, civilizations include analogous elements, that is, formally universal systems of values (*quincunx*). But, secondly, a globalized world is not possible, because such a world would have to be internally contradictory, and thus afflicted with a practical paralysis and doomed to destruction. I guess it has become clear by now that on Koneczny's take, the concepts of "universality" and (hypothetical) "globalization" are unrelated and do not side with each other at all. Of course, it is so because, in Koneczny, "universality" denotes in fact a *formal universality*, while (hypothetical) globalization is understood as a *material* (substantive) *synthesis*. The situation might be different if individual civilizations contained universal elements not only formally but also materially (substantively). But, as Koneczny stresses, they have no such elements.

What are we supposed to make of Koneczny's framework? Phrasings such as "it is not possible to be civilized in two ways" or "civilizational mixtures are a slippery slope" sound impressive and undoubtedly stir the imagination (especially that Koneczny is an accomplished and compelling writer). At the same time, however, they embody the fallacy of axiological non-differentiation, or the fallacy of axiological homogeneity. Such errors are committed when one does not differentiate values in respect to their rank and the nature of this rank. Koneczny is guilty of such a mistake. Otherwise, he would not have been able to aver that a synthesis in the realm of values was impossible. Such a synthesis is certainly possible, but in the scope of supplementary, non-fundamental values rather than basic values. This term may not be the most felicitous one, and it perhaps needs further specifying ad explaining. But as detailed elucidations of values are not my point here, I will only state that non-fundamental values constitute their meaning exclusively in relation to basic values. Therefore, if basic values are universal, supplementary values are not so and, as such, are not subject to the requirement of synthesis. If we endorse this way of thinking, synthesis (and globalization processes) will not be impossible despite differing *quincunxes*. However, we must bear in mind that such a conclusion is based on delimiting the scope of values which are subject to synthesis to basic values and, obviously, distinguishing basic values from non-fundamental values. It is by making this distinction and subsequently circumscribing the field of globalization to basic values that we can explain how cultural syntheses, therein globalization processes, are possible in this respect.

Another solution to the problem of the relation between the universal and the singular can be found in Hare's ethics. In his search for the ways to defend the ethical concept both against the threat of casuistry and against excessive schematism and generalization, Hare proposed refining moral principles by supplementing the general formulation of a principle with detailed variants in which it is valid or loses its validity. The rule "do not lie" is overly general as it needs qualifying, such as in "unless another person's life depends on it," "unless you are being interrogated by an occupier," "unless in this way you contribute to salvaging a higher value," etc. In this way, moral principles acquire a more particular, detailed, and individualized character, without forfeiting their universal resonance. In the spirit of Kant's categorical imperative, they can be treated as generalizable, i.e., as such that could be endorsed by anybody who found themselves in a concrete corresponding situation (depicted in the particularizing clauses appended to the general rule). In other words, Hare's proposition means that a person who finds themselves in such a situation cannot arbitrarily decide what is right or wrong, but can only recognize what conforms to the thus-specified rule (Hare 2000, 456–457; Hare 1981, 107–117; Saja 2008, 154–172). Moral injunctions of this kind are not general, but they are generalizable. This distinction is both lucid and needed.

How can Hare's position, which he called universal prescriptivism, be used in the study of the foundations of globalization? Firstly, his framework can of course be applied to the areas of culture which are of moral character or are directly or indirectly related to morality. The divisions proposed by Hare can serve as the basis for accurately defining types, ranks, and hierarchies of values and our attitudes to them. Such a definition could foster a globalized, though at the same time not McDonaldized or mass, morality (I outlined this idea in Kopciuch 2012c, 67–76). Secondly, Hare's concept can be employed in two different approaches to globalization. One of them is that globalization is conceptually bound up with processes of cultural homogenization and assimilation, which is understandable also on the global scale and made familiar, for example, by the theory of the McDonaldization of culture (Ritzer 1993). The other (more precise) notion is that globalization denotes processes in which connections, contacts, and interdependences among various spheres of cultural life multiply, globally of course. With the latter (in my view, more apposite) notion, we are not faced with homogeneity, but with links among elements which retain their diversity. This is where Hare's proposition can effectively be applied, as its major tenet envisages a diversity of people's situations in life. These culturally diverse elements can be negotiated on the basis of distinction into basic and non-fundamental values. Universal prescriptivism is applicable to the sphere of basic values.

If used in the context of socio-cultural issues, Hare's position would represent a balanced and moderate attitude, in the sense that it combines the universal and the common with the singular and the individual. A radically different attitude was intrinsic to early theories of cultural plurality, especially to Oswald Spengler's catastrophic concept. Spengler, namely, ruled out any possibility of contact and communication between civilizations, which he envisaged as Leibnizian monads – without windows and incapable of relating to each other. In Leibniz, however, the situation of the monads was not hopeless, because the pre-established harmony he envisioned enabled the isolated monads to function efficiently and non-conflictually. Yet this problem was unresolved in Spengler, only provoking one to ask Spengler himself how it was possible in the first place for him, as a member of the separate Western civilization, to comprehend other distinct civilizations, such as Ancient civilization guided by the Apollonian spirit, if his Western civilization was informed by the Faustian spirit. But, even though Spengler's historiosophical speculation pushed them to the background, we could identify some solutions relevant to the issues discussed here even in Spengler, who would probably be really hard pressed to explain how civilizations could contact each other, while the possibility of such contact is indeed reasserted by globalization processes. Such solutions are suggested by analogies and homologies which Spengler discerned in various civilizations (Diec 2002, 155–157). Such correspondences between elements of civilizations (regarding the position they take or the function they fulfill in the bigger whole) can after all be interpreted as examples of universal (structural or functional) patterns enacted in individual, materially differentiated, and separate civilizations. Clearly, it is the same idea which was also developed by Koneczny.

The implications of this reasoning for the understanding of universality and generality in globalization processes can be articulated as follows:

1) It is exigent and expedient to seek to precisely define the meaning we attribute to the term globalization when we use it. The multiplication of meanings in the literature can further obscure the problem situation, because depending on the intended meaning of globalization, the relation among globalization, generality, and universality can be framed differently.

2) If we adopt the precise definition of globalization as an increase in the worldwide interconnections within particular spheres of life, our analysis shows that while the processes as such are universal, their object can retain individuality and diversity. Both the process and its object are of universal character only if we identify globalization with cultural unification.

3) The paradox of universality and diversity on the one hand and the paradox of universality and generality on the other both exemplify merely ostensible paradoxes. They disappear when our analysis takes into account various meanings of globalization and, most importantly, when we consider various levels and aspects of the cultural sphere. There is no other way in which to solve these paradoxes. The reason for this is that the world itself is diverse.

Bibliography

Diec, Joachim. *Cywilizacje bez okien. Teoria Mikołaja Danilewskiego i późniejsze koncepcje monadycznych formacji socjokulturowych.* Cracow: Wydawnictwo Uniwersytetu Jagielońskiego, 2002.

Hare, Richard M. *Moral Thinking: Its Levels, Methods and Point.* Oxford and New York: Oxford University Press, 1981.

Hare, Richard M. "Universal Prescriptivism." In *A Companion to Ethics*. Edited by Peter Singer. Oxford and Malden: Blackwell, 2000, pp. 451–63.

Hegel, Georg W. F. *Lectures on the Philosophy of World History: Introduction. Reason in History.* Translated by Hugh Barr Nisbet. Cambridge, New York and Melbourne: Cambridge University Press, 1998.

Koneczny, Feliks. *O ład w historii*. London: Wydawnictwa Towarzystwa Imienia Romana Dmowskiego, no 13, 1997.

Koneczny, Feliks. *On the Plurality of Civilisations*. London: Polonia Publications, 1962.

Kopciuch, Leszek. "Zmienność historyczno-kulturowa a poznawanie wartości." *Kultura-Historia- Globalizacja*, no. 11, 2012a.

Kopciuch, Leszek. "Globalizacja i lokalność w kontekście zagadnień filozofii dziejów." *Kultura- Historia-Globalizacja*, no. 12, 2012b.

Kopciuch, Leszek. "Głos w debacie *Dlaczego nie wystarczy być*." *Kultura i Wartości*, no. 2, 2012c.

Majbroda, Katarzyna. "Antropolog(ia) wobec globalizującego się świata. Globalizacja – nowa nazwa dla starych stylów myślenia w antropologii kulturowej?." *Kultura-Historia-Globalizacja*, no. 9, 2011.

Nobis, Adam. "Złożoność globalizacji, czyli różne globalne historie." *Kultura-Historia-Globalizacja*, no. 5, 2009.

Ritzer, George. *The McDonaldization of Society*. Thousand Oaks: Pine Forge Press, 1993.

Saja, Krzysztof. *Język etyki a utylitaryzm. Filozofia moralna Richarda M. Hare'a*. Cracow: Aureus, 2008.

CHAPTER 2

The Status of Global Studies and Transformations in the Social Sciences

Franciszek Czech

In his article in the *Annual Review of Sociology*, Mauro F. Guillén has presented an interesting comparison concerning the intensification of globalization processes. Specifically, he compared changes in the values of various globalization indices between 1980 and 1998. The data he had collected implied, for example, that the value of international trade, direct foreign investment, the number of international organizations, and the rates of foreign travel had increased. All the statistics cited by Guillén attest to an intensification of economic, financial, social, and political processes that contribute to globalization. The most important insight suggested by his comparisons concerns the sector in which the globalization index registered the greatest increase over the timeframe he studied. Interestingly, it was neither the nearly tripled increase in the number of international organizations nor any of the frequently cited economic figures. Guillén's data show that the globalization-related index which was changing most dynamically between 1980 and 1998 concerned an increase in the number of research studies on globalization. While in 1980 journal databases included 89 sociological articles which featured the notions of "globalization" or "global," in 1998 as many as 1009 such articles were published. This means an over eleven-fold increase. Over the same period, the number of books addressing global processes rocketed from 48 to 589, recording a twelve-fold increase (Guillén 2001). The rate of the intensification of selected globalization indices is presented in Figure 2.1 below.

Ronald Robertson proposed a definition of globalization in which globalization denotes "the compression of the world and the intensification of the consciousness of the world as a whole" (Robertson 2004, 93). If this approach is endorsed, globalization studies can indeed be regarded as a valid dimension of globalization. Such research is indisputably global and expresses an awareness of the changes at hand. Without a doubt, ideas on globalization are globally circulated and negotiated. Scholars from across the world attend international congresses together, read the same papers, and cite data published in the same sources. For one, the data included in the Figure above (in the Polish journal *Kultura – Historia – Globalizacja* [*Culture – History – Globalization*]) come from

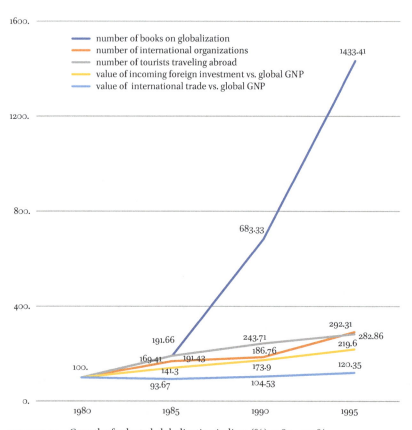

FIGURE 2.1 Growth of selected globalization indices (%), 1985 = 100%

a paper by Guillén, a Spanish scholar who works in the U.S. and publishes in an internationally read journal. No wonder that, if viewed from this perspective, science and scholarship as such are sometimes deemed to be transnational. This position is embraced by Piotr Sztompka in his article "Czy istnieje socjologia polska" ["Is There a Polish Sociology"], which appeared in *Studia Socjologiczne*. Sztompka argues that

> the internationalization of research means firstly that the organization of this field of activity is similar across the world, with sociology primarily practiced at universities, research institutes, and "think tanks." Secondly, the international mobility of scholars has developed on a mass scale, and networks of scholarly connections have become extremely dense and global. As a result, most researchers are no longer Merton's "locals" and are turning increasingly "cosmopolitan" (Merton 1973, 374). Thirdly,

research methods are informed by uniform standards: in the natural sciences, they are defined by the dominant paradigm, and in the social sciences, they are part of the shared "tool box," which includes useful techniques and procedures.[1]

SZTOMPKA 2011, 44.

If globalization studies as such can be considered a global phenomenon, it certainly makes sense to scrutinize its distinctive characteristics. I propose applying a metatheoretical perspective (a theory of globalization theory) and attempting to establish the status of this kind of research. What is actually the meaning of the label "global studies," and what is specific about such research? How can the ensemble of theories and studies on globalization and globality be described? Is this just a fleeting vogue, a new research paradigm, or perhaps a separate research discipline *in statu nascendi*? Briefly, what is the status of the study of global processes within the social sciences?

Claims that globalization theory, as well as globalization processes as such, is a temporary intellectual trend were articulated relatively early. As early as in 1999, Kenneth Waltz, an influential theorist of international relations, opined that "globalization is a fad of the 1990s" (Waltz 1999, 694). Indeed, globalization processes were extraordinarily abrupt and vehement in that period. They were mainly fueled by dynamically developing technologies (the Internet) and by the transformations precipitated by the end of the Cold War, which resulted in a deeper, more robust, and topographically expanded supranational political and economic collaboration. The scale of these processes could not but

---

1   Sztompka earlier presented the major ideas of this article in his conference paper at the 14th Congress of the Polish Sociological Society in Cracow in 2010. The presentation invited a polemic from Andrzej Zybertowicz, who insisted that despite obvious international influences and interdependencies, it was certainly possible to delineate a Polish sociology (and thus other national disciplines as well), which was practiced with Poland (or other countries) in mind. This dispute fits into an ongoing debate within globalization studies over the extent to which certain developments are global or local. To a degree, this resembles the argument over the nature of man, which Durkheim tried to settle by proposing the concept of *homo duplex*, where the human being is simultaneously a biopsychical and moral being, exceeding pure animality. Of course, neither of the two aspects should be ignored, and scholarship must not be reduced either to its national or its global dimension. Nevertheless, we must notice that various disciplines can be globalized to different degrees and in different ways. While research on the social, economic, or political situation in Poland – or, for that matter, any other country/region – is conducted either from an insider position or from an outsider perspective (which, as methodologists insist, has relevant cognitive consequences), studies on global processes are always carried out by insiders. In this sense, globalization studies is more globalized than national sociologies are.

affect social awareness. The number of scholarly publications on globalization surged, as attested by Guillén's data, and – perhaps more importantly – the very term globalization started to be commonly used outside academic discourse. Emphatically, what Waltz meant by globalization theories were only the theories of international relations which pointed at the decreasing role of the state and the increasing role of the economic system, which was becoming growingly independent of state structures. This was actually a very restricted understanding of globalization. As shown by David Held, Anthony McGrew, and colleagues, such definitions were in fact popular at the onset of theorizing on globalization. Nevertheless, such positions were largely abandoned later, and several globalization models currently register not so much the decline of the state as rather changes in the role the state plays in the contemporary world (Held, McGrew 1999, 3–10). In this sense, Waltz was right, and the type of globalization theories which he referred to indeed soon proved a momentary intellectual fad.

To prove that the globalization theory as a whole was a temporary vogue would be a far more challenging thing to do. Such claims are disproved, for example, by the data on the number of research papers which address globalization. For this paper, I have analyzed the contents of twenty-five important journals on anthropology, political sciences, and sociology (e.g., *Anthropology Quarterly*, *Current Anthropology*, *Journal of Anthropological Research*, *International Journal of Politics, Culture and Society*, *Political Theory*, *Social Research*, and *American Sociological Review*), whose articles from 1985–2009 are catalogued in the jstor database. I have found that within this timeframe, the number of papers which either mentioned globalization at least once or focused on it as their key thematic concern (signaled by the inclusion of "globalization" in their titles) was incessantly growing. Given this, it would be untenable to insist that the study of global processes is but a fleeting fad (Figure 2.2).

The term "globalization" used throughout an article (the scale on the left-hand side)

James Mittelman, another theorist of international relations, took Waltz's assertion as his starting point and set out to establish the status of globalization theory more accurately. He concluded that

> although globalization studies entails a putting together of bold attempts to theorize structural change, it would be wrong both to underestimate or to exaggerate the achievements. Judging the arguments in the debate, on balance, a modest thesis is in order. The efforts to theorize globalization have produced a patchwork, an intellectual move rather than a movement, and more of a potential than worked-out alternatives to accepted

STATUS OF GLOBAL STUDIES AND TRANSFORMATIONS 25

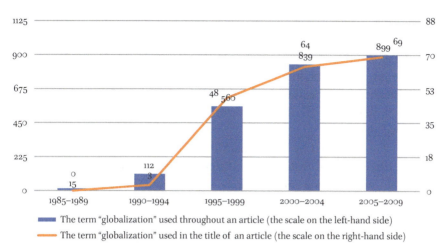

FIGURE 2.2 The number of articles addressing globalization in the selected twenty-five journals in 1985–2009

ways of thinking in international studies. In sum, this fledgling may be regarded as a proto-paradigm.

MITTELMAN 2002, 12

In evoking a proto-paradigm, Mittelman relies on the conceptual apparatus specific to the theory of international relations, which is governed by a handful of basic theoretical perspectives, such as realism, liberalism, and constructivism. According to Mittleman, the globalization (proto)paradigm can soon join them. It is my impression that the notion of paradigm is not appropriately applied here (and not only here). Thomas Kuhn, to whom Mittleman himself refers as it were, reserved this term for philosophic-methodological or epistemological and ontological concepts of science and its goals, and resultant research approaches. Despite this, the term paradigm tends to be used in academic practice to describe theories of slightly above-average complexity. Instead of sharing a set of research premises characteristic of paradigms, what globalization theories in fact have in common is a group of phenomena which they seek to explain. On the one hand, globalization is studied quantitatively by using neopositivist models and not infrequently applying complicated procedures to ensure the objectivity and reliability of data. This is exemplified in globalization indices which I have discussed elsewhere (Czech 2011). On the other hand, globalization is equally frequently studied within postmodernist frameworks, as a series of disconnected inquiries, and/or through metaphors as a basically non-operationalizable state of affairs (cf. e.g., Czech 2010, 129–164). If so divergent approaches together contribute to the field of globalization studies, even a proto-paradigm seems an exaggerated and misleading moniker. Mittelman comes to other conclusions, because his analysis is only limited to the positions on globalization which have been developed within the theory of international relations, where disparities in the theorization of globalization are not as glaring as those briefly described above.

The views espoused by Waltz and Mittelman share the same defect. Both authors discuss solely he discourse on globalization which unfolds within the theory of international relations, whereas globalization studies is a profoundly and intrinsically interdisciplinary field. Globalization is co-produced by multifarious processes which lie within the research focus of multiple social-scientific disciplines, such as anthropology, economy, geography, political science, and sociology, to name but a few. Each of these disciplines studies different, though often parallel, developments. By default, each of them has also developed its own, at least somewhat separate traditions of theorizing. This is reflected in various takes on and approaches to globalization which appear in the interdisciplinary space of research on global phenomena. This heterogeneity is perfectly captured in the well-known typology of globalization definitions proposed by Jan Aart Scholte. Scholte divided a plethora of definitions used in research discourse into five groups, in which globalization is understood respectively as: internationalization, liberalization, universalization, Westernization, modernization, and re-spatialization (Scholte 2005, 15–17). Table 2.1 below includes a synthetic depiction of these approaches to globalization. The manners of grasping globalization which were discussed by Scholte are accompanied by my clues as to the disciplines in which a given type of definition is particularly widespread. This helps perceive how the multidimensional space of globalization studies is co-produced by researchers who embrace different and sometimes widely divergent research traditions.

Scholte does not bind his respective ways of defining globalization to any particular disciplines, and further in his study he proceeds to spell out why the last of the models is superior to the other ones. However, in my view, the specificity of and limits to each of the approaches result from nothing else than different research premises and goals of the various social-scientific disciplines. Political scientists and theorists of international relations are usually satisfied with notions in which globalization is reduced to internationalization, because their research as a rule focuses on what happens with states in the time of globalization. For their part, economists who explore contemporary economic international relations will employ the definition of globalization

TABLE 2.1 Selected ways of defining globalization as identified by Jan Aart Scholte

Definition type	Characteristics	Symbol	Selected theorists	Scope of popularity
Liberalization	Reducing barriers in international traffic and the rise of common markets	WTO, IMF	Harald Sander, Kenichi Ohmae	Economy
Universalization	Worldwide dissemination of values and commodities; homogenization of culture	"global village"	Olivier Reiser, Blodwen Davies, Marshall McLuhan Martin Albrow	Various disciplines (especially older approaches)
Internationalization	Increasing interdependence among states	UNO	Kenneth Waltz, Paul Hirst, Grahame Thompson	Political sciences
Modernization Westernization (Americanization)	Dissemination of Western values, organizations and products in other parts of the world	McDonald, Coca-Cola	Martin Khor, George Ritzer	Sociology (especially critical approaches)
Re-spatialization (Re-configuration of space)	Changes in the spatial organization of social relations: remote communication in real time, rapid movement of people and goods	Internet, Airplane,	David Held, Anthony McGrew, Anthony Giddens, Jan Aart Scholte	Sociology

as liberalization, which usefully furthers their pursuits. We can conclude that even if syntheses and more general models appear, globalization theory will remain multi-layered and interdisciplinary.

Symptomatically, this interdisciplinary research space is being institutionalized. The first harbingers of the crystallization of this space are provided by regular conferences and congresses. The Global Studies Conference, which is held in a different country each year, is an excellent case in point. Another manifestation of the institutionalization of globalization studies is to be found in the dissemination of journals, such as *Globalizations*, *Global Governance*, and *Global Networks: A Journal of Transnational Affairs*. An even stronger indicator of institutionalization is provided by the establishment of research centers and university departments dedicated to the study of globalization; the Centre for the Study of Globalisation and Regionalisation (CSGR) at Warwick University (with which Scholte is affiliated), the Centre for the Study of Global Governance at the London School of Economics, and the Center on Globalization and Sustainable Development at New York's Columbia University are but a small sample of relevant examples. The steadily increasing number of study programs and degree courses in which students are educated in global studies serves perhaps as the most telling sign of the institutionalization of the discipline. This means that heis worldwide produce graduates who have earned their degrees not in any of the traditional disciplines, such as anthropology, sociology, economy, or political sciences, but in an interdisciplinary field which draws on the legacy of all these disciplines and trains students in the study of global processes and interdependences.

I believe that globalization studies courses and programs offered by various universities deserve a separate analysis of their own. Since what I can do here is a brief outline of this new tendency, I will only cite two examples of such programs. The website of the University of Freiburg describes its degree program in Global Studies as follows:

> The Global Studies Programme (GSP) is a two-year Master's degree programme in Social Sciences. The programme is jointly organized by Albert-Ludwigs-University (Freiburg), Chulalongkorn University (Bangkok), FLACSO Argentina (Buenos Aires), Jawaharlal Nehru University (New Delhi) and University of Cape Town (Cape Town). [...] This programme's curriculum includes sociology, political science, anthropology and geography. Since 2002, more than 200 students from more than 60 countries have travelled to the participating institutions to gain a rounded perspective on globalization with special emphasis on the Global South.
> http://www.gsp.uni-freiburg.de

For the sake of comparison, ucla advertises its program in Global Studies as an inter-faculty program which gives first-cycle students an opportunity to acquire specialized interdisciplinary knowledge on the central problems confronting the contemporary globalized world:

> Global Studies students are given the tools to understand the processes of globalization and their consequences, and they are empowered to shape their world as the next generation of global leaders in business, education, government, and the non-profit sector. The Global Studies curriculum focuses on three thematic pillars of globalization: *Culture & Society* [...], *Governance & Conflict* [...], *Markets & Resources* [...] These three pillars of globalization capture the principal dimensions of the multifaceted interconnections increasingly defining the world we live in. Global Studies examines the ways in which people across the globe are affected every day by an unprecedented array of linkages that defy geographic and political boundaries. Global Studies draws on insights from disciplines across the humanities and social sciences to give students the theoretical and methodological skills and the knowledge base necessary to understand this complex and rapidly changing world.
> http://www.international.ucla.edu/idps/globalstudies/article.asp?parentid=20069

Even this very cursory look at how global studies curricula are composed confirms that globalization studies is a profoundly interdisciplinary movement. Another testimony to the emergence of an interdisciplinary research field is supplied by the formation of a canon of the literature on globalization, which features publications in several different fields. This is perhaps best exemplified in collected volumes largely intended as academic textbooks, such as *The Globalization Reader*, edited by Frank Lechner and John Boli (Lechner, Boli 2004). The anthology assembles contributions by prominent globalization researchers affiliated with an array of disciplines: anthropology, economy, history, theory of international relations, sociology, political sciences, religion studies, musicology, and media studies. An equally varied range of texts can also be found in *The Global Transformation Reader*, edited by David Held and Anthony McGrew (Held, McGrew 2000). That both volumes include papers by the same authors (Dani Rodrik, Robert O. Keohane, Joseph S. Nye, Joseph Stiglitz, Susan Strange, and John Tomlinson) also confirms that an interdisciplinary canon of globalization studies is in the making.

In Poland, these institutionalization processes are slower than in the West. Polish textbooks introducing the themes of global studies based on the interdisciplinary literature are admittedly available, but there are no equivalent readers in Polish yet. While conferences are held to discuss global issues, they usually feature merely one session dedicated to globalization as such. There may be journals which publish articles on global problems, but the themes they examine are as a rule far wider and more comprehensive. Basically, only one among the point-scoring journals included in the recognized list of the Ministry of Science and Higher Education is largely devoted to global issues. *Kultura-Historia-Globalizacja* is this journal. Admittedly, research on globalization is done at some universities, but except the Institute of Global and Regional Studies at the University of Warsaw, such pursuits are confined to much smaller academic units, such as chairs or sections subsumed within and subordinated to bigger university structures (e.g., Chair for Globalization and Economic Integration at the Jagiellonian University, Section on Global Economic Relations at the sgh Warsaw School of Economics, and Global Studies Group at the Institute of Cultural Studies, University of Wroclaw). Finally, there are subject courses and specialization programs linked to globalization (e.g., specialization in Markets and Competition in the Globalized World at the Economic University in Katowice, or specialization in The Globalization of Culture at the Institute of Cultural Studies, University of Wroclaw), yet no Polish hei offers a complete, comprehensive, integrated, and interdisciplinary first- or second-cycle degree program in global studies. Importantly, until recently, it was basically impossible to offer global studies courses at all, because there had been a mandatory, fixed list of degree courses, which only changed in 2012, when the National Qualification Framework was put in place, enabling faculties, departments, and institutes to construct their curricula more freely and to offer degree courses in new fields. Given this, the institutionalization processes of global studies may well accelerate in the coming years. Until now, however, they have been relatively slow.

So far, we have not addressed another essential condition which must be met for a research field to become fully institutionalized. Having a recognizable and widely accepted name is this condition. A commonly used name speaks to the existence in a given community of a belief that practices, procedures, and traditions comprised under this label are distinct and unique. If such a name is missing, a given phenomenon, a set of practices, or a category of things can be regarded as not relevant to a given social group. Without a name, it is a challenge to fashion a disciplinary identity which can be shared by a group of researchers who believe that their research concerns and methodologies are autonomous to a degree. Although in Poland global studies is developing rather slowly, a name for the research field has already been proposed. Nevertheless, this term – *globalistyka* (*globalistics*), which was first coined, I guess, by Janusz Gnitecki – has won a very scant appreciation (Gnitecki 2002). The label is usually understood to be an equivalent of the far more widespread English coinage of *global studies*. This is confirmed by Mirosława Czerny and colleagues, who explain:

> As early as in the 1990s, Western – chiefly American – universities founded interdisciplinary degree courses referred to as *global studies*. They enjoy enormous popularity and attract throngs of students who crave knowledge about the so rapidly mutating world, which is so challenging to comprehend. Having long deliberated over what to call studies on globalization in Polish, we have eventually chosen the already familiar term *globalistyka/globalistics* which has been used in our academic communities for quite a while now. I believe that there is a clear analogy in it to *europeistyka* [*Europeistics*, i.e. European studies], which has recently appeared at Polish universities as a new major.
>
> CZERNY, ŁUCZAK, MAKOWSKI 2007, 7–8

As already mentioned, the term *globalistics*, which Czerny endorses, is hardly common currency in Polish academia. Sometimes, an alternative name, i.e., *studia globalne*, a literal translation of English "global studies," is used, which is not a universal practice either. This alternative is employed, for example, on the website of *Kultura-Historia-Globalizacja*. Such terminological ambiguity also explicitly indicates that globalization studies has not become a fully emancipated research discipline in Poland yet. This is corroborated by a comparison with sociology. In the early stages of the institutionalization of this discipline, various phrasings (therein, for example, social physics) were proposed as names for it, but finally one – sociology – came to be commonly recognized and used. Undoubtedly, *global studies* is now an entrenched term in English, but in Polish no coherent linguistic convention of referring to the research field we are discussing here has evolved yet.

There is one more important aspect concerning the name and its scope. The term global studies in its Polish version (*studia globalne*) is indeed used in Poland, while the Polish equivalent of globalization studies (*studia globalizacyjne*) is not, as confirmed by Google search (1,260 entries for the former, 0 entries for the latter). There is also a disproportion in the English usage, with *global studies* being a far more frequent choice than *globalization studies* (1,680,000 and 91,800 records, respectively). The two similar-sounding names may denote two different research fields. The term *globalization studies* is narrower and may entail constraining the research field to the study of globalization processes. For its part, *global studies* is a far more universal term, because it implies that its focus is on the developments on the global scale, whether or not globalization processes intensify or abate. Global studies is thus devoted to researching the social, political, and cultural condition of the contemporary world. This label suggests not only the object of research but also some methodological tenets. They have been aptly grasped by Robertson, who has identified four major levels of the exploration of the social world, specifically: the individual, society, the system of societies, and humankind as such (Robertson 1992, 25, 49–52). Robertson emphasizes that the main task lies in establishing how these four factors, which together make up the global system, interact with each other. He argues that without discerning the latter component, i.e., the global level, any analysis of contemporary realities is bound to be incomplete. In other words, global studies denotes research on the situation of the world as a whole and on the network of interdependencies among the global situation, the situation in regions and states, and the life situation of individual people. Given this, global studies goes beyond the investigation of the advancement of globalization processes. Rather, the field offers an interdisciplinary reflection on social, cultural, political, and economic relations on the global scale. Such research draws on several social sciences and offers a very general, holistic knowledge of today's world. We can easily imagine that some globalization processes will considerably subside (for example, if various hazards compel states to radically seal their borders), and the very catchphrase of globalization, extremely popular in the 1990s as it was, will go out of fashion. Nevertheless, I believe that even such developments will not bring about a decline of global studies, because such a general research perspective on the global situation seems simply indispensable at the current level of our civilization's development.

If global studies has its distinct and relevant object of research, perhaps it represents not so much a proto-paradigm (as Mittleman would have it) as rather a proto-discipline. Are the institutionalization processes described above capable of breeding a separate scholarly discipline, such as culturology, sociology, or economy? To answer this question, we need to consider the current context in which the social sciences are positioned. In methodological terms, there are at least two conditions which usually have to be met for a scholarly discipline to be recognized as such. These conditions are: a distinct object of research and corresponding research methods. These criteria, however, are anything but sharp. This is vividly evinced by the reformulation of the title of a celebrated methodology textbook authored by Stefan Nowak. In 1970, the textbook was published as *Metodologia badań socjologicznych* (*The Methodology of Sociological Research*), and a dozen years later its slightly revised edition was released with the title *Metodologia badań społecznych* (*The Methodology of Social Research*). In the opening sentences of the Introduction, Nowak explained that:

> the previous title read *Metodologia badań socjologicznych* (*The Methodology of Sociological Research*), which was probably related to the author's formal affiliation with the discipline called sociology, whatever the term might denote, and to the fact that its target readership – at least its implied target readership – was supposed to consist of sociology students. As it turned out later, the textbook attracted a reading public from beyond sociology and was used by representatives of rather varied social disciplines. This should not come as a surprise, considering that most sociologists have already acknowledged that any attempt to rigorously define principles for setting sociology apart from other social disciplines is by default doomed to failure.
>
> NOWAK 1985, 9

With clear substantive criteria for delimiting disciplines lacking, we must accept that, as Stanisław Ossowski insisted, "it is largely a matter of convention whether we regard a certain system of issues as a separate science, or whether we subsume them under another, more general science" (Ossowski 1967, 96). At the same time, heterogeneous and often incoherent conventions upheld by some research communities intersect with formal classifications of disciplines enumerated in fixed catalogues of scholarly fields and disciplines (as mentioned by Nowak), within which degree programs can be offered and academic titles and degrees can be conferred. Thus, on the one hand, there are conventions which allow even very narrow specializations and subdisciplines to be called disciplines, and on the other there, is a rigid catalogue of disciplines in place. This catalogue is itself quite arbitrarily constructed, which can be seen in the fact that classification systems vary across countries (and sometimes even within the same country). The arbitrariness behind formal classifications is brought into relief by changes introduced in them. For example, in 2011, a regulation by the Minister of Science and Higher Education recognized security studies, a field with no tradition to talk about in Poland, as a separate discipline and re-inscribed political sciences from the field of the humanities into the field of the social sciences.

This maze of academic tribes and territories, to use the eponymous coinage of the already classic study of Tony Becher and Paul Trowler, has been dynamically changing in recent years. Institutionalization processes which unfold in global studies take place in other areas of the social sciences as well, for example, in peace and conflict studies, development studies, media studies, area studies with its numerous varieties (e.g. Asian studies and European studies), and cultural studies, which is not identified either with more broadly conceived culture sciences or with culturology, which is formally recognized as a separate research discipline in Poland (Pankowicz, Rokicki, Plichta 2008). Research spaces which go beyond the social sciences are also institutionalized, as exemplified in health sciences and various attempts at integrating the natural sciences and the social sciences dedicated to ecology. Clearly, the institutionalization of global studies is part of more comprehensive changes in the organization of the social sciences. The research fields listed above differ in their objects of research and degrees of institutionalization. What they share is their inherently interdisciplinary investment. They all build on the theoretical legacy accumulated in various disciplines of the social sciences and the humanities, such as philosophy, history, culturology, sociology, anthropology, linguistics, and political sciences. All new research fields which are undergoing institutionalization also employ the same research methods shared by the social sciences and the humanities. The accumulation of institutionalization processes taking place in various research fields within the broadly understood social sciences heads towards what is referred to as trans-disciplinarity or even post-disciplinarity. In other words, disciplines are becoming more and more integrated. In fact, what we observe today is not so much a reliance on research traditions of individual disciplines, as rather the use of an emergent shared theoretical canon and a common research tool box.

There are many reasons why the social sciences are becoming increasingly interdisciplinary. One of them is certainly quick and incessant growth in the number of research staff and research projects. As research projects multiply, new labels are produced which often overlap, at least partly. This process encourages researchers to seek to give more precise headings to their studies in the ever denser and busier space of social research. In his discussion of globalization, Jarosław Rokicki observed that the cultural gap dividing young Poles who work for international corporations from elderly highlanders from the Podhale region can be bigger than any cultural differences between the latter and their Slovakian neighbors (Rokicki 2006, 32). A similar observation can easily be made about the social sciences, where a sociologists who studies family or sport may have less in common with a sociologist of politics, who finds more common ground with a political scientist, an economist, or a historian. Nevertheless, the motives behind some scholars' commitment to the development of institutionalizing research areas may involve more than just identification within a transdisciplinary community of interests. They may also be driven by the fact that every new research fields produces its own classics and masters, not to mention the fact that every label has its own marketing potential which can be tapped into in order to attract students and secure grants. Various motives are by no means mutually exclusive, and together they reinforce and fuel processes which contribute to the emergence of new research fields.

The transformations within the social sciences which are caused by the progressing institutionalization of research fields can be usefully summed up by referencing an analogy with theoretical debates on globalization. David Held and Anthony McGrew have once proposed that there are three major positions on globalization: hyperglobalism, skepticism, and transformationism. The debate was purportedly started by hyperglobalists, who believed, in very broad lines, that globalization meant entirely new processes leading to the disappearance of borders, the fall of nation states, and the formation of one global culture. They were opposed by skeptics, who argued that globalization processes had been occurring for a long time, albeit with a varying intensity, and they had neither abolished borders nor dismantled nation states. Transformationalists synthesized the two positions by concluding that while globalization processes were not a novel development, they had become unprecedentedly robust and were bound to contribute not so much to the collapse of states as rather to a transformation of political communities, generating a new architecture of the world order (Held, McGrew 1999; Czech 2010, 61–63). By analogy, we can imagine three corresponding scenarios for the development social-scientific disciplines. One of the scenarios envisions a radical change, with the currently existing disciplines losing their position and a post-disciplinary space of the social sciences replacing them. Another scenario insists that nothing is basically going to change. The disciplines formed at the turn of the 19th century and in the first half of the 20th century will continue to form the core of the social sciences. This will not mean a total petrification. Every now and then various shifts are bound to happen. For example, the progressing institutionalization of international relations, still considered a subdiscipline within the political sciences, will help it achieve a greater autonomy and the status of a legitimate distinct discipline. The third scenario strikes a balance between the former two. Traditional disciplines (e.g., sociology and economy) will not disappear, be it only because of the strength of the tradition and institutions. But the entrenched and formally fortified disciplinary classification will be marred by interdisciplinary research fields at various levels of institutionalization. Some of them will offer university programs and confer academic degrees (in conjunction with a general liberalization of educational and research policies in this respect), while other ones will remain more informal research communities. As many other people in the era of globalization, researchers will be free to identify with various fields: some will remain loyal to the sociological traditions, others will consider themselves sociologists-cum-globalists, and yet others will only perceive themselves as global studies specialists formally affiliated with sociology.

While arguments supporting each of the three scenarios can be found at the moment, I believe that the third of them is the most probable one. In my view, global studies will not obtain the formal status of a separate scholarly discipline, remaining one of the highly relevant interdisciplinary research fields which are becoming an increasingly widespread fixture in the social sciences. On the one hand, the institutionalization processes of global studies have advanced so far that to treat it as a temporary intellectual fad is profoundly misguided, all the more so that global interdependences and processes are certainly not going to become a less engaging or less relevant thematic concern. On the other hand, however, the institutionalization of international relations seems to have reached an even more advanced stage. Both research fields – international relations and global studies – overlap to a large extent (with the former being narrower, as it is largely limited to the political-scientific study of relations among states), which reduces chances for the establishment of two strong disciplines dedicated to very similar issues. The two fields will only be regarded as separate disciplines in very detailed typologies. The considerable interdisciplinary investment, which is an immanent characteristic of global studies, also undercuts its efforts to found an entirely distinct discipline (which is the case with other interdisciplinary research fields as well). Given this, what we are witnessing is the institutionalization of an interdisciplinary research field rather than of a new discipline or subdiscipline. The rise of this kind of supra-disciplinary collaboration makes for a new quality in the social sciences.

Bibliography

Czerny, Mirosława, Robert Łuczak, and Jerzy Makowski. *Globalistyka*. Warsaw: PWN, 2007.

Czech, Franciszek. *Koszmarne scenariusze. Socjologiczne studium konstruowania lękuw dyskursie globalizacyjnym*. Cracow: Wydawnictwo Uniwersytetu Jagiellońskiego, 2010.

Czech, Franciszek. "Indeksy globalizacji. Atuty i ułomności neopozytywistycznych pomiarów nasilenia procesów globalizacyjnych." *Kultura-Historia-Globalizacja*, no. 10, 2011, pp. 41–59.

Gnitecki, Janusz. *Globalistyka*. Poznań: Wydawnictwo Naukowe PTP, 2002.

Guillén, Mauro. "Is Globalization Civilizing, Destructive or Feeble? A Critique of Five Key Debates in the Social Science Literature." *Annual Review of Sociology*, vol. 27, 2001, ss. 235–260.

Held, David, Anthony McGrew, David Goldblatt, Jonathan Perraton. *Global Transformations: Politics, Economics and Culture*. Stanford: Stanford University Press, 1999.

Held David, Anthony McGrew. "The Great Globalization Debate: An Introduction." In *The Global Transformation Reader*. Edited by D. Held. Cambridge: Polity, 2000.

Lechner, Frank, John Boli (eds.). *The Globalization Reader*. Malden, Oxford and Carlton: Blackwell Publishing, 2004.
Merton, Robert. *Sociology of Science*. Chicago: University of Chicago Press, 1973.
Mittelman, James. "Globalization: An ascendant paradigm?." *International Studies Perspectives*, vol. 3, no. 1, 2002, ss. 1–14.
Nowak, Stefan; *Metodologia badań społecznych*. Warszawa: PWN, 1985.
Ossowski,Stanisław. "Nauka o nauce." In *O nauce*. Edited by S. Ossowki. Warsaw: PWN, 1967.
Pankowicz, Andrzej, Jarosław Rokicki, Paweł Plichta (eds.). *Tożsamość kulturoznawstwa*. Cracow: Wydawnictwo Uniwersytetu Jagiellońskiego, 2008.
Robertson, Roland. *Globalization. Social Theory and Global Culture*. London: Sage, 1992.
Robertson, Ronald. "Globalization as a Problem." In *The Globalization Reader*. Edited by Lechner, Frank, John Boli. Malden, Oxford and Carlton: Blackwell Publishing, 2004, pp. 93–99.
Rokicki, Jarosław. "O realności i złudzeniu *globalizacji, wielokulturowości i ponowoczesności*." In *Wzory wielokulturowości we współczesnym świecie*. Edited by K. Golemo, T. Paleczny, E. Wiącek. Cracow: Wydawnictwo Uniwersytetu Jagiellońskiego, 2006.
Scholte, Jan A. *Globalization: A Critical Introduction*. Basingstoke: Palgrave, 2005.
Sztompka, Piotr. "Czy istnieje polska socjologia?." *Studia Socjologiczne*, vol. 201, no 2, 2011, pp. 43–54.
Waltz, Kenneth. "Globalization and Governance." *Political Science & Politics*, vol. 32, no. 4, 1999, pp. 693–700.

CHAPTER 3

Musicology and Globalization

Bożena Muszkalska

In the early 21st century, we are living in what Marshall McLuhan has called a "global village." Over recent years, we have seen a rapid development of media which make music available to the entire world in defiance of geographical boundaries. The progressing expansion of tapes, CDs, and the Internet among musicians has propelled the mass production of music. The dissemination of electronic playing devices and supra-cultural music production have rendered national and state organizations unable to establish any coherent music systems. The boundaries of states have ceased to play the role they once had in determining the compass of musical cultures. As a result, "[c]ommodities of all sorts – including music – are being produced and consumed in multiple international contexts rather than one culturally-specific location" (Pacini 1993, 48). "Locations" in this context should be understood as referring to communities with common musical interests rather than to physically delimited spaces. Consequently, the belief that only one kind of music, for example so-called ethnic music, can represent a given group, a notion shared by musicologists (and not only them) until quite recently, is no longer tenable. As a rule, several kinds of such music exist side by side, bound up with countless imagined communities and invented traditions. Ceasing to be a marginal phenomenon, musical multiculturality has been elevated into one of the major characteristics of contemporary societies.

Among musicologists, the sociologists and anthropologists of music were quickest to respond to the advancing globalization of musical cultures. In the 1980s, they began to champion the idea that musics could no longer be studied exclusively in their historical homelands, but that the field of music research should be extended, while exploring the musically conveyed identities and ethnicities locally and transnationally at the same time.

This shift in research approaches called for defining new goals and coining a terminology which would promote more pertinent accounts of global musical cultures. To investigate the relationships and multiple interdependences between the global and the local in music came to be considered one of the main research goals in musicology. Most scholars applied themselves to the examination of contexts in which music appeared rather than of music itself. It should not come as a surprise, given that the theoretical perspectives of globality and locality are chiefly defined by sociologists, philosophers, and culture theorists. Ethnomusicologists have adopted the vocabulary employed in this interdisciplinary debate, whereby they have made several notions – such as fragmentation, totalization, commodification, imagined community, hybridity, Creolism, and the like – their own. Scholars who also analyze processes which unfold in music seek to establish whether and if so in what ways their findings can be useful to general social and cultural theories. Such endeavors are epitomized by Ingrid Monson, who has studied various types of repetitions in the music of the African diaspora and showed that by investigating interactive, multifaceted, and multidimensional musical practices which at the same time function as social and symbolic acts, one can contribute to these theories. According to Monson, juxtaposing certain musical elements which can be found in various species of so-called world music (funk, blues, zouk popular with the Creole-speaking Caribbean population, reggae, Senegal-derived mbalax, rumba, plena typical of Puerto Rico, and calypso-related soca) reveals how freely these elements are borrowed and circulate among and across different musical genres. If we envision these overlapping and accumulating music processes as analogies of social and cultural processes, we will grasp how the findings of research into music can be harnessed to further the theorizing of cultural globalization and studies on cultural hybridity (Monson 1999, 46).

In their search for parallels between musical and social processes, musicologists rely on two basic metaphors which are employed in sociology and philosophy. One of these metaphors emphasizes the fragmentation, while the other the systemic nature of global culture. The former approaches musical culture as a text, with language as a model for relationships occurring in culture. In the latter metaphor, the model of cultural interactions is provided by trade in goods in reference to the Marxist tradition and the theories developed by Theodor Adorno and Frederic Jameson. In both these frameworks, attempts are made to transfer emphasis from people's activity onto social forces which operate beyond human control. Studies underpinned by such interpretive perspectives are exemplified by Mark Slobin's "Micromusics of the West: A Comparative Approach" (1992) and Veit Erlmann's "The Aesthetics of the Global Imagination: Reflections on World Music in the 1990s" (1996), both articles serving as major points of reference for several later authors.

Slobin outlines a vision of the global circulation of music in Western Europe and the U.S. His aim is to capture new relations which emerge in the global system of cultures which he dubs supercultures, subcultures, and intercultures (1992, 2). He explores each level of this structure as a configuration of various spaces – "-scapes" (ethno-, media-, techno-, ideo-, and finanscapes)[1] – in particular musical contexts. He places the interactions of superculture and subculture at the center of research on the operations of the global cultural economy, especially focusing on interdependences of individual choices, group actions, and changes in the form and significance of local musics, i.e. micromusics,[2] engendered by global forces. According to Slobin, every individual lives at the intersection of subculture, interculture, and superculture, which add up to a complicated "cultural counterpoint" (ibid., 4). Navigating between the levels of this structure is possible if makers and performers of micromusics have mastered the skill of "code switching" (ibid., 61*pass.*).

Erlmann questions the utility of methodological procedures proposed by Slobin and claims that any attempt at integrating heterogeneous ad amorphous micromusics in one broader system, i.e., at systematizing what is in and of itself definitely unsystematic, is doomed to failure. Instead, he puts forward the concept of a "global cultural entity," which is founded on the Jamesonian idea of difference and the systemic character of late capitalist cultural production. Erlmann believes that because homogenization and differentiation are mutually related aspects of the global cultural economy, it must by default be assumed that disparate subsystems are elements of one system. Consequently, he dismisses the notion that maintaining the cultural differences of musics from the world music movement is an expression of opposition to the hegemony of the West (Erlmann 1996, 468). Drawing on Niklas Luhmann's framework of the autopoietic (self-reproducing) system, Erlmann argues that "a complex system such as [...] world music [...] thus gains integration not only on the basis of common values, norms, or power relations, but simply by providing an ordered environment" for its subsystems to self-develop and redefine in Erlmann (1996, 473).

Though embracing different positions, Slobin and Erlmann pursue the same aim. Both are looking for a "structure of conjuncture" (Sahlins) which helps explain how music performers, listeners, and sounds are involved in the processes of global circulation and how people behave vis-à-vis social forces which simultaneously fragment and totalize culture.

In between Slobin's fragmented world of "micromusics" and Erlmann's "panoramic specter of a local ecumene," there is a site for the image of the participants in the global musical repetitions and their combinations as

---

[1] These terms were coined by Arjun Appadurai in "Disjuncture and Difference in the Global Cultural Economy," *Public Culture*, vol. 2, 1990, part 2, pp. 1–24.

[2] Slobin defines micromusics as "the small musical units within big music-cultures" (Slobin 1992, 1).

portrayed by Monson. Monson delves into how these repetitions navigate across musical genres and what information they carry about the sphere of global reality which Slobin refers to as diasporic intercultures (1992, 44). In her interpretations, Monson builds on the concept of habitus, which was developed by Pierre Bourdieu to describe interactions among structures, bodily dispositions, and practices involved in the production and reproduction of culture (ibid., 49).

Musicologists most frequently explore globalization in relation to the current situation of musical cultures. Philip Bohlman's works stands out against this backdrop as he ponders the mobilizations of globalizing processes at particular moments in history. In his "World Music at the 'End of History'" (2002), Bohlman insists that such moments mainly coincide with the beginnings and ends of centuries, especially when they overlap with the turns of millennia. At such points, music serves to express the intensifying feeling of decline and the fear of the end of the world (endism), and as such it requires "global dimensions." Its meanings and functions change, with the strange and the exotic increasing in prominence (ibid., 2). As "the geographical and ontological distance between different musical practices" shrinks, the only remaining thing is the sense of separateness between "Self" and "Other" (ibid., 1). Bohlman grounds his argument on the old and currently existing musical genres, including prima and seconda prattica, North-American Amish hymns, Jewish music, popular songs, Marian songs of Medjugorje, and world music.

World music is the kind of music on which a considerable majority of researchers focus when studying global processes in contemporary musical culture. Although the term is commonly used, it is not unambiguous. Deborah Pacini points out that the name "world music" does not denote any musical genre as such. She claims that initially it served as "a marketing term describing the products of musical cross-fertilization between north – the U.S. and Western Europe, and south – primarily Africa and the Caribbean Basin, which began appearing on the popular music landscape in the early 1980s" (Pacini 1993, 48). Since 1985, world music has served as an umbrella term subsuming practically all musics of non-European cultures. It is a commercial ploy devised to conquer new markets by means of sounds and ideas which were once bound up with "ethnic music." As observed by Erlmann, who draws on Jameson's concept of "spatial historiographies," several musics within world music are characterized by "the pseudohistorical sound of pastness" (Erlmann 1996, 483). Musial idioms which are associated with world music are hybrid and exhibit an enhanced sensitivity to any changes unfolding in broadly conceived music as well as in the social and political domains. While world music was once classified and launched on the market as external to the mainstream musical production, currently it is actually nearing the top position in several cultures worldwide.

The concepts of hybridity and Creolism,[3] which are associated with new forms of self-awareness, stir a considerable interest among ethnomusicologists. This is neither an awareness of being "here" or "there" nor an awareness of being "us" or "them"; rather, it is an awareness of, to use Homi Bhabha's coinage, "in-betweenness," of being in "a third space" (2010). While the process of Creolization was once construed as a consequence of musical exchange between colonial metropolises of the North and earlier African and Caribbean colonies, since the 1980s researchers have identified new forms of Creolization. The process is exemplified in the rise of new, commercially interconnected infrastructures within which First-World listeners are recruited to listen to exotic sounds of the Third World (Pacini 1993, 50). Ceasing to be conceived in negative terms as a legacy of colonialism, Creolization has garnered positive appraisal, at least in some regions of the world (e.g. among local Caribbean communities) where musical mélanges function as a symptom of prosperity and openness to the world. Ethnomusicologists join the rife interdisciplinary debate on cultural identity by seeking to demonstrate that music offers special opportunities of reconfiguring elements of one's own structure as determinants of identity. This however requires a degree of compatibility among musical genres, without which they cannot possibly amalgamate. Rather than given in advance, such a congruity is decided by people. Hence utterly surprising combinations of rhythms, tunes, and sounds are sometimes bound to emerge (Guilbault 1997, 36).

The accelerated global circulation of music has prompted hew questions concerning cultures of diasporic communities and other "traveling cultures" (e.g. in places associated with tourism and pilgrimages). While modernist theoretical frameworks described such cultures by means of assimilation and acculturation models, showing the states "before" and "after" (interactions with other culture), current research approaches conceptualize such cultures in supranational categories. Thereby, the attention shifts from nation-related communities and nations as such to the spaces of which these groups are components. Discussions focus on historical processes which have led to marginalizing "travelers" and treating them as "others" as well as to fostering representations of authentic culture.

---

[3] These themes dominated the conference of the ICTM "Music and Minorities" Study Group, which was held in Varna in 2006.

Concluding my survey of the positions musicologists take on globalization in musical cultures, I will follow René Lysloff and evoke a cyberpunk story by Bruce Sterling and Lewis Shiner entitled "Mozart in Mirrorshades." Lysloff cites the story when reflecting on the dilemmas experienced by researchers of local cultures in the age of an advancing globalization of the technology of music-making and -playing. Though accepting modern inventions, researchers often fail to cast off the romantic vision of a native living far away from technical civilization. The Mozart story is supposed to invite reflection on the necessity of choice-making in the global, technology-ridden world and on the various possibilities of assessing the decisions made in this world and their consequences (Lysloff 1997, 206).

Young Mozart, the protagonist of the story, meets time travelers. The visitors from the future want to exploit the natural and cultural resources of 18th-century Europe, offering in return cheap mass-produced goods, trade exchange, and – severely limited – scientific knowledge. Similarly to his peers, Mozart is taken in by the appeal of media and popular music brought by the travelers. Listening to the radio and tapes, he quickly learns rock music. Under the influence of new impressions, he casts his wig and period garments away, puts on jeans and sunshades, and starts smoking hashish. Soon he becomes a rock star and enjoys far more success than his brilliant compositions earned him in real world. Finally, he receives a "green card," which enables him emigrate to the future, where his music makes it to top-ten charts.

One way to look at Mozart in this story is to regard him as a tragic character whose grand future as a brilliant composer of classical music is all but wrecked by the arrival of the time travelers. Researchers who adopt an analogous perspective believe that the development of technology empties cultures of symbolic meanings, while only offering fleeting entertainment fads in return. They construe the postcolonial age as a time of virtual colonization: traditional cultures and their musics, which are not sufficiently protected by copyright, are vulnerable to commercial colonizers who come armed with modern technologies.

However, another way to look at Mozart is to consider him a hero who wisely taps into this situation's possibilities: after all, he avoids death in poverty and even becomes a star of the future. Such a reading of the composer's character in the story is a metaphor for contemporary local communities whose musics had inevitable extinction prognosticated to them by anthropologists but a while ago. In fact, there are several instances which powerfully showcase the music of such groups as gaining an increasingly stronger position and reviving in global and transnational contexts.

Bibliography

Bhabha, Homi. *Miejsca kultury*. Translated by Tomasz Dobrogoszcz. Cracow: Wydawnictwo Uniwersytetu Jagiellońskiego, 2010.

Bohlman, Philip. "World Music at the *End of History.*" *Ethnomusicology*, vol. 46, part 1, 2002, pp. 1–32.

Erlmann, Veit. "The Aesthetics of the Global Imagination: Reflections on World Music in the 1990s." *Public Culture*, vol. 8, part 3, 1996, pp. 467–487.

Guilbault, Jocelyne. "Interpreting World Music: A Challenge in Theory and Practice." *Popular Music*, vol. 16, part 1, 1997, pp. 31–44.

Lysloff, René T. A. "Mozart in Mirrorshades: Ethnomusicology, Technology, and the Politics of Representation."; *Ethnomusicology*, vol. 41, part 2, 1997, pp. 206–219.

Monson, Ingrid. "Riffs, Repetition, and Theories of Globalization."; *Ethnomusicology*, vol. 43, part 1, 1999, p. 31–65.

Pacini, Deborah H. "A View from the South Spanish Caribbean Perspectives on World Beat." *The World of Music*, vol. 35, 1993, pp. 48–60.

Slobin, Mark; "Micromusics of the West: A Comparative Approach." *Ethnomusicology*, vol. 36, part 1, 1992, pp. 1–86.

PART 2

Cultural History of Globalization

∴

The authors of articles in the second part of the volume scrutinize cultural phenomena which are analyzed by means of tools used in global studies. Mirosław Kocur expands performance studies by adding a globally and historically oriented perspective. Stanisław Rosik uses the global-studies perspective to analyze medieval sources. Piotr Badyna looks for manifestations of globality in the work of Charles Darwin. Magdalena Barbaruk's article concerns the "Spanish Crisis of the 17th Century" and depicts two dominant approaches to this development, both of them associated with globalization in their separate ways. Tadeusz Paleczny's text is devoted to examining nation-building processes in Latin American countries.

CHAPTER 4

Towards Historical Performatics?

Gesture as the Origin of Speech. A Case Study

Mirosław Kocur

In its Anglo-American iteration, performatics focuses on the contemporary performance perceived in terms of an "event." I propose extending this field of study by including a historical perspective. The performative approach is perfectly suited for reconstructing past – even pre-historic – events. This, however, requires expanding research competences quite considerably. Since its very onset, the methodology of performance studies has been intrinsically eclectic. Historical performatics picks up and continues this tendency, for it is not a "historical" science in the strict sense of the term. The point is that, instead of interpreting and explaining events, performatics seeks to reconstruct them. Additionally, this reconstruction takes place at various levels and in various areas. To better grasp the strategies of the research method I put forward, let us use a case study, specifically, a short reconstruction of an event which was critical to the evolution of our species – the emergence of spoken language.

The use of speech is what sets humans apart from all other creatures that inhabit the Earth. Even the simplest material cultures, such as the Pirahã of the Amazon rainforest have developed their own speech (Everett 2005), whereas no ape species, not even the most intelligent primates, can talk, even though they relatively effectively communicate in other ways, including gestures. Could gesticulation be the source of speech? The findings of several recent studies suggest that this was exactly the case. Deriving speech form gesture also appears to be justified in the performatic perspective (Kocur 2008). A performer, after all, is not merely an orator, but above all an actor, in its original sense of a doer.

Research on the origin of the human species is a global phenomenon today. Concerted excavations are in progress in Africa, Europe, and Asia. Ethnographers study the behavior of peoples from the most remote corners of the inhabited world, collecting invaluable source materials for comparative studies. High-profile experiments are carried out and breakthrough discoveries are made at laboratories and universities across the globe. The findings are published in scores of increasingly more accessible journals and books. The disciplines whose insights point to gesture as the origin of speech range from paleoarcheology and paleoanthropology to primatology, developmental psychology, and neuroscience.

1 Apes and Humans

As perhaps the most obvious consequence of adopting an erect posture six to seven million years ago, the upper limbs no longer had to support the body while moving. What actions were the thus-freed arms and hands used to perform? Ardi, a recently famous early hominid specimen of the *Ardipithecus ramidus* species, spent a lot of time away from trees as early as 4.4 million years ago (for more information about Ardi, see *Science* 326, 2009). She did not construct tools. The earliest evidence of the use of worked stones dates back to 3.3 million years ago, which means that in all likelihood Lucy, an equally famous female Australopithecus that lived 3.2 million years ago (Johanson, Edey 1982), could produce tools. Without a doubt, hands were invaluably useful for gathering food or carrying infants. But could Lucy communicate with other Australopithecines by gestures?

Humans, as all primates, are predominantly visualizers. This may be a heritage of adaptation to living in the forest. Ardi spent most of her life up in the trees. The reasons for the domination of sight seem banal. Unable to see branches well when jumping, an individual with poor eyesight was likely to fall on the ground, possibly crashing dead and in this way preventing his or her genes from reproducing (Armstrong et al. 1995, 48). Performances corrected and stimulated evolutionary processes.

In primates, vision plays the key role in collecting information about the surrounding world (Armstrong, Wilcox 2007, 13). It also facilitates the establishment of relations among individuals. Primates regularly transmit and receive each other's messages by means of body postures, hand movements, and facial expressions. Inborn intentional gestures are ubiquitous in the animal world. They were already recognized by Darwin (1872), and first classified by Nikolaas "Niko" Tinbergen (1951), a Dutch ethologist and ornithologist who received the 1973 Nobel Prize, along with Karl von Frisch and Konrad Lorenz, for the work on animal behavior patterns. Intentional signals are as a rule but a first stage in a sequence of actions. An abbreviated token gesture is often enough to elicit the desired response, as illustrated by two males fighting for domination: one male forces the rival to budge by signaling biting through growling and baring his teeth, even though the actual biting rarely takes place. With such a signal behavior preceding a real attack and bite, both rivals enjoyed a considerable adaptive advantage. The weaker one had an opportunity to yield and survive, while the stronger one could avoid engaging in a risky showdown. Consequently, with time, fang-baring was evolutionarily inscribed in the genes as an instinctive gesture. Inborn behavior more often than not serves as a demonstration.

Pioneering comparative research on the behavior of apes and humans was carried out by Michael Tomasello of the Max Planck Institute of Evolutionary Anthropology in Leipzig. Besides instinctive gestures, Tomasello has identified ritual gestures of primate apes, i.e., specific intentional signals which must be learned and which serve communication (Tomasello et al. 1985, 1994, 1997, 1989; Call, Tomasello 2007; Tomasello 2008). The repertoire of ritual gestures is very rich and heterogeneous. Even within one species, multiple distinct signals can be developed by its members. Individuals as a rule use one gesture for various communication tasks and different gestures for the same task. Signals are only produced when their potential recipients are appropriately attentive, and their reactions are always monitored in expectation of their response. When the reactions are inappropriate, the sender of the signal repeats the gesture in rhythmic sequences or in combination with other gestures.

Tomasello has divided intentional gestures into attention-drawing activities and intentional signals proper (Call, Tomasello 2007). The former have so far been identified exclusively in primate apes. Chimpanzees summon their mates' attention by patting the ground, nudging, hurling an object, or clapping their hands. When they want to be groomed, they position themselves with their backs right in front of the selected individual's eyes. This strategy is also used by apes to evade an attention-calling gesture. In one experiment, a woman holding food behind her back turned to face an ape. The animal immediately gestured toward the woman. However, when she turned back on the animal, the ape moved round the woman and gestured again towards her face (Liebal et al. 2004).

Popular intentional signals which propose playing together include arm-raising and head-nodding. Young chimpanzees touch their parents' backs when they want a piggyback ride, and place their hands beneath their mothers' mouths when they are hungry. In order to initiate a shared stroll, the hand is put on a mate's back. Apes must learn all these gestures, but this happens through individual experimentation rather than through the imitation of other individuals. This is one of Tomasello's crucial findings.

New gestures are mastered through repetition and ritualization (Tomasello et al. 1994, 1997; Call, Tomasello 2007; Tomasello 2008). There are basically no systematic gestural differences between groups of primate apes in captivity, though differences in the behavior of individuals within a group are observable. Individuals often develop gestures which they have had no chance of watching. Young animals in captivity and at large perform several similar gestures not because they have picked them from their older mates, but because they engage in similar group activities, such as playing together. In an experiment, a young chimpanzee was separated from his group and trained to perform a new gesture in return for food. Having rejoined the group, the chimpanzee continued to use this gesture to obtain food, but none of the other apes took over this behavior from him (Tomasello et al. 1997).

All the conducted and reported experiments concern exclusively gesticulations. Primate apes that are in regular contact with humans easily invent or learn new kinds of gestures, but they are unable to master new ways of vocalization. Nobody has succeeded in teaching an ape to produce a new sound yet (Tomasello, Zuberbühler 2002). This is another paramount finding. Gesture appears to fulfill a more fundamental communicative function than voice does. Vocalizations predominantly serve primates to express emotions (Lieberman 1998; Premack 2004; Tomasello, Call 1997); however, these communications as a rule are not intended to turn other individuals' attention to an incident or an object. When perceiving danger, apes scream out, because they are scared, and not because they want to warn the group. Vocal displays of apes practically do not differ much from vocal displays of other mammals (Tomasello 2008, 53–54).

Intentional gesticulations of apes have limited applications. According to Tomasello, chimpanzees always communicate their intentions in the form of an imperative demand and can only understand others' gestures if they are imperatives as well. They do not collaborate with others towards a common goal to such an extent as young human children do. They are egoists. When chimpanzees hunt an animal together, there is no perceptible communication of intentions concerning the joint action among them. When the prey is killed, the individual closest to the carcass often tries to steal the meat, either chasing the others away or climbing to the top of the branch to block others access to it (Gilby 2006; cf. Goodall 1986). Their competitive nature, makes it difficult for chimpanzees to share food and to cooperate. As Tomasello argues in several studies, this lack of collaboration differentiates apes from humans. Humans are capable of implementing undertakings which are underpinned by common intentions and geared to a shared goal. Therein Tomasello draws on the classic theory of human communication acts proposed years ago by Paul Grice (1957), an eminent philosopher of language, born in Birmingham and deceased in Berkeley. Grice observed that when a human being directs another human being's attention toward an object or an event, s/he simultaneously communicates his/her own desire for attention, for example, to his/her enthusiasm or need of support. In this respect, the behavior of apes is not straightforward. Chimpanzees seem to be capable of altruism (Warneken, Tomasello 2006; Warneken et al. 2006) and even of interaction (de Waal, Lutrell 1988).

Adam Kendon (2004, 107), the world's most renowned body language specialist today, regards pointing and pantomiming (i.e., iconic gesture) as the most natural and typical human gestures. Pointing directs the recipient's attention to something that is usually visible. Pantomiming directs the recipient's imagination toward something that as a rule cannot be seen through a behavior which simulates an action, a relationship, or an object (Tomasello 2008, 61). Despite several attempts which have continued since the ancient Roman times (Kocur 2018, 180–195), a more precise and more universally endorsed classification of human gestures has not been developed yet.

2   Deictic Gesture: Pointing

Pointing is a complete communicative act. The effectiveness of pointing is vividly exemplified by one of the most famous American posters in which Uncle Sam, his index finger extended, appeals to Americans to join the army. According to the official website of the U.S. Congress Library, the recruitment image of Uncle Sam made its first appearance on 6th July, 1916. Designed by James Montgomery Flagg (1877–1960), it was put on the cover of *Leslie's Weekly*. First copies of the poster began to be mass-produced in 1917, just before the U.S. joined World War One. By the end of the war, over four million copies had been made. Because the image on the poster enjoyed enormous popularity, it was also used during World War Two. "Uncle Sam" is one of the most widespread personifications of the U.S. Its historical model was probably provided by a meat packer who worked for supply services during the British-American war of 1812. His name was Samuel (Uncle Sam) Wilson (1766–1854), and he was purportedly characterized by exceptional fairness, honesty, and love of his homeland. Today, the famous poster is one of the greatest treasures of the U.S. Congress Library.

The indicating gesture has been conventionally associated with an extended index finger since Antiquity. Quintilian (*Institutio oratoria* 11.3.94) emphasized that the Latin name of the finger (*index*) was derived from its major function of pointing. *Digitus index* also features in Horace's texts (*Saturae* 2.8.26).

Andrea de Jorio, a pioneer of modern gesture research and the author of the now classic study *La mimica degli antichi invetsigata nel gestire napoletano* (published in 1832), identified seven pointing or indicating gestures (Italian: *additare*) which were used by his contemporary Neapolitans and, partly at least, already recognized by ancient Romans (de Jorio 2000, 70–74; cf. Kendon, Versante 2003):

1. The index finger only extended and directed to some object.
2. Eyes turned toward the object.
3. The elbow tap. To argue for the ancient roots of this gesture, de Jorio cites Horace (*Saturae* 1.9.63): "*Vellere coepi et pressare manu lentissima*

bracchia, nutans, distorquens oculos, ut me eriperet" / "I began to twitch his cloak and squeeze his arms – they were quite unfeeling – nodding and winking hard for him to save me."
4. Light tapping of the feet.
5. Cough, which was already known as such to Ovid (*Heroides* 21.24): *"Excreat, et ficta dat mihi signa nota"*/"She clears her throat and thus gives me the sign agreed upon."
6. The thumb directed toward the object, a gesture mentioned by Quintilian (*Institutio oratoria* 11.3.104-15): *"Verso pollice demonstrare aliquid, receptum magis puto, quam oratori decorum"*/"To point at something with the thumb turned back is a gesture which is in general use, but is not in my opinion, becoming to an orator."
7. The index finger being moved upwards many times.

As early as two centuries ago, de Jorio, a canon at the Cathedral of Naples, noticed that not all pointing is done by the index finger. The head, the eyes, and/or the thumb could also be used. An indigenous people of Panama, the Cuna, who inhabit the San Blas Islands, perform this gesture with their lips. They raise their heads, their eyes fixed in the direction to which they want to turn somebody's attention, and at the same time open their mouths wide. At the end, they close their mouths and lower their heads to the initial position (Sherzer 1973).

The indicating, deictic gesture (from Greek *deíknumai*, "to show") is known in all human communities. Leonard Rolfe (1995, 1996) has identified three criteria of deixis:
1. dialogicity – the gesture presupposes an audience and is advantageous to another person;
2. referentiality – the gesture singles out something that the addressee comprehends as an object of reference;
3. directionality – the direction of pointing is perceived as an extension of the stretched-out hand.

Thus-defined pointing is one of the earliest means of communication used by infants. It appears around eleven months of age, a few weeks before first spoken words. From the twelfth month of age on, pointings are accompanied by vocalizations (Butterworth 2003; Masataka 2003). How this gesture is used by infants affects their later language competences (Goldin-Meadow, Butcher 2003). The lack of such a behavior is an important factor in diagnosing autism in children (Baron-Cohen 1993). Midway through the second year of life, infants become capable of following gestures and sight of other people who point to distant objects (Adamson 1996; Butterworth 2003; Franco, Butterworth 1996). Called "joint attention" by developmental psychologists, this capacity is recognized by multiple scholars as critical to the emergence of language (Bruner 1983; Baldwin, Moses 1996; Hauser et al. 2002; Davidson 2003; Tomasello 2003) and as a distinctively and exclusively human adaptation (Butterworth, Grover 1988; Corbalis 1991; Donald 1991; Gómez et al. 1993; Tomasello 2002, 87; Povinelli et al. 2003).

Joint attention is reported to have appeared along with the first hominids, that is, about seven million years ago, when chimpanzees split off from the Hominidae (Hauser et al. 2002). As an erect posture was adopted and the mass of the brain increased, the period of infants' dependence on caregivers extended, which radically modified the conditions of learning and knowledge transmission. Bipedalism favored a slim body with the narrow pelvis, resulting in the reduction of the diameter of the birth canal. Endurance running, which was a major hunting method, reinforced these adaptations. At the same time, moving on two legs stimulated the development of the brain. As a consequence, babies had to be born increasingly earlier for their growing neurocrania to pass through the narrowing birth canal. The protracted and stronger dependence of the infant on the mother promoted the development of joint attention.

This scenario envisages distinct evolutionary trajectories of hominids and primate apes. Researchers, such as Tomasello, stress that exclusively humans can perform complete deictic gestures, because apes do not share joint attention. Nevertheless, empirical observations are less than unambiguous in this respect. Certain behavior patterns displayed by wild apes at large can be interpreted as spontaneous pointing gestures (Inoue-Nakamura, Matsuzawa 1997; Veà, Sabater-Pi 1998). For example, Simone Pika and John Mitani (2006, 2009), who observed apes in Uganda and saw them scratch the exact spots they wanted their mates to groom, concluded that this gesture was deictic.

Wild apes seem to be capable of manipulation in order to obtain something in possession of their mates. Mothers sometimes share food with their young, but it is never their own initiative (Ueno 2006; Nishida, Turner 1996; Bard 1992; Goodall 1986). Yet wild apes have never been observed to give each other clear signals concerning object remote from the two communicating individuals.

Apes' gesticulations in captivity resemble human behavior far more than at large (Leavens et al. 2009). Like human children, apes (Golinkoff 1986) are not discouraged by failures in communication (Cartmill, Byrne 2007; Leavens et al. 2004, 2005; Poss et al. 2006), and likewise (Bakeman, Adamson 1986; O'Neill 1996) modify their behavior depending on the degree of their mates' attention (Bodamer, Gardner 2002; Hostetter et al. 2001; Krause, Fouts 1997; Leavens et al. 2004; Liebal et al. 2004; Pika et al. 2003, 2005; Tomasello et al. 1994). When alone, apes do not extend their hands to food beyond their reach, so their pointing gestures are not a desperate attempt at grabbing food (Leavens et al. 1996, 2004; Poss et al. 2006). Most of the observed behavior of apes is spontaneous.

These research findings suggest that apes use deictic gestures when circumstances compel such behavior. In captivity, their movement opportunities are limited. Human infants around one year of age find themselves in similar circumstances, as they are capable of joint attention and of recognizing remote objects, but their motor capacities are still restricted (Leavens et al. 1996, 2009). In such conditions, pointing is perfectly useful. As apes in captivity and at large often belong to the same groups, and their gene pools are identical, the development of deictic gestures in captivity is affected environmentally rather than genetically. The capacity to direct another individual's attention to a specific object may be a skill which primate apes and humans share. Evolutionary adaptation to joint attention could have occurred long before language (Hauser et al. 2002; Leavens et al. 2009). The last common ancestor of all primates lived about fifteen million years ago (Schrago, Russo 2003). Infants are capable of joint attention before they make their first pointing gesture (Carpenter et al. 1998).

3 Iconic Gesture: Pantomiming

On 30th July 1980, the superb Polish athlete Władysław Kozakiewicz won the gold medal in pole vault at the summer Olympics in Moscow. The Russians left no stone unturned to help their home favorite Konstantin Volkov win the competition. When the Polish pole vaulter was taking his jumps, the organizers tried to change the wind direction by opening and closing the stadium gates. The public was booing and whistling. Despite that, Kozakiewicz not only defeated his heavily favored rival, but also broke the world record by clearing 5.78 meters. After his winning attempt, the Pole showed to the hostile Russian crowd and TV viewers worldwide what has since come to be referred to as "Kozakiewicz's gesture" – a classic iconic gesture expressing his resentment of the stratagems of the hosts. Specifically, with his left arm outstretched and his fist clenched, he raised his underarm at the same time energetically slamming his right hand in his left inner elbow. The very term "Kozakiewicz's gesture," conveying protest and disdain, has become a permanent and popular fixture among Polish colloquial lexemes (Lubaś 2004, 54).

Kozakiewicz's gesture is a typical phallic sign. In antiquity, a fully extended thumb fulfilled a similar function. According to Macrobius (*Saturnalia* 7.13.14), the thumb was called *pollex* (from *polleo*) "because of its strength." Stretching one's thumb up was associated with the phallus in erection. This was the gesture which the audience at Rome's amphitheater used to demand that a gladiator be killed. Poking one's thumb between the middle and index finger – i.e. a popular "fig sign" – was supposed to protect one's against evil (Kocur 2018, 188).

To properly interpret iconic gestures, one must understand relevant contexts, though the comprehension of gestures as such does not depend on language. Iconic gestures precede speech. Deaf children freely communicate using them, long before they master sign language (Goldin-Meadow 2003). As several iconic gestures consist in imitating activities or actions, such behavior is often called pantomiming. Common examples of pantomiming include the gesture performed by the airport security control staff when they make a circle with their hand to suggest that a passenger should turn around. Iconic gestures may also evoke objects. In Moscow, Kozakiewicz "showed" a phallus in erection.

Contrary to the deictic gesture, which as a rule refers to a present and visible object or event, the iconic gesture – pantomiming – generally evokes something that is not there. This gesture presents and represents something by means of body movements. Tomasello (2008) states that it takes special mental competences to perform a pantomime which is understandable to others; for example one must be able to differentiate between a real event and an imitation of it. Merlin Donald (1991) has called the culture of primate apes episodic as opposed to the imitational, mimetic culture of humans. Episodic culture is founded on episodic and procedural memory. Animals are capable of repeating a series of activities (especially if it leads to obtaining food), remembering an event, and making a meaningful gesture, but this behavior will always be linked to particular situations and will never be combined into one model of reality conveyable in an iconic gesture.

According to Tomasello, pantomiming was partly replaced by conventions of spoken language, which channeled the creative explosion of modern humans. Creativity is a very important dimension of iconic gestures (Tomasello 2008; Magno Caldognetto, Poggi 1995; Crais et al. 2009). It often takes considerable ingenuity to perform a short pantomime. Several years ago, I set out on a cycling trip to visit the utopian city of Auroville near Puducherry in South India. Having ridden a few kilometers, I had to dismount and push the bike through tall grass, as the road disappeared. Suddenly, a man emerged from a grove and started pantomiming energetically to me. His display involved bouncing, throwing his arms up and down, putting the hand to the mouth, and constantly repeating a waving arm movement concluded with the freezing of the extended hand. I understood his message right away. I froze and did not even try to say a word. The man immediately calmed down. Now, he commanded me to keep still and slowly lower my head. I looked down. A huge cobra was crawling between my legs.

Mastering iconic gestures effectively enhances communicative skills. Imitation plays a number of important social roles (Užgiris 1981; Carpenter 2006). It is one of the major engines driving efficient and fast education. Around one year of age, children develop the capacity to understand adults' behavior. They can identify actions as well as their outcomes and purposes, also recognizing their situational contexts. This information serves them later to imitate observed behavior. As a rule, children faithfully re-enact actions performed by adults. According to researchers from the mentalist movement, human imitation includes two components which are absent from animal behavior: understanding other people's mental states and motivation to share mental states with others (Carpenter, Call 2009). For their part, apes only exhibit a limited understanding of others and little motivation for co-feeling (Behne et al. 2008). Given this, apes appear to imitate instrumentally in order to benefit from it (Carpenter, Call 2002; Tomasello, Carpenter 2007).

Repeating others' behavior is a key factor in the transmission of fundamental cultural practices, such as beliefs, rituals, and language conventions (Gergely, Csibra 2006; Tomasello 2002). Recognizing that others are similar to me reinforces my cultural identity (Meltzoff 1995, 2005). Perhaps the chief difference between humans and all other animals lies not so much in that humans speak, but rather in that they are capable of imitation (Blackmore 1999), of *mimesis*, which as was acknowledge as the source of all arts as early as in ancient Greece.

4 Gesture as the Origin of Language

In broad lines, there are two major scientific positions on the origin of human language. Some scholars consider language a unique achievement of the human species, while others view language as deriving from the gesticulation or vocalization of primate apes. The former position was somewhat reformulated a few years ago. Marc Hauser, Noam Chomsky, and Tecumseh Fitch (2002) stated that human language differed from animal language in one crucial property, specifically in recursion, which made it possible to produce an infinite number of expressions using a finite set of elements. They also concluded that the recursive system had developed as a result of natural selection from prior structures which had evolved for other reasons than communication. Two other American scholars, Steven Pinker and Ray Jackendoff (2005), argued that recursion must be complemented with other aspects of language, which they believed were distinctively human, such as phonology (articulation of speech sounds), morphology (principles for combining words and suffixes into longer words), and the anatomical features of the vocal apparatus.

To posit that gesture was the primary language of humans is not a novel idea. This stance has long been embraced by eminent thinkers and researchers, including the French philosopher Étienne Bonnot de Condillac (1746), the Scottish economic theorist and researcher of Polynesian languages John Rae (1862), the British anthropologist Edward Burnett Tylor (1868, 1871), the American anthropologist Lewis Henry Morgan (1877, 35–36), the British naturalist Alfred Russel Wallace (1881, 1895), the Canadian-born evolutionary biologist George John Romanes (1888), the German founder of experimental psychology Wilhelm Wundt (1912), the British baronet and lawyer Sir Richard Arthur Surtees Paget (1930, 1944), and the Rector of Reykjavik's University of Iceland Jóhannesson (1944, 1949, 1950). Following Wallace, Paget and Jóhannesson believed that lips, teeth, and the tongue "imitated" movements of the hand and other body parts engaged in communication or manipulation. This hypothesis gained a considerable popularity, and several scholars sought to corroborate it by pointing out similarities of word roots in unrelated languages. This was supposed to prove the existence of semantic and phonetic universals (Taylor, Taylor 1962; Holland, Wertheimer 1964; Weiss 1966).

In the second part he 20th century, another chapter in the debate on the genesis of language was commenced by the American anthropologist Gordon Hewes (1973), whose "Primate communications and gestural origin of language" appeared in *Current Anthropology*. In response to this paper, the Dutch ethologist Adriaan Kortlandt cited an illuminating anecdote from his own field research in Congo. In spring 1960, Kortlandt began regular observations of chimpanzees, himself hiding in two observation stations constructed among trees at the edge of the rainforest and a papaya plantation. From his concealment, he could freely watch the behavior of animals who were searching for food at the plantation. There was a human settlement about two hundred meters away. While observing chimpanzees, Kortlandt could hear the shouts and laughs of children at play. Young chimpanzees also indulged in similar and equally vivacious play, yet they always did that in silence. Solely grown-up individual erupted in hoots, shrieks, and howls every now and then, unlike adults in the village, whom Kortlad almost never heard. Why were the young chimps silent? After all, they coo soon after they are born, just as human infants do. They fall silent when they begin to crawl on their fours. Kortlandt supposed that it was an evolutionary adaptation, as young chimpanzees are hunted by leopards. Village children make noise because they feel safe. The terrifying clamor raised by adult chimpanzees was interpreted by Kortlandt as a deterring measure. To prove this hypothesis, he carried out a series of experiments using a stuffed leopard. At the sight of the dummy, the apes would raise a terrible din, and when it was too close to the chimpanzees' current abode, the adult individuals attacked it with enormous aggression and annihilated it, smashing it with powerful clubs (Kortlandt 1966, 1967).

This episode makes the impact of environmental conditions on primate behavior palpable indeed. Vocalizations have a limited range of functions in natural conditions. In the evolution of chimpanzees, silence could have had a significant impact on the formation of the language of communication. Of course, one anecdote is by far not enough to draw any legitimate conclusions about the behavior of early hominids. Kortlandt was tempted into this trap when he claimed that Australopithecines communicated by whispering. The discovery and reconstruction of Ardi's skeleton vividly admonish us not to jump to conclusions based on analogies between humans and primate apes. When walking on their fours, hominids did not lean on their knuckles, unlike most apes.

Several experiments have confirmed that apes learn and use gestures in varied and creative ways, which stands in stark contrast with their fixed and stereotypical repertoire of vocalizations. Is this enough evidence to claim, as for example Tomasello (2008, 329) does, that apes' behavior powerfully substantiates the idea of the gestural origin of our distant ancestors' speech? Stronger evidence seems to be offered by the behavior of humans themselves. Initiated by William Stokoe (1960), breakthrough research on sign language has shown that the language of gestures may have structures and grammar as complex as spoken language does.

When the Nicaraguan Sign Language appeared in the 1980s, i.e., relatively recently, scholars had an opportunity to follow "live" the birth of a mature language (Polich 2005). Before the Sandinistas acceded to power in 1979, Nicaragua did not have a sign language. The Nicaraguan deaf did not form any community and lived in isolation. Admittedly, the first special school was founded as early as in 1946, but it had merely ten students. It was only in 1980 that the Sandinistas opened a trade school for deaf youngsters from all over the country in Managua, Nicaragua's capital and biggest city. Education was primarily based on oral instruction, and its effects were rather paltry. The children, however, gesticulated and used gestures to communicate behind their teachers' backs and outside of school. They quickly developed their own communication system. While their first gestures resembled iconic signs, i.e., pantomiming (Spanish: *mimicas*), after 1983 the students had a fully-fledged sign language at their disposal (Kegl et al. 1999). The development of the Nicaraguan Sign Language (*Idioma de Señas Nikaragüense*) was the first documented birth of a natural human language. The process itself was surprisingly quick.

The second generation of the users of this language could already freely use hand movements in space to give their utterances a grammatical structure, which is typical of sign language. Most enunciations ended with a verb, resembling the convention of another sign language which has recently been invented at a small Bedouin village in the Negev Desert, Israel (Sandler et al. 2005). Examples of spontaneous births of sign languages in our times strongly indicate that similar processes could also have taken place in the past. Inferably, gesticulations can easily morph into a complete communicative system of complex grammar.

How could gesture language transform into speech? This continues to be "Achilles' heel" of the hypothesis that gesture preceded vocalization. Perhaps enhanced motor activity stimulated some genetic mutations which promoted the development of vocalization (Armstrong, Wilcox 2007, 38). Human vocal capabilities are predicated on motor capacities which are not found in great apes (Lieberman 1984). This involves the monitoring and correction of operations of such organs as the larynx, the tongue, and the mouth. The human vocal apparatus as a whole is comprised of about forty muscles. Their effective working is linked to the correct function of FOXP2 protein, a gene which regulates the functions of other genes (Lai et al. 2001). FOXP2 was discovered by chance. A London-based family, dubbed KE, has reported serious speech and language impairments over three generations (Hurst et al. 1990). They have difficulty controlling and coordinating facial and mouth muscles, which fundamentally thwarts their correct sound articulation. They also have problems with writing and grammar. They cannot pull in the tongue while closing the lips. They struggle when trying to repeat two-word sentences; nor can they identify phonemes in a word. They score low in intelligence tests (Vargha-Kadem et al. 1995; Alcock et al. 2000a; Watkins et al. 2002). They are better at recognizing and repeating tunes, but their sense of rhythm is disturbed, and they are unable to reproduce a sequence of sounds either vocally or manually. Rhythm disorders seem to be the major source of their language difficulties (Alcock et al. 2000b).

The gene whose dysfunction causes these problems in half of the KE family has been identified by researchers from Oxford's Trust Center for Human Genetics. FOXP2 is this gene. It is located on 7q31(Fisher et al. 1998; Lai et al. 2001). Researchers named it FOXP2 because of its similarity to DNA-binding proteins from the family called the "winged helix" or the *forkhead box*, hence the FOX abbreviation (Carlsson, Mahlapuu 2002). The FOXP2 gene consists of sequences of about one hundred amino acids which control the expression of other genes, i.e., the decoding and transcription of genetic information. In the KE family, one of the two copies of FOXP2 inherited from parents is damaged, so only half of the gene is decoded and reproduced (Diller, Cann 2009).

The FOXP2 gene regulates the embryonic development of basal ganglia (Lai et al. 2003; Haesler et al. 2004), i.e., the part of the brain which is a key factor in language-related cognitive and motor operations (Lieberman 2000). It is also responsible for the development of other vital organs, therein of the lungs, the heart, and the intestines (Lai et al. 2001; Shu et al. 2001). Experiments using functional brain imaging have confirmed that FOXP2 plays a critical role in the development of language and speech (Liégeois et al. 2003; Vargha-Khadem et al. 2005). Damage of this gene prevents neural networks from carrying out complex sequential tasks.

FOXP2 is the first gene known to be involved in the development of vocalization. It has also been identified in birds (Haesler et al. 2004), mice (Shu et al. 2005), and echo-locating bats (Li et al. 2007). In songbirds, the FOXP2 gene controls the regions of the brain which are responsible for learning their song sequences (Haesler et al. 2004; see Teramitsu et al. 2004; see Wada et al. 2006). If one copy of it is removed from a newly born mouse, its ultrasound capacity is severely reduced, and if both copies are removed, vocalization is entirely missing and the animal soon dies. FOXP2 in mice and in humans only differs by three mutations (Enard et al. 2002). There are only two mutations dividing humans from chimpanzees, and we share one of them with wolves and tigers (Zhang et al. 2002). Comparisons of the sequences of FOXP2 nucleotides and amino acids in humans, great apes, and other placentalia have shown that the FOXP2 gene is among five percent of the most conservative and thus little mutating proteins, which implies that the gene plays a fundamental role in mammals. It is even more crucial to humans. Various human populations do not exhibit any variations in the amino acid configuration: the FOXP2 gene is fixed and identical in all humans (Enard et al. 2002; Zhang et al. 2002).

The FOXP2 gene is dated to about 70 million years ago, when the common ancestor of mice and primates lived. When did the two crucial mutations appear in humans? Researchers initially supposed that language had been part of the "creative explosion" (Pfeiffer 1982), which occurred fifty thousand years ago. However, a human version of the FOXP2 gene has recently been found in the remains of Neanderthals. Consequently, the dating of the mutation had to be moved back to the times of the common ancestor of *Homo sapiens* and *Homo neanderthalensis*, that is, about 660,000 years ago. The idea of the revolution thus gave way to an evolutionary process. Karl Diller and Rebecca Cann (2009) of the University of Hawai'i comprehensively argued for dating the mutation even earlier – to 1.8 or even 1.9 million years ago. This was when a tool-producing *Homo erectus* appeared, fully capable of endurance running and furnished with a brain at least three times as big as the brain of the chimpanzee or of the Australopithecus. New anatomical adaptations not only promoted the capacity to run long, but also stimulated the development of manual skills. *Homo erectus* could hew stones into perfectly symmetrical forms. Enhanced gesticulations could have fostered the activity of facial muscles. In apes, hand motions are often accompanied by facial grimacing and vocalizations (Pollick, de Waal 2007). Though compelling, this analogy alone cannot lend grounding to a reliable theory.

The emergence of FOXP2 mutations nearly two million years ago may suggest not so much a hereditary speech organ (Hauser et al. 2002) as rather the evolutionary adaptation of hominid anatomy to richer and more complex communication. Speech made it possible to give names to individuals and objects, consumed less energy than manual gestures, freed hands for the production of tools and the development of technology, was an effective means of communication in darkness and challenging conditions, and did not require special attention from the recipient (Corballis 2002, 186–192; Armstrong, Wilcox 2007, 38). By means of speech, humans are capable of transmitting phonetic signals at the speed of twenty to thirty segments per second (Liberman et al. 1967).

Of course, the FOXP2 gene could not guarantee the emergence and development of speech all by itself. Nevertheless, its discovery seems to prove that syntax and human creativity are determined by neural mechanisms which were initially adapted to motor control and stimulated by endurance running. Similar nerve-cell systems fostered the human capacity for cultural practices as different as dancing or composing music (Lieberman 2007).

Summing up, the case for the gestural origin of language is grounded on the following findings:

1. Primate apes inherit vocalization, but they learn gesticulation.
2. Fundamentally different brain mechanisms control vocalization in people and in great apes (Jürgens 2002).
3. Human gestures – pointing and pantomiming – developed as a result of cooperation/socialization.
4. Pointing is a natural gesture and originates in the natural human tendency to follow sight.
5. Pantomiming stimulates imitating.
6. Language conventions are arbitrary and could develop faster from the complex structures produced while gesticulating than from modest and little flexible vocalizations.
7. FOXP-2, a gene that controls "vocal gestures," mutated 1.9 million years ago, enabling hominids to more efficiently use their bodies and facial muscles in communication.
8. New spectacular discoveries in neuroscience prove that cognitive processes are inseparable from motor performances.

5 Conclusion

This survey of major arguments supporting the hypothesis that speech originated from gesture was meant to showcase the richness and multifariousness of the contemporary science of man. The study of culture cannot be limited to axiology alone. Culture also develops through linguistic and bodily performances. In order to understand the source of these performances today, we must study anatomy, genetics, anthropology, and even archaeology. Performatics, an eclectic and weakly defined science, may excellently complement the classic knowledge of culture. The perception of the world as a network of events stimulates the development of new competences.

Bibliography

Adamson, Lauren N. *Communication Development During Infancy*. Boulder, Colorado: Westview Press, 1996.

Alcock, Katherine J., Richard E. Passingham, Kate Watkins, and Faraneh Vargha-Khadem. "Oral Dyspraxia in Inherited Speech and Language Impairment and Acquired Dysphasia." *Brain and Language*, vol. 75, 2000a, pp. 17–33.

Alcock, Katherine, Richard E. Passingham, Kate Watkins, and Faraneh Vargha-Khadem. "Pitch and Timing Abilities in Inherited Speech and Language Impairment." *Brain and Language*, vol. 75, 2000b, pp. 34–46.

Ambrosius Aurelius Theodosius Macrobius. *The Saturnalia*. Translated by P. V. Davies. London and New York: Columbia University Press, 1969.

Armstrong, David F., William C. Stokoe, and Sherman E. Wilcox. *Gesture and the Nature of Language*. Cambridge: Cambridge University Press 1995.

Armstrong, David F., and Sherman E. Wilcox. *The gestural origin of language*. Oxford: Oxford University Press 2007.

Bakeman, Robert, and Lauren B. Adamson. "Infants' Conventionalized Acts. Gestures and Words with Mothers and Peers." *Infant Behavior and Development*, no. 9, 1986, pp. 215–230.

Baldwin, Dare A., and Louis J. Moses. "The Ontogeny of Social Information Gathering." *Child Development*, vol. 67, no. 5, 1996, pp. 1915–1939.

Bard, Kim A. "Intentional Behavior and Intentional Communication in Young Free-Ranging Orangutans." *Child Development*, vol. 62, no. 5, 1992, pp. 1186–1197.

Baron-Cohen, Simon. "From Attention-Goal Psychology to Belief-Desire Psychology. The Development of the Theory of Mind and its Dysfunction." In *Understanding Other Minds: Perspectives from Autism*. Edited by S. Baron-Cohen, H. Tager-Flusberg and D.J. Cohen. New York: Oxford University Press, 1993, pp. 59–82.

Behne, Tanya, Malinda Carpenter, Maria Gräfenhain, Kristian Liebal, Ulf Liszkowski, Henrike Moll, Hannes Rakoczy, Michael Tomasello, Felix Warneken, and Emily Wyman. "Cultural Learning and Cultural Creation." In *Social Life and Social Knowledge: Toward a Process Account of Development*. Edited by U. Müller, J.I.M. Carpendale, N. Budwig and B. Sokol. New York: Lawrence Erlbaum, 2008, pp. 65–101.

Blackmore, Susan. *The Meme Machine.* Oxford: Oxford University Press 1999.

Bodamer, Mark D., and Allen R. Gardner. "How Cross-Fostered Chimpanzees (Pan Troglodytes) Initiate and Maintain Conversations." *Journal of Comparative Psychology*, vol. 116, no. 1, 2002, pp. 12–26.

Bruner, Jerome S. *Child's Talk: Learning to Use Language.* Norton, New York: Oxford University Press, 1983.

Butterworth, George. "Pointing Is the Royal Road to Language for Babies." In *Pointing: Where Language, Culture, and Cognition Meet*. Edited by S. Kita. Mahwah. New Jersey: Lawrence Erlbaum, 2003, pp. 9–34.

Butterworth, George, and Lesley Grover. "The Origins of Referential Communication in Human Infancy." In *Thought Without Language*. Edited by L. Weiskrantz. Oxford: Clarendon Press, 1988, pp. 5–24.

Call, Josep, and Michael Tomasello M. (eds.). *The Gestural Communication of Apes and Monkeys*. Mahwah, New Jersey: Lawrence Erlbaum, 2007.

Carlsson, Peter, and Margit Mahlapuu; "Forkhead Transcription Factors. Key Players in Development and Metabolism." *Developmental Biology*, vol. 250, no. 1, 2002, pp. 1–23.

Carpenter, Malinda.; "Instrumental, Social, and Shared Goals and Intentions in Imitation" In *Imitation and the Development of the Social Mind: Lessons from Typical Development and Autism*. Edited by S.J. Rogers, and J. Williams. New York: Guilford, 2006, pp. 48–70.

Carpenter, Malinda, and Josep Call. "The Chemistry of Social Learning." *Developmental Science*, 2002, no. 5, pp. 22–24.

Carpenter, Malinda, and Josep Call. "Comparing the Imitative Skills of Children and Nonhuman Apes." *Revue de Primatologie*, no. 1, 2009, pp. 1–17.

Carpenter, Malinda, Katherine Nagell, and Michael Tomasello. "Social Cognition, Joint Attention and Communicative Competence from 9 to 15 Months of Age." *Monograph for the Society for Research in Child Development*, vol. 63, 1998.

Cartmill, Erica A., and Richard W. Byre. "Orangutans Modify Their Gesturing Signaling According to Their Audience's Comprehension." *Current Biology*, vol. 17, no. 15, 2007, pp. 1345–1348.

Condillac, Étienne B. de. *Essai sur l'origine des connaissances humaines, ouvrage ou l'on réduit à un seul principe tout ce concerne l'entendement*. Amsterdam: P. Mortier, 1746.

Corballis, Michael C. *The Lopsided Ape: Evolution of the Generative Mind*. New York: Oxford University Press, 1991.

Corballis, Michael C. *From Hand to Mouth: The Origin of Language*. Princeton: Princeton University Press, 2002.

Corballis, Michael C., and Carlos E. Roldan. "Detection of Symmetry as a Function of Angular Orientation." *Journal of Experimental Psychology. Human Perception and Performance*, vol. 3, no. 1, 1975, pp. 221–230.

Crais, Elizabeth R., Linda R. Watson, and Grace T. Baranek. "Use of Gestural Development in Profiling Children's Prelinguistic Communication Skills." *American Journal of Speech-Language Pathology*, vol. 18, 2009, pp. 95–108.

Darwin, Charles. *The Expression of Emotion in Man and Animals*. London: John Murray, Albemarle Street, 1872.

Davidson, Iain. "The Archeological Evidence of Language Origins. State of Art." In *Language evolution*. Edited by M.H. Christiansen, and S. Kirby. Oxford: Oxford University Press, 2003, pp. 140–157.

de Jorio, Andrea. *Gesture in Naples and Gesture in Classical Antiquity. A Translation of Andrea de Jorio's La Mimica Degli Antichi Investigate Nel Gestire Napoletano*. With an introduction and notes by A. Kendon. Bloomington and Indianapolis: Andrea Indiana University Press, 2000.

de Waal, Frans B.M., and Lesleigh Lutrell."Mechanisms of Social Reciprocity in Three Primate Species. Symmetrical Relationship Characteristics or Cognition?." *Ethology and Sociobiology*, no. 9, 1988, pp. 101–118.

Diller, Karl C., and Rebecca L. Cann. "Evidence Against a Genetic-Based Revolution in Language 50 000 Years Ago." In *The Cradle of Language*. Edited by R. Botha, and C. Knight. Oxford: Oxford University Press, 2009, pp. 135–149.

Donald, Merlin. *Origins of the Modern Mind. Three Stages in the Evolution of Culture and Cognition*. Cambridge, MA: Harvard University Press, 1991.

Enard, Wolfgang, Molly Przeworski, Simon E. Fisher, Cecilia S. L. Lai, Victor Wiebe, Takashi Kitano, Anthony P. Monaco, and Svante Pääbo. "Molecular Evolution of Foxp2, a Gene Involved in Speech and Language." *Nature*, vol. 418, 2002, pp. 869–872.

Everett, Daniel. "Cultural Constraints on Grammar and Cognition in Piraha: Another Look at the Design Features of Human Language." *Current Anthropology*, vol. 46, 2005, pp. 621–646.

Fisher, Simon E., Faraneh Vargha-Khadem, Kate E. Watkins, Anthony P. Monaco, and Marcus E. Pembrey. "Localisation of a Gene Implicated in a Severe Speech and Language Disorder." *Nature Genetics*, no. 18, 1998, pp. 168–170.

Franco, Fabia, and Georg Butterworth. "Pointing and Social Awareness. Declaring and Requesting in the Second Year." *Journal of Child Language*, vol. 23, no. 2, 1996, pp. 307–336.

Gergely, György, and Gergely Csibra. "Sylvia's Recipe. The Role of Imitation and Pedagogy in the Transmission of Cultural Knowledge." In *Roots of Human Sociality: Culture,*

Cognition, and Interaction. Edited by N. Enfield, and S. Levinson. Oxford: Berg, 2006, pp. 229–255.

Gilby, Ian C. "Meat Sharing Among the Gombe Chimpanzees. Harassment and Reciprocal Exchange." *Animal Behavior*, vol. 71, no. 4, 2006, pp. 953–963.

Goldin-Meadow, Susan. *The Resilience on Language: What Gesture Creation in Deaf Children Can Tell Us About How All Children Learn Language*. New York: Psychology Press, 2003.

Goldin-Meadow, Susan, and Cynthia Butcher. "Pointing Toward Two-Word Speech." In *Pointing: Where Language, Culture, and Cognition Meet*. Edited by S. Kita. Mahwah, New Jersey: Lawrence Erlbaum, 2003, pp. 85–107.

Golinkoff, Roberta M. "*I Beg You Pardon?* The Preverbal Negotiation of Failed Messages." *Journal of Child Language*, no. 13, 1986, pp. 455–476.

Gómez, J.C., E. Sarriá, and J. Tamari J. "The Comparative Study of Early Communication and Theories of Mind. Ontogeny, Phylogeny And Pathology." In *Understanding Other Minds: Perspectives from Autism*. Edited by S. Baron-Cohen, H. Tager-Flusberg and D.J. Cohen. New York: Oxford University Press, 1993, pp. 397–426.

Goodall, Jane. *The Chimpanzees of Gombe: Patterns of Behavior*. Cambridge, MA: Harvard University Press, 1986.

Grice, Paul. "Meaning." *Philosophical Review*, vol. 64, 1957, pp. 377–388.

Haesler, Sebastian, Kazuhiro Wada, A. Nshdejan, Edward E. Morrisey, Thierry Lints, Eric D. Jarvis, and Constance Scharff. "FoxP2 Expression in Avian Vocal Learners and Non-learners." *Journal of Neuroscience*, vol. 24, no. 13, 2004, pp. 3164–3175.

Hauser, Marc D., Noam Chomsky, and W. Tecumseh Fitch. "The Faculty of Language. What Is It, Who Has It, and How Did It Evolve?." *Science*, vol. 298, 2002, pp. 1569–1579.

Hewes, Gordon W. "Primate Communication and the Gestural Origin of Language." *Current Anthropology*, vol. 14, no. 1/2, 1973, pp. 5–24.

Holland, Morris K., and Michael Wertheimer. "Some Physiognomic Aspects of Naming, or *Maluna* and *Takete* Revisited." *Perceptual and Motor Skills*, vol. 19, 1964, pp. 111–17.

Hostetter, Autumn B., Monica Cantero, and William D. Hopkins. "Differential Use of Vocal and Gestural Communication by Chimpanzees (Pan Troglodytes) in Response to the Attentional Status of Human (Homo Sapiens)." *Journal of Comparative Psychology*, vol. 115, no. 4, 2001, pp. 337–343.

Hurst, Jane A., Michael Baraitser, Emmanuel Auger, Fred K. Graham, and Staffann E. Norell. "An Extended Family with a Dominantly Inherited Speech Disorder." *Developmental Medicine and Child Neurology*, vol.32, no. 4, 1990, pp. 352–355.

Inoue-Nakamura, Noriko, and Tetsuro Matsuzawa. "Development of Stone Tool Use by Wild Chimpanzees (Pan Troglodytes)." *Journal of Comparative Psychology*, vol. 111, 1997, pp. 159–173.

Jóhannesson, Alexsander. "Gesture Origin of Indo-European Languages." *Nature*, vol. 153, 1944, pp. 171–172.

Jóhannesson, Alexander. *Origin of language: Four essays*. Reykjavik: Leiftur, 1949.

Jóhannesson, Alexander. 1950. "The Gestural Origin of Language." *Nature*, vol. 166, 1950, pp. 60–61.

Johanson, Donald C., and Maitland A. Edey. *Lucy: The Beginning of Humankind*. New York: Warner Books, 1982.

Jürgens, Uwe. "Neural Pathways Underlying Vocal Control." *Neuroscience and Behavioral Review*, vol. 26, no. 2, 2002, pp. 235–258.

Kegl, Judy, Ann Senghas, and Marie Coppola. "Creation Through Contact: Sign Language Emergence and Sign Language Change in Nicaragua." In *Language Creation and Language Change: Creolization, Diachrony, and Development*. Edited by M. DeGraff. Cambridge, MA: MIT Press, 1999, pp. 179–237.

Kendon, Adam. *Gesture: Visible Action as Utterance*. Cambridge: Cambridge University Press, 2004.

Kendon, Adam, and Laura Versante. "Pointing by Hand in *Neapolitan*." In *Pointing: Where Language, Culture, and Cognition Meet*. Edited by S. Kita. Mahwah. New Jersey: Lawrence Erlbaum, 2003, pp. 109–137.

Kocur, Mirosław. "Taniec jako źródło kultury." *Kultura-Historia-Globalizacja*, no. 2, 2008, pp. 15–25.

Kocur, Mirosław. *The Power of Theater: Actors and Spectators in Ancient Rome* (Interdisciplinary Studies in Performance 11). Translated by D. Malcolm. Franfurt am Main: Peter Lang, 2018.

Kortlandt, Adriaan. "On Tool-use Among Primates." *Current Anthropology*, vol. 7, 1966, pp. 215–16.

Kortlandt, Adriaan. "Experimentation with Chimpanzees in the Wild." In *Progress in Primatology*. Edited by D. Starck, R. Schnelder, and H.J. Kohn. Stuttgart: Gustav Fischer, 1967, pp. 208–224.

Krause, Mark A., and Roger S. Fouts. "Chimpanzee (Pan Troglodytes) Pointing. Hand Shapes, Accuracy, nad the Role of Eye Gaze." *Journal of Comparative Psychology*, vol. 111, 1997, pp. 330–336.

Lai, Cecilia S.L., Simon E. Fisher, Jane A. Hurst, Faraneh Vargha-Khadem, and Anthony P. Monaco. "A Forkhead-Domain Gene Is Mutated in a Severe Speech and Language Disorder." *Nature*, vol. 413, 2001, pp. 519–523.

Lai, Cecilia S.L., Gerrelli, Diane, Anthony P. Monaco, Simon E. Fisher and Andrew J. Copp. "FOXP2 Expression During Brain Development Coincides with Adult Sites of Pathology in a Severe Speech and Language Disorder." *Brain*, vol. 126, 2003, pp. 2455–2462.

Leavens, David A., and William D. Hopkins. "Communication by Chimpanzees. A Cross-sectional Study of the Use of Referential Gestures." *Developmental Psychology*, vol. 34, 1998, pp. 813–822.

Leavens, David A., William D. Hopkins, and Kim A. Bard. "Indexical and Referential Pointing in Chimpanzees (Pan Troglodytes)." *Journal of Comparative Psychology*, vol. 110, 1996, pp. 346–353.

Leavens, David A., Autumn B. Hostetter, Michael Wesley, and William D. Hopkins. "Tactical Use of Unimodal and Bimodal Communication by Chimpanzees, *Pan Troglodytes*." *Animal Behaviour*, vol. 67, no. 3, 2004, pp. 467–476.

Leavens, David A., Timothy P. Racine, and William D. Hopkins. "The Ontogeny and Phylogeny of Non-Verbal Deixis." In *The Prehistory of Language*. Edited by R. Botha, and C. Knight. Oxford: Oxford University, 2009, pp. 142–165.

Leavens, David A., Jamie L. Russell, and William D. Hopkins. "Intentionality as Measured in the Persistence and Elaboration of Communication by Chimpanzees (Pan Troglodytes)." *Child Development*, vol. 76, no. 1, 2005, pp. 291–306.

Li Gang, Jinhong Wang, Stephen J. Rossiter, Gareth Jones and Shuyi Zhang. "Accelerated FOXP2 Evolution in Echolocating Bats." *PLoS ONE*, vol. 2, no. 9, 2007, p. e900.

Liebal, Katja, Simone S. Pika, Jospeh Call, and Michael Tomasello. "To Move or Not to Move: How Apes Adjust to the Attentional State of Others." *Interaction Studies*, vol. 5, no. 2, 2004, pp. 199–219.

Libermam, Alvin M., Franklin S. Cooper, Donald P. Shankweiler, and Michael Studdert-Kennedy. "Perception of the Speech Code." *Psychological Review*, vol. 74, no. 6, 1967, pp. 431–61.

Lieberman, Daniel E. "Homing in on Early Homo." *Nature*, vol. 436, 2007, pp. 291–292.

Lieberman, Philip. *The Biology and Evolution of Language*. Cambridge, MA: Harvard University Press, 1984.

Lieberman, Philip. *Eve Spoke: Human Language and Human Evolution*. New York: Norton, 1998.

Lieberman, Philip. *Human Language and Our Reptilian Brain: The Subcortical Bases of Speech, Syntax, and Thought*. Cambridge, MA: Harvard University Press, 2000.

Liégeois, Frédérique, Torsten Baldeweg, Alan Connelly, David G. Gadian, Mortimer Mishkin and Faraneh Vargha-Khadem. "Language fMRI Abnormalities Associated With FOXP2 Gene Mutation." *Nature Neuroscience*, vol. 6, 2003, pp. 1230–1237.

Lubaś, Władysław (ed.). *Słownik polskich leksemów potocznych*, vol. 3: G-J. Kraków: Wydawnictwo: "Lexis," 2004.

Magno Caldognetto, Emmanuela, and Isabella Poggi. "Creative Iconic Gesture. Some Evidence from Aphasics." In *Iconicity in Language*. Edited by R. Simone. Amsterdam: John Benjamins, 1995, pp. 257–276.

Masataka, Nobuo. "From Index-Finger Extension to Index-Pointing. Ontogenesis of Pointing in Preverbal Infants." In *Pointing: Where language, culture, and cognition meet*. Edited by S. Kita. Mahwah, New Jersey: Lawrence Erlbaum, 2003, pp. 69–84.

Meltzoff, Andrew N. "Understanding the Intentions of Others. Re-enactment of Intended Acts by 18-Month-Old Children." *Developmental Psychology*, vol. 31, 1995, pp. 1–16.

Morgan, Lewis H. *Ancient Society*. New York: Holt, 1877.

Nishida, Toshisada, and Linda A. Turner. "Food Transfer Between Mother and Infant Chimpanzees of the Mahale Mountains National Park, Tanzania." *International Journal of Primatology*, vol. 17, 1996, pp. 947–968.

O'Neill, Daniela K. "Two-Year-Old Children's Sensitivity to Parent's Knowledge State When Making Request." *Child Development*, vol. 67, no. 2, 1996, pp. 659–677.

Paget, Richard A.S. *Human Speech: Some Observations, Experiments and Conclusions as to the Nature, Origin, Purpose and Possible Improvement of Human Speech*, London: Routledge and Kegan Paul, 1930.

Paget, Richard A.S. "The Origin of Language." *Science*, vol. 99, 1944, pp. 14–15.

Pfeiffer, John E. *The Creative Explosion: an Inquiry into the Origins of Art and Religion*. New York: Harper and Row, 1982.

Pika, Simone S., Katja Liebal, and Michael Tomasello. "Gestural Communication on Young Gorillas (Gorilla Gorilla). Gestural Repertoire, Learning, and Use." *American Journal of Primatology*, vol. 60, no. 3, 2003, pp. 95–111.

Pika, Simone S., Katja Liebal, and Michael Tomasello. "The Gestural Repertoire of Bonobos (Pan Paniscus). Flexibility and Use." *American Journal of Primatology*, vol. 65, 2005, pp. 36–61.

Pika, Simone S., and John C. Mitani. "Referential Gesturing in Wild Chimpanzees (Pan Troglodytes)." *Current Biology*, vol. 16, no. 6, 2006, pp. 191–192.

Pika, Simone S., and John C. Mitani. "The Directed Scratch: Evidence for a Referential Gesture in Chimpanzees?." In *The Prehistory of Language*. Edited by R. Botha and C. Knight. Oxford: Oxford University Press, pp. 166-180.

Pinker, Steven, and Ray Jackendoff. "The Faculty of Language. What's Special about It?." *Cognition*, vol. 95, no. 2, 2005, pp. 201–236.

Polich, Laura. *The Emergence of the Deaf Community in Nicaragua: "With Sign Language You Can Learn So Much."* Washington D.C.: Gallaudet University Press, 2005.

Pollick, Amy S., and Frans B. M. de Waal. "Ape Gesture and Language Evolution." *Proceedings of the National Academy of Sciences, USA*, vol 104, no. 19, 2007, pp. 8184–8189.

Poss, Sarah R., Chris Kuhar, Tara S. Stoinski, and William D. Hopkins. "Differential Use of Attentional and Visual Communicative Signaling by Orangutans (Pongo Pygmaeus) and Gorillas (Gorilla Gorilla) in Response to the Attentional Status of a Human." *American Journal of Primatology*, vol. 68, no. 10, 2006, pp. 978–992.

Povinelli, Daniel J., Jesse M. Bering, and Steve Giambrone. "Chimpanzees' "Pointing." Another Error of the Argument by Analogy?." In *Pointing: Where Language, Culture, and Cognition Meet*. Edited by S. Kita. Mahwah. New Jersey: Lawrence Erlbaum, 2003, pp. 35–68.

Premack, David. "Is Language the Key to Human Intelligence?." *Science*, vol. 303, 2004, pp. 318–320.

Rae, John. "Polynesian Language." 1862. [repr. in] R.A.S. Paget. *Human Speech. Some Observations, Experiments and Conclusions as to the Nature, Origin, Purpose and Possible Improvement of Human Speech*. London: Routledge and Kegan Paul, 1930, pp. 318–361.

Rolfe, Leonard H. "Deixis as an Iconic Element of Syntax." In *Syntactic Iconicity and Linguistic Freezes. The Human Dimension* (Studies In Anthropological Linguistic 9). Edited by M.E. Landsberg. Berlin, New York: Mouton de Gruyter, 1995, pp. 117–130.

Rolfe, Leonard H. "Theoretical Stages in the Prehistory of Grammar." In *Handbook of Human Symbolic Revolution*. Edited by Lock A., and C.R. Peters. Hove: Blackwell, 1996, pp. 776–792.

Romanes, George J. *Mental Evolution in Man. Origin of Human Faculty*. London: Kegan Paul, 1888.

Sandler, Wendy, Irit Meir, Carol Padden, and Mark Aronoff. "The Emergence of Grammar. Systematic Structure in a New Language." *Proceedings of the National Academy of Science*, vol. 102, no. 7, 2005, pp. 2661–2665.

Schrago, Carlos G., and Claudia A.M. Russo. "Timing the Origin of New World Monkeys." *Molecular Biology and Evolution*, vol. 20, no. 10, 2003, pp. 1620–1625.

Sherzer, Joel. "Verbal and Nonverbal Deixis. The Pointed Lip Gesture Among the San Blas Cuna." *Language in Society*, vol. 2, no. 1, 1973, pp. 117–131.

Shu, Weigo G., Julie Y. Cho, Yuhui Jiang, Minhua Zhang, Donald Weisz, Gregory A. Elder, James Schmeidler, Rita de Gasperi, Miguel A. Gama Sosa, Donald Rabidou, Anthony C. Santucci, Daniel P. Perl, Edward Morrisey, and Joseph D. Buxbaum. "Altered Ultrasonic Vocalization in Mice with a Disruption in the FOXP2 Gene." *Proceedings of the National Academy of Sciences, USA*, vol. 102, 2005, pp. 9643–9648.

Shu, Weiguo, Hua Yang, Lili Zhang, Min Min Lu, and Edward E. Morrisey. "Characterization of a New Subfamily of Winged-helix/Forkhead (Fox) Genes That Are Expressed in the Lung and Act as Transcriptional Repressors." *Journal of Biological Chemistry*, vol. 276, 2001, pp. 27488–27497.

Stokoe, William C. *Sign Language Structure. An Outline of the Visual Communication Systems of the American Deaf* (Studies in Linguistics, Occasional papers 8). Buffalo: University of Buffalo, 1960.

Taylor, Insup K., and Martha M. Taylor. "Phonetic Symbolism in Four Unrelated Languages." *Canadian Journal of Psychology*, vol. 76, 1962, pp. 344–56.

Teramitsu, Ikuko, Lili C. Kudo, Sarah E. London, Daniel H. Geschwind, and Stephanie A. White. "Parallel FoxP1 and FoxP2 Expression in Songbird and Human Brain Predicts Functional Interaction." *Journal of Neuroscience*, vol. 24, no. 13, 2004, pp. 3152–3163.

Tinbergen, Nikolaas. *The Study of Instincts*. Oxford: Clarendon Press, 1951.

Tomasello, Michael. *Kulturowe źródła ludzkiego poznania*. Translated by J. Rączaszek. Warsaw: PIW, 2002.

Tomasello, Michael. *Constructing a Language*. Cambridge, Massachusetts: Harvard University Press, 2003.

Tomasello, Michael. *Origins of Human Communication*. Cambridge, Massachusetts: MIT Press, 2008.

Tomasello, Michael, Josep Call, Katherine Nagell, Kelly Jaakkola, and Malinda Carpernter. "The Learning and Use of Gestural Signals by Young Chimpanzees. A Trans-Generational Study." *Primates*, vol. 35, 1994, pp. 137–154.

Tomasello, Michael, Josep Call, Jennifer Warren, G. Thomas Frost, Malinda Carpenter, and Katherine Nagell. "The Ontogeny of Chimpanzee Gestural Signals. A Comparison Across Groups and Generations." *Evolution of Communication*, vol. 1, 1997, pp. 223–259.

Tomasello, Michael, Malinda Carpenter. "Shared Intentionality." *Developmental Science*, vol. 10, 2007, pp. 121-125.

Tomasello, Michael, Barbara L. George, Ann C. Kruger, M. Farrar, and Andrea Evans. "The Development of Gestural Communication in Young Chimpanzees." *Journal of Human Evolution*, vol. 14, no. 2, 1985, pp. 175–186.

Tomasello, Michael, Deborah A. Gust, and G. Thomas Frost. "A Longitudinal Investigation of Gestural Communication in Chimpanzees." *Primates*, vol. 30, 1989, pp. 35–50.

Tomasello, Michael, and Klaus Zuberbühler. "Primate Vocal and Gestural Communication." In *The Cognitive Animal: Empirical and Theoretical Perspectives on Animal Cognition*. Edited by M. Bekoff, C. Allen, and G. Burghardt. Cambridge, Massachusetts: MIT Press, 2002, pp. 293–300.

Tylor, Edward B. "On the Origin of Language." *Fortnightly Review*, vol. 1, 1868, pp. 22.

Tylor, Edward B. *Primitive Culture*, vol. 1. London: Murray, 1871.

Ueno, Ari. "Food Sharing and Referencing Behavior in Chimpanzee Mother and Infant." In *Cognitive Development in Chimpanzees*. Edited by T. Matsuzawa, M. Tomonaga, and M. Tanaka. Tokio: Springer, 2006, pp. 172–181.

Užgiris, Ina C. "Two Functions of Imitation During Infancy." *International Journal of Behavioral Development*, vol. 4, 1981, pp. 1–12.

Vargha-Khadem, Faraneh, David G. Gadian, Andrew Copp, and Mortimer Mishkin. "FOXP2 and the Neuroanatomy of Speech and Language." *Nature Review of Neuroscience*, vol. 6, 2005, pp. 131–138.

Vargha-Khadem, Faraneh, Kate Watkins, Katie Alcock, Paul Fletcher, and Richard Passingham. "Praxic and Nonverbal Cognitive Deficits in a Large Family with Genetically Transmitted Speech and Language Disorder." *Proceedings of the National Academy of Sciences, USA*, vol. 92, 1995, pp. 930–933.

Veà, Joaquim J., and Jordi Sabater-Pi. "Spontaneous Pointing Behavior in the Wild Pygmy Chimpanzee (Pan Paniscus)." *Folia Primatologica*, vol. 69, no. 5, 1998, pp. 289–290.

Wada, Kazuhiro, Jason T. Howard, Patrick McConnell, Osceola Whitney, Thierry Lints, Miriam Rivas, Haruhito Horita, Michael A. Patterson, Stephanie A. White, Constance Scharff, Sebastian Haesler, Shengli Zhao, Hironobu Sakaguchi, Masatoshi Hagiwara, Toshiyuki Shiraki, Tomoko Hirozane-Kishikawa, Pate Skene, Yoshihide Hayashizaki, Piero Carninci, and Erich D. Jarvis. "A Molecular Neuroethological Approach for Identifying and Characterizing a Cascade of Behaviorally Regulated Genes." *Proceedings of the National Academy of Science, USA*, vol. 103, no. 41, 2006, pp. 15212–15217.

Wallace, Alfred R. "Review of *Anthropology* by Edward B. Tylor." *Nature*, vol. 24, 1881, pp. 242–45.

Wallace, Alfred R. "Expressiveness of Speech, or, Mouth Gesture as a Factor in the Origin of Language." *Fortnightly Review*, n.s. 64, 1895, pp. 528–43.

Warneken, Felix, Frances Chen, and Michael Tomasello. "Cooperative Activities in Young Children and Chimpanzees." *Child Development*, vol. 77, 2006, pp. 640–663.

Warneken, Felix, and Michael Tomasello. "Altruistic Helping in Human Infants and Young Chimpanzees." *Science*, vol. 31, 2006, pp. 1301–1303.

Watkins, Kate E., Nina F. Dronkers, and Faraneh Vargha-Khadem. "Behavioural Analysis of an Inherited Speech and Language Disorder. Comparison with Acquired Aphasia." *Brain*, vol. 125, 2002, pp. 452–464.

Weiss, Jonathan H. "A Study of the Ability of English Speakers to Guess the Meanings of Non-antonym Foreign Words." *Journal of General Psychology*, vol. 74, 1966, pp. 97-106.

Wundt, Wilhelm. *Völkerpsychologie. Eine Untersuchung der Entwicklunsgesetze von Sprache, Mythos, und Sitte*, vols. 1–2. Leipzig: Wilhelm Engelmann, 1912.

Zhang, Jianzhi, David M. Webb, and Ondrej Podlaha. "Accelerated Protein Evolution and Origins of Human-Specific Features. FOXP2 as an Example." *Genetics*, vol. 162, no. 4, 2002, pp. 1825–1835.

CHAPTER 5

"There Is Neither Barbarian Nor Greek ..."

On the Tools of the Globalist Interpretation of History in Medieval Thought. An Example of the Reception of New-Testamental Ideas in the Historiography of the 11th and 12th Centuries

Stanisław Rosik

The earliest history of archbishops of Hamburg (from 831), who were simultaneously bishops of Bremen (from 845), was written by the local capitular Adamus Bremensis in the 1070s, when the Christianization of Northern peoples initiated under Charlemagne's reign was well underway. The chronicler witnessed the efforts that Adalbert (d. 1072), the archbishop of Hamburg-Bremen, launched to build the Patriarchate of the North and to extend his supremacy over Scandinavia and some of the Slavic peoples living near the coastline of the Baltic Sea in the area of the Peene, which flows into the Baltic Sea near the island of Usedom. The designs of founding the "second Rome" in the Latin world – i.e., the patriarchate – did not succeed, and the chronicler himself approached them with remarkable restraint, even though his work frames Hamburg as a major hub of Christianizing missions to the North, and with some reason too, as historical research confirms (see particularly Adam 1917, I, 16; for the basic information about Adam of Bremen, his chronicle, its editions, and the relevant literature, see Trillmich 1961; Rosik 2000, 180–191).

In Adam's times, the conversion of Scandinavian kingdoms was recognized as a fact in public life (e.g., Kulesza 2007), while North-Polabian and coastline Slavic communities still officially cultivated pagan worship. The early attempts at converting them were wrecked by insurgencies of Polabian tribes at the turn of the 10th century. Outlining a panorama of these peoples, the Bremen capitular pointed out two major centers: Rethra with its famous temple of Radegast, which earned the name of "the capital of idolatry" (Adam 1917 II, 18), and the town of *Iumne* (Adam 1917, II, 19), that is, in all likelihood, Wolin (e.g., Filipowiak 2000, 154), which is of special interest to us in this chapter. Adam portrayed *Iumne* as the biggest town in Europe [sic!], with an equally impressive composition of its population:

Est sane maxima omnium quas Europa claudit civitatum, quam incolunt Sclavi cum aliis gentibus, Graecis et Barbaris. Nam et advenae Saxones parem cohabitandi legem acceperunt, si tamen christianitatis titulum ibi morantes non publicaverint. Omnes enim adhuc paganicis ritibus oberrant, ceterum moribus et hospi-talitate nulla gens honestior aut benignior poterit inveniri. Urbs illa mercibus omnium septentrionalium nationum locuples, nichil non habet iocundi aut rari. Ibi est Olla Vul-cani, quod incolae Graecum ignem vocant (…). Ibi cernitur Neptunus triplicis natu-rae: tribus enim fretis alluitur illa insula, quorum aiunt unum esse viridissimae spe-ciei, alterum subalbidae, tertium motu furi-bundo perpetuis saevit tempestatibus. (Adam 1917, II, 19)	Indeed, it is the biggest of towns to be found in Europe, and it is populated by Slavs together with other peoples, Greeks, and Barbarians. For the arriving Saxons also received the equal right of cohabitation on condition that while dwelling there they would not indulge in Christian worship publicly. For all of them still sinfully practice pagan rites, though except that, in customs and hospitality there is hardly any people that could match their uprightness and civility. The town is replete with merchandise brought from all the nations of the North; it does not lack anything that is enjoyable or rare. There is Vulcan's cauldron there, which the dwellers call the Greek fire (…). Neptune is split there into a threefold form, for the island is circumvented by three see waters, one of which is bright green, another one whiteish, and the third rages in its seething billows due to incessant tempests.

While the inclusion of Slavs or their Saxon neighbors in this enumeration of peoples is not surprising, the mention of Greeks is indeed eyebrow-raising. The wording of the description itself is captivating. The phrase "Sclavi cum aliis gentibus, Grecis et Barbaris" pictures Slavs as the main force in the town. However, adding that they are accompanied by "other peoples" – included here under the umbrella term of "Greeks and Barbarians" – refers to the concepts that organized the perception of the world in Antiquity and is an exception in Adam's entire work, where the basic functional division pits Christians against Barbarians (Rosik 2000, 188). What is the meaning of inserting this anachronic fossil at this point of the chronicling narrative? When answering this question, it makes sense to recall the essential context in which this fossil appears. The point is that the erudite author imbued his depiction of heathendom with the undertones of *interpretatio Romana* in the Old-Roman spirit.

Neptune as a personification of the marine element is evoked side by side with Vulcan, who features in the name of a device referred to as a cauldron which holds a blazing substance called "Greek fire." The widespread construal of this passage as a confirmation that *Iumne* boasted a lighthouse (e.g., Filipowiak 2000, 154) resonates well with the previous sentence, which extols the barbarians' extraordinary hospitality and noble-mindedness: the luminous point shows the way to newcomers from afar, and the town owes its worldwide recognition to merchants from remote corners of the world. At the same time, the praise of barbarian virtues is to a large extent an entrenched topos, one which was used by writers as early as in the Antiquity. When describing foreign peoples, ancient authors tended to laud the unspoiled nature of the barbarians and in this way to brand the Romans' degenerate attitudes (Modzelewski 2004, 17–44). It was thus not for no reason that Adam of Bremen was recognized as the "Tacitus of the North" (e.g., Witkowski 1995, 10).

The phrase "Greeks and Barbarians" in his account is similarly redolent of a certain topos. Although Greeks in this phrase may very well have been mentioned by way of association with Eastern Christian church worshipers (perhaps merchants from Ruthenia), the very concept of talking about peoples as such in this way dates back to the New Testament and, specifically, to St. Paul's writings. In his *Letter to the Romans* (1, 14; cf. *King James Bible*, all other references to the Bible are based on this edition), St. Paul portrayed himself as having a mission to preach the gospel to "the Geeks and to the Barbarians." In this way, the horizon of apostleship comprising all peoples was delineated. As Adam of Bremen's primary focus was the Christianization of the Northern peoples, there is good reason to believe that the wording *Greci et Barbari*, employed to depict the most famous town of pagan Slavs, was meant to refer to the establishment of this worldwide horizon of Evangelization in the New Testament's epistolography. This horizon also encompassed Scythians (cf. *Colossians* 3, 11), whom Adam of Bremen mentioned as well (11, 19), when specifying that *Iumne* was located on an island where the Oder flows into the Scythian Marshes (*Scythice Paludes*). The chronicler stressed that by outlining this image he sought to rein in fantastic notions about *Iumne* (which he most likely failed to do); still, if what he described was indeed Wolin, there is no reason to have any doubts about its world-important commercial position, which is also borne out by its multi-ethnic population (Filipowiak 2000). This multi-ethnic character underpins the evoked image of "Greeks and Barbarians," which determined the fundamental framework for the ancient Greeks' perception of strangers and as such was utilized by St. Paul in his epistles. In the writings of Adamus Bremensis, the image became an allegory serving as a tool of the globalist interpretation of the totality of peoples, which was well harmonized (also by means of the Scythian motif) with the New Testament's vision of eschatological reality enveloping the world (Rosik 2008).

On this take, its origin in time is associated with the incarnation of Logos in Christ, which is treated as the foundation of the Church. The endorsement of this vision resulted in revaluing relations among human beings as such, a change informed by the abolishment of ethically, culturally, and socially conditioned antinomies: "there is no Greek, nor Jew, Barbarian, Scythian, bond nor free" (*Colossians* 3, 11). This is how the community of Christian worshippers was supposed to enact here, in this world, the eschatological aspect of the Church as a community destined to assemble the whole of humanity at the end of time. This heralded the resumption of the original unity, whose fragmentation was conveyed in the mythical image of Noe's offspring splitting and losing the common language at the tower of Babel (e.g., Strzelczyk 2001).

As no explicit expression of this idea is to be found in the work of Adam of Bremen, it is evoked here in order to emphasize the epoch's universal understanding of the meaning of history. Given the theme of the chronicle, the glaringly anachronic usage of the global take on humanity (*Greci-Barbari*) can justifiably be interpreted as a reference to this circle of representations. As a matter of fact, the formulation not so much cites a specific passage from Paul's writings as it rather evokes a certain general idea in the context of reflection on the missions among pagans – barbarians. The point does not lie in trying to understand "strangers" but in accepting their presence in the world in the perspective of realizing values regarded as ones of the future and eternal in theological assessment.

In this framework, the presentation of the customs of barbarian peoples comes across as ambivalent. On the one hand, their foreignness, hostility, and savagery are highlighted, but on the other they are recognized as displaying the ultimately human attributes. This is exactly how Adam of Bremen (VI, 18) painted Old Prussians, whom he admired as "the most human of humans," citing their care for shipwrecks and contempt of wealth. At the same time, he dwelled on St. Adalbert's martyrdom at their hands and in this context condemned their persistent paganism. This was generally analogous to his earlier appraisal of the residents of *Iumne*. The good, "natural" virtues qualified barbarians as human beings who were called on to participate in the eschatological unity and thus accepted and showered with pastoral care by missionaries in the practice of conversion.

As a matter of fact, Christianity took hold in *Iumne*/Wolin over half a century after Adam wrote his chronicle. The feat was accomplished by the missions under the command of St. Otto of Bamberg in the Duchy of West Pomerania in 1124–1125 and in 1128 (Petersohn 1979, 213–232; Rębkowski 2007, 25–40; Rosik

2010, 126–496). Within two decades after St. Otto's death in 1139, three version of his *vita* were produced in Bavaria's monastic circles: the earliest one, called *Vita Priflingensis*, was written by an anonymous author in Prüfening near Regensburg (VP, 1999), and two later versions were respectively authored by Ebo at the Michlesberg Abbey near Bamberg (1969) and by his polemicist Herbord (1974). Engaged in disseminating the cult of the famous missionary, these works are superb literary monuments (for a concise review of studies on and editions of the *vitae* in the 19th and 20th centuries, see e.g., Haarländer 2000, 527–535; Strzelczyk 2005, 18*ff*, 23–26) and offer several examples of ambivalent attitudes to barbarians espoused in the debate on their conversion.

In St. Otto's *vitae*, Wolin, whose Latinized name *Julin* apocryphally tied it with Julius Caesar as its founder (VP 1999, II, 5; Ebo 1969, II, 1) and which was to become the first capital of the bishopric for Pomeranian neophytes starting in 1140 (recently Rosik 2010, 496–511, see there for the literature review), is framed as a site of considerable relevance to the success of Otto's ventures. Before Otto actually embarked on his mission, Wolin witnessed the debacle of conversion efforts undertaken by bishop Bernard, a zealous ascetic of Spain (Ebo 1969, II, 1). On seeing the evangelizer barefoot and in tatters, the dwellers of the affluent town responded derisively, quite unable to believe that such a wretch could possibly be an envoy of the Supreme God he claimed to be. According to the hagiographist's account, before Bernard shared his experiences with Otto – which essentially shaped the latter's missionary methods discouraging him from any ostentatious poverty (e.g., Bracha 2000) – he had complained about the Wolinians to Boleslaus II Wrymouth at Gniezno. This episode is striking for its animalistic connotations in the depiction of the barbarians' attitude, as the Spaniard argued that they remained insensitive to "spiritual gifts" because of their beastliness (literally: "animales sunt" – "they are animals"), and the Duke of Poland reportedly begged him not to expose himself to risks by triggering their "canine bitterness" (Ebo 1969, II, 1).

The coloring of the portrayal of the Pomeranian pagans changes in episodes which describe their receptivity to religion preached by the Bamberg missionary. The beauty and intelligence of Szczecin adolescents, who even before the town's official conversion eagerly listen to Otto's teachings, embody the beauty of man as an image of the Creator (VP 1999, II, 9), and special praises are lavished on people, in particular on women, who offer hospitality and care to the ministers of the gospel (e.g., Ebo 1969, III, 7; Herbord 1974, II, 19). Moreover, in a heart-wrenching episode of families being torn apart by slave traffickers (trading in pagan captives), Otto, his charity prompted by their "human condition," exerts himself to save the unfortunates and later begs the Pomeranian ruler to set them free, baptize them, and send them back home (Herbord 1974, III, 2).

Nevertheless, in the hagiographic narratives, such scenes are only a component which on particular occasions supports the core drive of the missionary motivation.

This drive is particularly vividly indicated at the onset of narratives about Otto's expeditions among the pagans by reiterating the New Testament's injunction to spread the gospel among all peoples before the end of the world comes: "In omnes gentes primum oportet predicari euangelium" (Ebo 1969, II, 1; cf. e.g., *Gospel according to Mark* 13, 10). The *vitae* mentioned above relate the theological justification of this imperative to an inner compulsion in the form of Christ's *caritas*, a variety of love which purportedly compelled the protagonist to engage in ministerial activity even when faced with the hostility and total defiance of the barbarians (VP 1999, II, 8). *Caritas* is again understood here in terms defined by St. Paul (e.g., *Letter to the Romans* 5, 5; *First Letter to Thessalonians* 2, 19), that is, not as a liking for another person, but as a reality of relations binding people with each other and primarily with God, which is also reistically rendered in the image of grace or charity "spilling over in the hearts" (Rosik 2010, 537, 556; cf. VP 1999, II, 8; Ebo 1969, II, 12). In this conceptual context, the meaning of evangelization lies in extending this reality across the world, including communities and individuals into it, which is exemplified in the hagiographic accounts of Otto's pursuits in the hubs along the Baltic coastline (Rosik 2010, 560–644).

Highly relevant to reliance on such a concept as a justification of commencing a Christianizing mission was framing humankind in categories which on the one hand highlighted barriers (Greek vs. barbarian, free vs. slave, Christian vs. barbarian, or even German vs. barbarian in one of the lives of Otto [e.g., Ebo 1969, III, 1; cf. Rosik 2010, 365]), but on the other made it possible to encompass the whole of humanity. In the context of narratives about missions to pagans discussed here, this inclusive vision of the human totality, inspired by the anthropological opposition of "self" vs. "other," became an element of the conceptual model within which the missionary pursuits became meaningful by overcoming thus-defined barriers through the implementation of a new social order.

In this concept, the enactment of the idea of global unity involves the establishment of an individually and collectively conceived human community together with institutional connections. All this relies on a particular system of values, some of which are identified in societies which as yet do not but are supposed to make up this unity. This general formula entails a specific iteration of social attitudes that promote globalization processes, but preclude any genuine exploration of diversity and characters of other cultures. This is responsible for a specific conceptual mechanism of overcoming otherness: the stress is put not so much on knowing "others" as rather on involving them in giving the world a new shape which one endorses as optimal.

Bibliography

Adam . "Magistri Adam Bremensis Gesta Hammmaburgensis Ecclesiae Pontificum." Edited by B. Schmeidler. In *Monumenta Germaniae Historica, Scriptores rerum Germanicarum in usum scholarum*. Hannover-Lepzig, 1917.

Bracha, Krzysztof. "Sztuka misyjnej perswazji. Przykład św. Wojciecha i Ottona z Bambergu." *Almanach Historyczny*, no. 2, 2000, pp. 11–24.

Ebo. "Żywot św. Ottona biskupa bamberskiego." Edited by J. Wikarjak. In *Monumenta Poloniae Historica. Nova series*, vol. 7, part 2, introduced and edited by K. Liman. Warsaw: PWN, 1969.

Filipowiak, Władysław. "Wollin – ein frühmittelalterliches Zentrum an der Ostsee." In *Europasmitte um 1000. Beiträge zur Geschichte, Kunst und Archäologie. Handbuch zur Ausstellung*, vol. 1. Edited by Alfred Wiec-zorek, Hans-Martin Hinz. Stuttgart: Theiss, 2000.

Haarländer, Stephanie. *Vitae episcoporum. Eine Quellengattung zwischen Hagiographie und Histo-riographie, untersucht an Lebensbeschreibungen von Bischöfen des Regnum Teutonicum im Zeital-ter der Ottonen und Salier*. Stuttgart: Hiersemann, 2000.

Herbord . "Dialog o życiu św. Ottona biskupa bamberskiego." Edited by J. Wikarjak. In *Monumenta Poloniae Historica. Nova series*, vol. 7, part 2, introduced and edited by K. Liman. Warsaw: PWN, 1974.

King James Bible. https://www.kingjamesbibleonline.org. Accessed on December 2, 2019.

Kulesza, Przemysław. *Normanowie a chrześcijaństwo. Recepcja nowej wiary w Skandynawii w IX i X wieku*. Wrocław-Racibórz: Wydawnictwo i Agencja Informacyjna waw, 2007.

Modzelewski, Karol. *Barbarzyńska Europa*. Warszawa: Iskry 2004.

Petersohn, Jürgen. *Der südliche Ostseeraum im kirchlich-politischen Kräftespiel des Reichs, Polens und Dänmarks vom 10. bis 13. Jahrhundert. Mission – Kirchenorganisation – Kultpolitik*. Köln-Wien: Böhlau Verlag GmbH, 1979.

Rębkowski, Marian. Chrystianizacja Pomorza Zachodniego. Studium archeologiczne. Szczecin: Instytut Archeologii i Etnologii PAN, Oddział w Szczecinie, 2007.

Rosik, Stanisław. *Interpretacja chrześcijańska religii pogańskich Słowian w świetle kronik niemieckich XI–XII wieku (Thietmar, Adam z Bremy, Helmold)*. Wrocław: Wydawnictwo Uniwersytetu Wrocławskiego, 2000.

Rosik, Stanisław. *Conversio gentis Pomeranorum. Studium świadectwa o wydarzeniu (XII wiek)*. Wrocław: Chronicon, 2010.

Strzelczyk, Jerzy. "Rajskie początki i upadek człowieka w świadomości ludzi średniowiecza." In *Origines mundi, gentium et civitatum*. Edited by S. Rosik, P. Wiszewski. Wroclaw: Wydawnictwo Uniwersytetu Wrocławskiego, 2001.

Strzelczyk, Jerzy. "Einleitung." In *Ausgewählte Quellen zur Deutschen Geschichte des Mittelalters*, vol. 23. Edited by H.W. Goetz. Darmstadt: Wissenschaftliche Buchgesellschaft, 2005.

Trillmich, Werner. "Einleitung." In "Gesta Hammaburgensis ecclesiae pontificum." Edited by Werner Trillmich. In *Quellen des 9. und 11. Jahrhunderts zur Geschichte der hamburgischen Kirche und des Reiches, Ausgewählte Quellen zur deutschen Geschichte des Mittelalters. Freiherr vom Stein-Gedächtnisausgabe*, vol. 11. Darmstadt: Wissenschaftliche Buchgesellschaft, 1961.

VP; "Die Prüfeninger Vita Bischof Ottos I. von Bamberg nach der Fassung des Großen Österreichi-schen Legendars." Edited by J. Petersohn. In *Monumenta Germaniae Historica, Scriptores rerum Germanicarum in usum scholarum*, Hannover, 1999.

Witkowski, Grzegorz. "Opis wysp Północy Adama Bremeńskiego jako dzieło etnografii wczesnośredniowiecznej." In *Studia z dziejów Europy Zachodniej i Śląska, Prace Historyczne XVI*. Edited by R. Żerelik. Wrocław: Instytut Historyczny Uniwersytetu Wrocławskiego i Wrocławskie Towarzystwo Miłośników Historii, 1995.

CHAPTER 6

Were the Natural Sciences Global in the 19th Century? The Case of Charles Darwin

Piotr Badyna

21st-century science and scholarship appear to be a global phenomenon, especially as far as the natural sciences are concerned. The biggest research projects are not single-handedly funded by any individual countries, but by groups of states which, rather than being neighbors or sharing the same continent, are often scattered across the world. Within such projects, huge collaborating research teams assemble scholars from multiple countries, nations, and ethnic groups. Even research teams "authorized" by one state not infrequently include members from various citizen, national, or ethnic backgrounds. This is emphatically exemplified by teams affiliated with U.S. universities. Such transnational collaborative undertakings are perhaps best epitomized by projects such as LISA (www.lisa.nasa.gov), under which U.S-based scholars (from Stanford University, University of Florida, JPL, and Caltech) cooperate with researchers from Hannover's AEI – Max Planck Institute for Gravitational Physics on observations of gravitational waves. Another excellent example of international research collaboration is provided by the HÚYÁ Bioscience International (www.huyabio.com), which is becoming a worldwide leader in developing and implementing new biopharmaceuticals. Its branches predominantly employ Chinese researches from Guangzhou and Shanghai, but the project has also an office in San Diego (U.S.). The North Greenland Ice Core Project, which is conducted by the Ice and Climate Centre at the Niels Bohr Institute, University of Copenhagen, represents another huge research enterprise scheduled for several years. So far, the research has involved seventeen research teams from Europe, one from Japan, and two from the U.S. These are but a mere handful of examples of a plethora of transnational research initiatives.

Such collaborations of scholars and researchers from various corners of the world inevitably entail migrations of academics. They traverse the globe to perform measurements, carry out explorations, or share their findings at numerous conferences. While some of these trips take a few days, other ones take them away from their home institutions for several years.

Importantly, not only people migrate. Thoughts, concepts, and research ideas do as well, for they practically crisscross the entire globe. This mobility is

© PIOTR BADYNA, 2021 | DOI:10.1163/9789004443792_008

undoubtedly promoted by the means and tools of electronic communication, which were invented in the 20th century. Traditional correspondence, therein letters handwritten or printed on paper, has been ousted by e-mails, which are now a veritably natural manner of communication in the world of science. They make it possible to share information in a blink of an eye, which contributes to accelerating scientific advancement. Of course, the development of electronic media has benefited not only correspondence among scholars, research teams, and academic hubs. The Internet has also boosted the establishment of multiple science-related websites and portals which offer easy access to information useful in research work. The Internet has further bolstered the development of research publishing, for example by promoting the foundation of online journals. This impact is not limited to the newly emerging journals, but has affected traditional, long-standing, even reputed research periodicals as well. Dedicated websites are established in order to collect and systematize data about research in progress, latest findings, and journals. One of them is, for example, e! Science News: "Its sole purpose is to ensure that you have access to the very latest and popular science breakthroughs" (www.esciencenews.com). For this purpose, the Internet is constantly combed for the latest information from various disciplinary fields, whereby highly advanced mathematical techniques (e.g., vectoral algorithms) are used to optimize information search by establishing with which disciplines given data are associated, how significant they are, how they are rated, etc. The e! Science News website also includes a list of important scientific journals, such as *21th-Century Science and Technology* (www.21stcenturysciencetech.com), *American Scientist* (www.americanscientist.org), *Discover Magazine* (www.discovermagazine.com), and renowned and prestigious *Nature* (www.nature.com).

As this very brief survey implies, the notion that science is not a global phenomenon is quite untenable. Arjun Appadurai asserts that "[t]his mobile and unforeseeable relationship between mass-mediated events and migratory audiences defines the core of the link between globalization and the modern" (2003, 4). As Appadurai insists, the globality of phenomena is predicated upon migrations and information flows in modern media. Admittedly, he developed his framework to analyze contemporary culture, but his criteria seem quite well applicable to science and scholarship as well. Appadurai makes it clear that the globality he addresses concerns the developments of the 20th century (or, more precisely, of the second half of the 20th century), and he argues that these phenomena in our times differ from their counterparts in earlier historical periods. Prior ages, preceding the 20th century, indeed knew migrations and information flows, but "electronic mediation and mass migration mark the world of the present not as technically new forces but as ones that seem to impel (and sometimes compel) the work of the imagination" (ibid.). Whether thus-conceived globalization is indeed identical with our present moment is a debatable issue. If we discard the trappings of modernity and contemporary technologies, will we not perceive similar phenomena (migrations and information flows) in bygone epochs? Was science not global, by any chance, for example as early as in the 19th century?

In this chapter, I examine science in the 19th century, that is, a time when a major revolution in the study of animate nature took place. From the 16th century till the end of the 18th century, empirical resources and approaches staggeringly expanded, triggering doubts as to the accuracy and reliability of the concepts of nature espoused by the natural sciences of the day. Previously unchallenged authorities, with Aristotle (384–322 B.C.) as one of notable examples, came under intense, questioning scrutiny. A major search was underway for new modes of describing nature, as emphatically pointed out by Alfred Rupert Hall, a pre-eminent historian of science (1966, 10–12). Nevertheless, until the end of the 18th century, all these changes could not put an end to the crisis. In was only in the 19th century that the realization that the development of empirical foundations alone would not effect a key and indispensable change in the understanding of the natural world triggered fundamental transformations. Obviously, a broad array of factors contributed to changes in science and in the study of nature. Besides cultural components, the English historian of science John Henry (2005) cites, for example, the confluence of changes in science and scientific worldviews on the on the one hand and the increasingly pragmatic application of the knowledge of nature (ibid., 44) and the development of capitalism (ibid.) on the other. We would be well advised to inquire whether, side by side with these and probably several other factors, the transformations – and, consequently, the revolutionary change that was Charles Darwin's concept – were not perhaps affected by the growingly global character of science.

Further in this paper, I will primarily focus on arguments supporting the notion of the global character of 19th-century science. I will also probe into the influence of thus-shaped science on the greatest biological concept since Aristotle, which was developed at that time.

My analysis is based on the life and work of Charles Darwin (1809–1882), the founder of the theory of evolution through natural selection. While Darwin is but an individual case, I believe that this case is highly representative of the processes I discuss. Darwin was a rather typical representative of the English scholars of the 19th century, which obviously does not detract anything from the brilliance of his mind, which excelled his contemporaries. When calling Darwin's career typical, I have in mind the modes and paths of scientific development at that time. Darwin was born into an affluent family as a son of a leading pottery entrepreneur. He started studying to be a clergyman at Christ College in Cambridge, but he did not display any particular aptitude either for ancient languages or for theology. He was far more into hunting, horse-riding, and collecting insects. From 1831 to 1836, Darwin traveled around the world aboard the brig HMS "Beagle." After the voyage, he settled on an estate he had bought at Down near Farnborough. This was where he spent the rest of his science-filled life, studying the wealth of empirical resources he had collected during his voyage, conducting observations of the local fauna and flora, studying barnacles, and writing his greatest works. His life did not differ much from the lives of his middle-class peers or of other naturalists of his day (Mägdefrau 2004; Thomson 2009; White, Gribbin 1998).

However, while the course and style of his private life were not particularly revolutionary, what this life produced was revolutionary indeed. Given this, it makes sense to have a closer look at Darwin's intellectual achievements and investigate how his voyage around the world could have contributed to them.

Darwin's Introduction to his paramount work *On the Origin of Species*, which marked a turning point for European civilization, opens in a very modest way: "When on board H.M.S 'Beagle,' as naturalist, I was much struck with certain facts in the distribution of the inhabitants of South America, and in the geological relations of the present to the past inhabitants of that continent" (1859, n.p.). The significance of Darwin's voyage aboard the "Beagle" has been discussed in volumes upon volumes of studies, scrutinizing each day of the expedition addressed in the available sources. Many authors have examined the journey itself, with its crucial moments and less known episodes as described by Darwin himself (1960). Attention has been devoted to how Darwin's skill as a research writer perfected during and under the influence of his traveling experiences (Tallmadge 1980). Yet, the most concerted effort has been invested in attempts to pinpoint the moment when Darwin became an evolutionist, with plentiful disputes over whether this shift took place while traveling or only after the trip (Sulloway 1980). The key question in terms of my argument in this paper is whether such a voyage was something standard and regularly practiced at that time. Educational travel became very fashionable among aristocrats and intellectuals of 17th-century England and was referred to as "the Grand Tour" (Black 2003). A vogue for this type of journey spread among the elites across Europe in the 18th century, and towards the end of this age traveling for education and knowledge became a common practice. Basically, there was no eminent natural scientist at the turn of the 18th century who did not go on such a journey. For one, Alexander von Humboldt (1769–1859) traveled to South America in 1799–1804 and to the Ural, Siberia and Dzungaria in 1829

(Magee 2009). English scholars of this period also made similar research journeys all over the world; suffice it to mention personages such as Charles Lyell (1797–1875) and his trip to South America (Cook 2009), and Alfred R. Wallace (1823–1913), who traveled to South America and the Malay Archipelago (Knapp 2009). As similar examples could easily be multiplied, I believe there is no exaggeration in concluding that such journeys were a mass phenomenon in the community of 19th-century English naturalists.

So far, no study has attempted to analyze the impact of the voyage itself – as a voyage of such a global compass – on Darwin's work as a scientist and on an exceptionally broad perspective which he adopted and which could formatively influence the general nature of his concept. Copious notes which he made after his return clearly express the impact this long journey had had on him. In one of the notes he literally wrote: "In July opened first note Book on 'transmutation of Species.' – Had been greatly struck from about month of previous March – on character of South American fossils – & species on Galapagos Archipelago. – These facts origin (especially latter) of all my views" (2008, 63). In his letters, there is hardly any passage on research issues that does not refer to the knowledge he acquired when traveling. From the moment the "Beagle" entered the first roadstead in South America and Darwin set his foot on land on, he thought in terms of empirical findings he came across at various locations of the southern hemisphere. All his letters to scholars were saturated with his knowledge of the flora and primarily the fauna of the southern outskirts of the globe. This mindset was to continue basically until the end of his long and scientifically prolific life, certainly at least until 1859. When solving problems, he juxtaposed data from various geographical regions, rather than relying on his knowledge of the local fauna. This can be seen for example, in a dispute in which he engaged with Alfred Wallace over the colonization of oceanic islands by animals. In a letter dated to 9th August, 1859, Darwin wrote: "Are you aware that *annually* birds are blown to Madeira, to Azores (& to Bermuda from America)" (1859, n.p.).

Importantly, this more general (global) perspective only makes its way to the forefront in Darwin's correspondence after the return from his voyage around the world. His earlier statements are very tentative and rather offer modest suggestions. This is clearly embodied in the correspondence with John S. Henslow (1796–1861), Darwin's mentor and long-time friend. In a letter sent to Henslow on 11th April, 1833, Darwin wrote: "I had here the high good fortune, to find amongst most primitive looking rocks, a bed of micaceous sandstone abounding with Terebratula [brachiopods] & its subgenera & Entrochitus, I think the comparison of these impressions, with those of the oldest fossiliferous rocks of Europe will be preeminently interesting" (2008, 32). Darwin's later letters, written after he returned to England and thoroughly studied the wealth of data he had compiled, clearly indicate that whatever doubts he had entertained before disappeared for good. The only way to understand the entire abundance of nature leads through explanations applicable to the fauna and the flora both in Europe and in South America. We can conclude that he increasingly tended, at least in his correspondence, to perceive nature and its opulence in more and more general terms. The experience he had acquired, the empirical material he had collected, and primarily the observations of wildlife he had conducted at various locations across the globe transformed his perception of nature and its mechanisms.

It is also interesting to examine how this concept of nature as a worldwide phenomenon was articulated in Darwin's most important work, in his *opus vitae – On the Origin of Species*. In Chapter 12, which discusses the geographical distribution of animal and vegetal species, Darwin refutes the idea of a strict interdependence between geographical/climatic conditions and biodiversity. He unambiguously asserts that such an interdependence has not been found, and his counterargument is based on a juxtaposition of data from various, often very distant areas of the planet: "In the southern hemisphere, if we compare large tracts of land in Australia, South Africa, and western South America, between latitudes 25 deg and 35 deg, we shall find parts extremely similar in all their conditions, yeti t would not be possible to point out three faunas and floras more utterly dissimilar" (1859, n.p.). This passage directly shows where Darwin's knowledge about these geographical areas came from. It is enough to correlate this excerpt with the route of the "Beagle." Admittedly, the ship spent most time in South America, but it also stopped at the shores of New Zealand, Australia (its southern part: Hobart and King Georg), and Africa (Cape Good Hope). Darwin thus compared the areas of which he had hands-on knowledge from observations he had been carrying out during the breaks in the voyage. He started writing his grand work after returning from the journey of his life and having an immense wealth of experiences and empirical data at his disposal. Most importantly, perhaps, he also had a more general perspective which encompassed not just one continent, but basically the entire southern hemisphere.

To avoid an erroneous conclusion that Darwin's assertions only concerned the southern part of our globe, we should remember that he often juxtaposed the data about this region with information about the flora and the fauna of the northern hemisphere. For example, when describing birds he had seen in Tierra del Fuego, he wrote: "Petrels are the most aerial and oceanic of birds, yet in the quiet Sounds of Tierra del Fuego, the Puffinuria berardi, in its general habits, in its astonishing power of diving, its manner of swimming, and of flying when unwillingly takes flight, would be mistaken by any one for an auk or grebe" (ibid.). This clearly shows that his mind was inclined to synthesize data coming from various geographical areas.

He took a similar approach to another issue, specifically to the kinship of organisms inhabiting the same area of the same continent: "A third great fact, partly included in the foregoing statements, is the affinity of the productions of the same continent or sea [...] It is a law of the widest generality, and every continent offers innumerable instances" (ibid.). Evidently, Darwin's way of thinking in this respect was also influenced by his holistic, global take on the empirical data.

How deeply this conceptual approach to nature was entrenched in Darwin's mind is attested to by the fact that in he devoted much of Chapter 10 to reflection on yawning gaps in the empirical material. Thereby, he did not believe the problem was only the matter of inadequate explorations of Europe: "Only a small portion of the surface of the earth has been geologically explored, and no part with sufficient care [...]" (ibid.). It was only a small step from there to insisting that a fuller picture offering tangible cognitive benefits could only be obtained through researching as large areas of the Earth as possible.

The several-year-long voyage on board the "Beagle," the material collected then, and the insights gleaned from it had their far-reaching impact on Darwin's worldview. They not only influenced the domain of Darwin's scientific explorations but also deeply affected his religious outlooks. Namely, they persuaded him to negate the concepts of creation by God. He extensively dwelled on such thoughts in the last part of *On the Origin of Species*, where he discussed one of important components of the evolution of organisms, that is, "a rule" [sic!] of affinity between organisms and their ancestral forms coming from other regions: "We see this in nearly all plants and animals of the Galapagos archipelago, of Juan Fernandez, and of the other American islands being related in the most striking manner to the plants and animals of the neighbouring American mainland; and those of the Cape Verde archipelago and other African islands to the African mainland. It must be admitted that these facts receive no explanation on the theory of creation" (ibid.). This observation laid the foundation for transformations which quickly occurred in his closest circles among the supporters of his concept. However, it not only re-cast the perception of the role of religion in explaining nature among many people, even those who were not directly associated with Darwin, as early as in the 1860s. That the concept of evolution through natural selection triggered a genuine ideological storm can be seen, for example, in the immediate response of the Universal Church: "The authorities obviously condemned the theory powerfully and irrevocably, whereby they cited reasons entirely unrelated to science.

As early as in 1860, *On the Origin of Species* was translated into German and was repudiated by the Episcopate at the synod at Köln, where the doctrine deriving the human body from animal species was repeatedly and emphatically proclaimed to be contradictory to the Scriptures and irreconcilable with the Catholic faith" (Minois 1996, 208). Such responses were not restricted to Germany. After 1865, the Catholic clergy and thinkers in Italy reacted in a very similar way to Darwin's concept. An immense "production of works" commenced with the sole aim of defending the concept of creation by proving the erroneousness of Darwinism. The arguments which were advanced in such polemics predominantly focused on the divergence of Darwin's theory from the Bible (ibid., 209–213). Given this, Darwin's work cannot be denied having had a wide-ranging resonance and having re-fashioned ideas about human beings and their position in nature.

Information flow in Darwin's times is another point we can usefully scrutinize. It has already been addressed above. It can clearly be seen that information flow was very intense back then; in fact, we can say that it was at its most intense within the "technical" possibilities of the times. As Stephen Jay Gould claims in his Foreword to Darwin's selected letters: "Charles Darwin's life (1809–1882) falls squarely into an intermediary time of maximal information – after an older time of too much information lost (and no adequate postal service), and before our modern age of electronic obliteration. The intellectual leaders of Darwin's day wrote voluminous letters" (2008, ix). This concerned Darwin himself, his friends and acquaintances, and his contemporary scholars. The robustness and vigor of epistolary investment are perhaps most spectacularly exemplified in the everyday correspondence of Adam Sedgwick (1785–1873) and Roderick Murchison (1792–1871) from the period when they worked to establish the scale of geological time. Darwin himself left a huge body of letters, which have been studied and collected in as many as twenty seven volumes (www.darwinproject.ac.uk). Darwin corresponded practically with all scholars who could support his work in one way or another. The group included, for example, the American botanist Asa Gray (1810–1888) of Harvard University and Alfred R. Wallace, who did research in the Malaya. The sole, albeit serious, constraint to Darwin's letter-writing was that he only knew English, and consequently the circle of his correspondents was limited to those who could use this language. Darwin basically wrote whenever he was at leisure and was not afflicted by his cumbersome illness. When traveling, he literally used every opportunity to contrive and dispatch an epistle to his family, friends, or other scholars.

Discussing information flow, we cannot possibly omit Darwin's works as such or ignore how quickly they circulated across and resonated in the world of academia and not only academia. As mentioned above, a translation of *On the Origin of Species* appeared in Germany as early as in 186, and in Italy the work already made ripples in 1865. This attests to the staggering pace at which information included in Darwin's works was disseminated. As for the resonance of Darwin's concept, it was immediate and immense. More importantly, it was not just local. The theory of evolution through natural selection came under attacks not only in England but also across Europe and in several religious hubs in the U.S. I believe that this justifies positing that the Darwinian concept already resonated in the entire culture of the West in the 19th century. Consequently, it is quite legitimate to argue that it compelled "the work of the imagination" (to use Appadurai's coinage) of all those who came in touch with it. Without a doubt, such encounters were not limited merely to the local, English area of scholarship and ideology.

The aim of this paper was to examine the natural science of the 19th century and establish whether it can be considered to have been a global phenomenon. For this purpose, globality was defined on the basis of the concept proposed by Appadurai, who lists mass migrations and information flows in electronic media as distinctive factors in contemporary globality. In this context, the question was posed whether these components are indeed only characteristic of our times and, consequently, whether phenomena can be thought of as global exclusively in our times. The argument of this paper discarded the trappings of modern technologies to show that mass migrations were observable as early as in the 19th-century natural sciences. An overwhelming majority of the community of scholars and naturalists was involved in such migrations for education, knowledge, and research. Natural scientists went on shorter and longer journeys, many of which lasted longer than contemporary seasonal trips which Turkish *Gastarbeiters* make to gather strawberries or cucumbers in Germany. As far as information flow among 19th-century naturalists is concerned, their concept-sharing through correspondence was very intense. Research findings were also quickly announced and published, while responses to them tended to be very rapid. It seems that present-day scholars may be in a worse position, inundated as they are with science-related information, which makes selection of valuable and important data more time-consuming than in the 19th century. For this reason, responses to weighty problems and issues are sometimes offered later than in Darwin's day. The last important issue emphasized by Appadurai is the powerful impact of information and migrations on the social imagination. I argue that Darwin's *On the Origin of Species* epitomizes such a profound and far-ranging influence. I do not believe that we can find any present-day concept which has more vividly and vigorously impressed itself on people's imaginations. Of course, Darwin's work is a spectacular case, but the history of science at the turn of the 19th century without a doubt contains several other powerful accelerators of the imagination of entire communities scattered across our globe. All this suggests that science can be considered to have already been a global phenomenon in the 19th century.

The last issue to address is the impact of globality on the way in which scholars – Darwin in this case – thought. A voyage around the world alone does not seem to have been a sufficient stimulus to produce as astute and comprehensive a theory as Darwin's evolutionism. Undoubtedly, Darwin was not exceptional in terms of traveling. However, the historical literature on Darwin produces an irresistible impression that his view of nature profoundly transformed under the influence of his voyage. After 1836, he was no longer able to perceive nature as an amalgam of geographically isolated phenomena. This is quite clear, for example, in his refutation of the notion that the geographical location is correlated with the type of wild- and plant-life. One cannot miss the fact that, triggered among others by the journey, Darwin's inquiries changed the perception not only of nature as such but also of the human place in it. The shift concerned Darwin himself as well, who changed from a believer to an agnostic, to an atheist, as his biographers recount (Thomson 2009, 273). Though not the sole factor in these processes, Darwin's voyage in all likelihood bolstered and enhanced his conviction that nature must be explained in ways which took into account all emanations of natural life on the Earth.

Bibliography

Appadurai, Arjun. *Modernity at Large: Cultural Dimensions of Globalization*. Minneapolis and London: University of Minnesota Press, 2003.

Black, Jeremy. *The British Abroad. The Grand Tour in the Eighteenth Century*. Sutton Publishing, 2003.

Cook, Jill. "Charles Lyell." In *Wielcy przyrodnicy. Od Arystotelesa do Darwina*. Edited by R. Huxley. Translated by R. Milanowski. Warsaw: PWN, 2009.

Darwin, Charles. *Origins: Selected Letters of Charles Darwin, 1822–1859*. Edited by F. Burkhardt. Cambridge, UK, et al.: Cambridge University Press, 2008.

Darwin, Charles. "Darwin as a Traveller." *The Geographical Journal*, vol. 126, no. 2, 1960, pp. 129–136.

Darwin, Charles. *On the Origin of Species: Or the Preservation of Favoured Races in the Struggle for Life*. London: John Murray, 1859. The Project Gutenberg E-Book, https://www.gutenberg.org/files/1228/1228-h/1228-h.htm. Accessed October 24, 2019.

Gould, Stephen Jay. "Foreword: A Life's Epistolary Drama." In Charles Darwin, *Origins* …, pp. ix–xxii.

Hall, Alfred Rupert. *Rewolucja naukowa 1500–1800. Kształtowanie się nowożytnej postawy naukowej*. Translated by T. Zembrzuski, Warsaw: Pax, 1966.

Henry, John. *The Scientific Revolution and the Origins of Modern Science*. Third edition. New York: Palgrave, 2005.

Knapp, Sandra. "Alfred Russel Wallace." In *Wielcy* ... .

Mägdefrau, Karl. *Historia botaniki. życie i dokonania wielkich badaczy*. Translated by M. Mularczyk. Wroclaw: Wydawnictwo Uniwersytetu Wrocławskiego, 2004.

Magee, Judith. "Alexander von Humboldt." In Wielcy przyrodnicy. Od Arystotelesa do Darwina. Edited by R. Huxley. Translated by R. Milanowski. Warsaw: pwn, 2009

Minois, Georges. *Kościół i nauka. Dzieje pewnego niezrozumienia. Od Galileusza do Jana Pawła II*. Translated by A. Szymanowski. Warsaw: Bellona, 1996.

Rosik, Stanisław. „Barbari et Greci w Iumne : "Europa barbarzyńska" jako koncepcja w studiach nad formowaniem się kulturowego oblicza Kontynentu". In Europa barbarica, Europa christiana: studia mediaevalia Carolo Modzelewski dedicata. Edited by Roman Michałowski. Warszawa: Wydawnictwo "Dig", 2008.

Sulloway, Frank J. "Darwin's Conversion: The Beagle Voyage and Its Aftermath." *Journal of the History of Biology*, vol. 15, no. 3, 1980, pp. 325–396.

Tallmadge, John. "From Chronicle to Quest: The Shaping of Darwin's *Voyage of the Beagle*." *Victorian Studies*, vol. 23, no. 3, 1980, pp. 325–345.

Thomson, Keith; "Karol Darwin." In Wielcy przyrodnicy. Od Arystotelesa do Darwina. Edited by R. Huxley. Translated by R. Milanowski. Warsaw: pwn, 2009

White, Michael and John Gribbin. *Darwin. żywot uczonego*. Translated by H. Pawlikowska-Gannon. Warsaw: Prószynski i S-ka, 1998.

CHAPTER 7

The Spanish "Crisis of the 17th Century"

Magdalena Barbaruk

1   The Crisis Myth

The history of Spain offers a "horrendous example of a suicide of a nation, an example which other nations should long ponder," wrote Alfred Fouillée in his *Esquisse psychologique des peuples* (Lewandowski 2005, 251). If we assume that histories of nations are a domain of myth and mythologization, the myth of a crisis, "malady,"[1] "decline," "decadence," or "incurable collapse" was one of the major formative factors of the dominant narrative on Spain's past. Having easily replaced the old imperial myth, this particular myth appears to thrive today on the fertile soil of the current economic crisis. The history of Spain holds something that history writers and historical philosophers of the Polish past of immoderation recognize as intimately familiar: successes seem too grand, while crises long-lasting, permanent, and knowing no end. Accounts of the past barely feature notions related to progress, an incremental but systematic growth of cities, or the civilizing process in institutions and customs.[2] Focused

---

1 Cf. Unamuno's famous declaration "Me duele España" (Spain hurts me).
2 Skepticism about the idea of progress was also expressed by Théophile Gautier, who traveled across Spain in the 19th century and had an opportunity to see the Grand Mosque in Córdoba: "It was the Caliph Abderama I., who laid the foundations of the Mosque at Cordova, towards the end of the eighth century, and the works were carried on with such activity that the whole edifice was completed at the commencement of the ninth; twenty-one years were found sufficient to terminate this gigantic monument! When we reflect that, a thousand years ago, so admirable a work, and one of such colossal proportions, was executed in so short a time by a people who have since fallen into a state of the most savage barbarism, the mind is lost in astonishment, and refuses to believe the pretended doctrines of human progress which are generally received at the present day; we even feel inclined to adopt an opinion diametrically opposite, when we visit those countries which formerly enjoyed a state of civilization which now exists no longer. I have always regretted, for my own part, that the Moors did not remain in possession of Spain, which certainly has only lost by their expulsion. Under their dominion, if we can believe the popular exaggerations so gravely collected and preserved by historians, Cordova contained two hundred thousand houses, eighty thousand palaces, and nine hundred baths, while its suburbs consisted of twelve thousand villages. At present it does not number forty thousand inhabitants, and appears almost deserted" (Gautier 1853, 249).

on "extremity," narratives on the past events and on the Spanish identity[3] make Spain into a rewarding material for reflection on the nature of crises and the essence of "crisis-ness". They are also interesting resources for the study of the links between crisis and globalization processes, as Spain was a major actor in at least one of the most important events in the modern history of Europe and the world – the conquest of America – and this fact has often been cited as the cause of Spain's economic decline. In one of her essays, Zofia Szmydtowa wondered: "How did it happen that as early as towards the end of the 16th century voices began to be heard (only to multiply later) that all spheres of the country's life were at risk of a severe crisis. The year 1492, which was first commonly regarded as the beginning of Spain's greatness and triumph, came to be deemed a fatal date in its history"[4] (1969, 114). Equally importantly, according to Ortega y Gasset, only events as momentous as the discovery of the New World, crusades, or the Reconquista, imbued this "invertebrate country" with cohesion, unity, and strength. "If I grasp [Ortega y Gasset's idea]," writes Michel del Castillo, "this country does not succeed in any average undertaking. It needs grand plans to implement. If Spaniards do not conquer America, they become nothing and Spain falls apart" (Castillo 1989, 20). In Castillo's view, the history of Spain represents a sequence of discontinuities – "moments of collapse" – which make it incomprehensible to external observers. Above all, the myth of crisis is the axis of the perception of the Spanish 17th century, when the country was ruled by the Hapsburgian *menores*, Philip III and Philip IV (and partly Charles II). Most history textbook chapters dedicated to this period are symptomatically entitled "The Crisis of the 17th Century," and Domínguez Ortiz, the author of one of them, addresses the popularity of the "crisis-inflected" perspective on history by highlighting the global aspect of the problem:

> The crisis of the 17th century has been an object of heated polemics for over twenty years now, and although we are yet very far from settling the dispute, the gap between the positions in it has been considerably

---

[3] Thoughts on the extremity and the dichotomous character of the Spanish soul, which is torn by the dueling forces of "utopism" and "nadism," were articulated by Unamuno in the notion of "agonism." The ambiguity of this word sounds particularly interesting in the context of the discourse on the decline of Spain.

[4] The year 1492 is only symbolic: "In January, the last kingdom of the Moors falls, and Boabdil is exiled. [...] in October, Columbus's ships reach the shores of America, which opens huge territories for the uncertain monarchy and simultaneously furnishes it with fantastical riches. This is a key date in the most poetic sense. In fact, the collapse of the policy of tolerance and assimilation [vis-à-vis Moors and Jews] for the sake of the policy of plunder had already begun two ages before. By 1492, the dice had already been cast" (Castillo 1989, 50).

bridged. The interest in the phenomenon itself results from the fact that it did not affect just one country, but had an all-European, perhaps even worldwide, resonance, and its causes are not quite clear yet. That unfortunate century got wedged between two centuries of vivid progress, which produces methodological, if not philosophical, problems as it contravenes the common notion of the uninterrupted development of the Western world. Misunderstandings are largely bred because crisis is conceived in abstract terms while Europe should rather be examined as an ensemble of independently developing territories; Europe looked different at the threshold of the century and at its end. The conjuncture was different in England and in Spain, and there were considerable disparities even within individual countries. Finally, we should bear in mind that although all historical processes are interrelated to a degree, they do not always unfold at the same pace: a country can go through a deep economic or demographic crisis, but simultaneously experience the apex of its cultural and scientific development. This is what was happening in 17th-century Europe, which is colloquially called Baroque Europe, in which human suffering and national demises coincided with splendid cultural accomplishments. These stark contrasts also concerned Spain.

DOMÍNGUEZ ORTIZ 2007, 309

The passage conveys an awareness of relatively autonomous orders of the human universe (with the cultural order largely independent of other spheres of reality), which is shared by many other researchers of Spanish history. This is highly relevant to the major thematic concerns of my argument. In this chapter, while analyzing the Spanish case, I seek to tackle two (differently) popular notions of the causes and functions of crisis. Each of these beliefs is associated with globalization-related issues in its own way. One of them holds that in certain economic-cultural circumstances "wealth" can be the cause of crisis, collapse, and poverty both of huge states and of individual people. The other envisages the concurrence of economic, political, and state crisis on the one hand and the thriving of culture – art, literature, philosophy, etc. – on the other (also as propelled by wider-ranging – European or global – ideas, such as Renaissance and Baroque movements). The birth of a masterpiece despite the fall of the state is vividly exemplified in Miguel de Cervantes's *Don Quixote* and the artistic grandeur of the Spanish Golden Age as well as in the intellectual revival associated with what has come to be called Generation'98 (which is also observable in other countries, such as Russia and Germany at the turn of the 19th century). Given that dynamics of culture have their specificity and distinctiveness, historians are faced with a considerable challenge when trying to establish the precise timeframes of epochs (or crises). Miłkowski, for one, insists that "[p]eriods of the greatest achievements in culture and art do not always coincide with the apogees of a nation's or a civilization's political power. According to the first of two interpretations, the Golden Age (*Siglo de Oro*) of Spanish culture extended over one and a half centuries and overlapped with Spain's domination in Europe (from the reign of Charles V till the mid-17th century). The second interpretation gives precedence to literary achievements and locates the Golden Age between the mid-16th century and the end of the third quarter of the 17th century" (Miłkowski 2009, 149).

In fact, this issue can also be approached in other ways. For example, Domínguez Ortiz, who admits that the economy, politics, and culture can develop autonomously, actually sides with the former option. He locates the Golden Age at the turn of the 16th century and views it as terminating in a crisis in the mid-17th century, which was concomitant with crises in other spheres of the country's life:

> The Spanish Golden Age (…) indisputable excelled in mystical ad ascetic thought and in literature: Fray Luis de Granada, Saint Teresa of Avila, Saint John of the Cross … It essentially and in some senses originally contributed to the development of historiography (above all through prolific writings of soldier-writers, especially of conquistadors from America). The initially bland theater reached the heights of art owing to such dramatists as Lope de Vega, Tirso de Molina, Ruiz de Alarcón, and Calderón de la Barca, not to mention a throng of lesser playwrights. Evoking these few names is enough to realize that the Golden Age does not overlap either with the 16th or with the 17th century, but it flourishes as one century passes into the next, with the chronology of particular timeframes largely depending on respective genres. Barring a few exceptions, Spanish art as a whole found itself in a profound crisis around the middle of the 17th century. This marks the moment when the deep economic meltdown, whose causes lay in previous epochs, twined with the decline of that powerful culture, which had long been able to pass for the most splendid one in Europe.
>
> DOMÍNGUEZ ORTIZ, 270

2 Economic Crisis vs. Cultural Crisis

"By a most peculiar whim of fate, the time of Spain's economic and political decadence coincided with the age of its most exquisite cultural development," states Leszek Biały, a distinguished translator of Calderón de la Barca, Spanish scholar, and art historian (1997, XXV). His assertion, which seconds the insights of historians, encapsulates a common disinterest in issues such as reflection on culture as an important agent behind human behavior and its outcomes (in this case, on the dynamics, functions, or autonomy of culture), which are fundamental in this matter. When the cited texts wax eloquent on the mysterious and peculiar flourishing of Spanish culture in the 17th century, they evidently rely on a popular, narrow, and evaluative understanding of culture, in which culture denotes all observable products of human activity (so-called achievements) in fine arts, music, theater,[5] and above all literature. Multiple examples and proofs of Spain's cultural ascendancy can to my knowledge be found in all studies of Spanish culture and history, irrespective of what discipline or period they represent. The flourishing seems to be one of the truths taken for granted and uncontested by anybody who has heard of the brilliance of Cervantes, Calderón, or Velázquez. *España en su historia* (1948), a classic study authored by the historian of culture and philologist Américo Castro, who rehearses and illustrates this idea, is evoked by Carlos Fuentes:

> Spain's politics and economy [...] were little effective; its contribution to science and technology, relative; but its talents in arts, enormous. I do not know whether it is an absolute rule that the greatest works of the Spanish genius coincide with the periods of the crisis and decadence of Spanish society. Be it as it may, *The Book of Good Love* salvages and translates into Spanish the influences of the Cordovan caliphate, when the grand world of the Umayads of al-Andalus was destroyed by the invasions of the Almoravides and Almohads. *The Celestina*, a masterpiece of the Hebrew Spain, was produced when Jews and convertites were exiled and persecuted. The Golden Age, with Cervantes, Lope, Quevedo, Góngora, and Calderón, comes into bloom as the power of Spain wilts. Velázquez is a painter of the declining court of Philip IV, and Goya paints in the times of the blind and mercenary Bourbons, whose crowns were taken away by Bonaparte and colonies by the rebelling Creoles. And after the particularly miserable 19th century, which Sarmiento, with a typical parricidal satisfaction [...] thus describes in 1864: "There are neither artists nor writers, neither scholars nor economists, politicians, historians nor anything of

---

5   The 17th-century theater mania is discussed by Leszek Biały in his introduction to Calderón de La Barca's famous *autos sacramentales*. As Biały notes, this century saw the staging of ten thousand dramas (comedies and tragedies) and about one thousand *autos sacramentales*: "It can easily be calculated that over that century a new play was performed every three or four days" (1997, XXVIII).

value at all," it was only the shock brought about by the loss of the remnants of the empire in the war with the United States that triggered a series of sequent effects. Generation '98, Unamuno, Valle-Inclán, Ramón y Cajal, Machado, Ortega, Guillén, García Lorca, Bunuel, Alberti, Cernuda, Prados – this is a magnificent explosion of culture, brutally interrupted by the Fascist dictatorship. What will arise from the Fascist pressure and oppression in the nearest future? I dare not prophesize. I'd rather limit myself to subversively citing the emphatic words of the enlightened libertine, the famed Casanova: "Oh, Spaniards ... Who will wrench you out of your lethargy? Oh, country so miserable and pitiable today ... What is it that you need? A powerful revolution, a total transformation, a terrible shock, a rejuvenating Conquista, because your stagnation can no longer be overcome by civilized means alone; fire is needed to burn out the gangrene that afflicts you."

FUENTES 1980, 227–228

Unamuno had something else in mind than these authors when he opined that Spain did not add anything to the world's legacy of ideas beyond the hegemonic facts in the order of culture (2014, 231): the Counter-Reformation, the Reconquista ("eight centuries of warfare against the Moors, during which she [Spain] defended Europe from Mohammedanism, her work of internal unification"), the discovery of America and the Indies (creating "a score of nations, reserving nothing for herself, and [begetting], like the Conquistadores did, free men on poor Indian slaves"), and Spanish mysticism (233). These examples represent specific values which defined the cultural identity of Spain. These manifestations of "stone spirituality" (Gondowicz) simultaneously point to some of the reasons behind the "crisis of the 17th century." In culturological explorations, it makes more sense to highlight the role of cultures in the crisis and collapse of Spain (values as a factor in the economic crisis) than to talk of a cultural heyday (of various arts) despite the crisis of the state. Of course, this observation does not oppose the notion of culture being relatively independent of the economy or politics.

3   "The Crisis of the 17th Century"

If "the crisis of the 17th century" is not by default a crisis in culture, we must ask what developments are subsumed under this heading in historical-cultural discourse. As these developments are amply and insightfully described in the literature (e.g., Miłkowski, Domínguez Ortiz, Castillo, Szmydtowa, Biały), it is enough to briefly characterize them here, for their robustness and extremity paint an exceptionally vivid picture of a country submerged in a total crisis. The deeds and events of which this image is comprised seem so improbable and fantastic to us that we are inclined to endorse the view articulated by M. G. de Cellorigo in 1600: "It looks as if this state had been turned into a commonwealth of enchanted people living outside the natural order of things" (Szmydtowa 1969, 116). A perceptive observer of Spain, De Cellorigo actually criticized Spain's illusory wealth, which was based on bonds rather than on production. Yet not so long before, still in the 16th century, hardly any country could match the economic and political power of Spain. Charles V "came closer to establishing a worldwide monarchy than any other ruler before or after him" (114), and thousands of tons of silver and gold were brought to the port of Seville.[6] At the peak of Spain's glory, the reign of Charles V, the king of Spain and the Holy Roman Emperor, extended over the Netherlands, half of Italy, Northern Africa and the New World, with the Mediterranean Sea customarily referred to as "our sea." As Biały reminds, "later, Montesquieu would compare this extraordinary fall of a superpower […] to the decadence of the Roman Empire" (1997, XXV). What was it that brought the country "over which the sun did not set" to bankruptcy so rapidly? The following factors are listed in contemporary discourse on the crisis of the 17th century:

1. Demographic crisis. The country became depopulated (plague, pestilence, a famine caused by the collapse of agriculture, emigration to America, the expulsion of the Moriscos in 1609). As Miłkowski explains, the scale of the demographic crisis "was unprecedented in Spain since the mid-14th century (the waves of Europe's most deadly epidemics). Although the statistics are not quite reliable, it is very likely that the population size which Spain boasted at the end of the 16th century (about eight million people) was only reached again in the mid-18th century" (Miłkowski 2009, 165).

2. Economic crisis. This involved production becoming unprofitable due to inflation; the collapse of wool production, which was Spain's most important industry (the destructive role of what is known as the Mesta), and

---

6 "After huge deposits of silver were discovered in Potosí (Peru, 1545) and Zacatecas (Mexico, 1546), silver was the chief cargo carried by Spanish argosies. The Silver Mountain in Potosi accounted for an estimated half of the world's silver production in the second half of the 16th century. For Spain, it entailed the capacity to fund its European wars, while for the Peruvian Indians, it meant human losses comparable with epidemics" (Miłkowski 2009, 138). The amount of silver in Europe is reported to have increased by 300% and of gold by 20% between 1531–1660 (Biały 1997, X).

the related decline of large trading hubs (Medina del Campo, Burgos); the breakdown of ship-building companies; crisis in agriculture (land being abandoned by peasants; in 1600, one-third of the fields which had been farmed a hundred years before were left untilled); and soaring prices. As succinctly summed up by Biały: "Gradually, Spain was becoming a bizarre country in which production was not profitable to anybody. Anybody except foreigners" (Biały, XII). This was exacerbated by the economic ramifications of the expulsion of Jews[7] and Moriscos.[8]

3. Financial meltdown (inflation caused by the influx of bullion from America).[9] This included factors such as the depletion of silver and gold supplies,[10] minting copper coins *vellón*,[11] state debt (state loans called *juros*),[12] and the lack of money to pay foreign debt and interest on state loans. The state was declared bankrupt in 1607 (under Philip III) as well as in 1627, 1647, 1652, and 1662 (under Philip IV): "The aberrancy (chronic malady) of the Spanish finances is best shown in the distribution of the state expenditures (in 1621–1640). Over 90% of the state revenues was used up to pay debts (and interest on loans) and to fund military operations" (Miłkowski 2009, 167). While tax exemptions were extensively

---

[7]   According to Domínguez Ortiz, the expulsion of Jews in 1492 was driven by purely religious motives. The *Reyes Católicos* "perfectly realized what they were losing as Jews were leaving. They knew that Jews were faithful subjects and a valuable source of the Crown's revenue. It is impossible to establish how many Jews chose to be baptized in order to avoid expulsion." Many Jews returned; and the estimated total number of the expelled stands at about 100,000. However, "[i]n economic terms, losses were far more damaging. Spain got rid of educated and industrious people, a considerable proportion of whom was made up of craftsmen and merchants, i.e., the bourgeois, who were not really numerous in Castile in the first place" (Domínguez Ortiz 2007, 223).

[8]   "Today, the economic losses caused by the expulsion of the Moriscos are assessed less critically than ten years after the expulsion. At that time, the common opinion was that the exodus of the Moriscos was the chief reason behind Spain's decline. Today, historians believe that the expulsion was a factor which only exacerbated the negative economic developments which had already been there for some time" (Miłkowski 2009, 156).

[9]   "Precious metals briefly appeared on the peninsula and triggered inflation only to disappear quickly in the strongboxes of Dutch banks" (Castillo 1989, 62).

[10] "In the period of the most sizeable supplies (1596–1600), ships brought in thirteen million ducats' worth of metals from America. Subsequently, in 1646–1659, the amount dropped to two million" (Miłkowski 2009, 167).

[11] "In the mid-17th century, the world's biggest producer of gold and silver did not have gold and silver coins in regular circulation. To purchase basic commodities, people used *vellón* in sacks of a given weight (official coin denomination was not counted), e.g., three kilos of *vellón* for five kilos of cheese" (Miłkowski 2009, 167).

[12] For example, *juros* amounted to 112 million ducats in 1623.

granted to several population,[13] the property of other groups, such as the Moriscos, was confiscated; at least 20% of the population made their living by begging or relied on the support of the church, the state, or private individuals (Miłkowski 2009, 141).

4. "Deep social crisis." Protests, riots, popular rebellions, and thuggery were rampant; the numbers of vagabonds and beggars soared. The crisis affected all the social strata, therein the noble aristocracy even though they possessed the wealth (staggering debts and interest payments devoured their revenues); noble titles began to lose their value and relevance (the selling of noble titles). The crisis afflicting the urban middle estate (merchants, craftsmen, etc.) had two reasons: firstly, they could not effectively compete with foreign merchants and products, and secondly, they invested in the state debt (a safer source of income).

4   Gold for the Bold

Because "overseas riches were viewed as the cause of poverty which Spain had not known before the discovery of America" (Szmydtowa 1969, 114), the impact of the Conquista and the influx of bullion from America on the Spanish way of life – or, more broadly, on Spanish culture, mentality, and identity – should be emphatically articulated. Special emphasis is also due to the role of cultural factors (values) which determined the dissipation of America's treasures. The point is that culture appears to have been the major factor in the fateful "crisis of Spain," which was not overcome before the end of the 19th century.

Although some historians have questioned the interdependence of the influx of gold and silver on the one hand and Spain's economic breakdown (inflation) on the other, Miłkowski insists that this very finding of the American historian Earl J. Hamilton is still indisputable[14]: "Accustomed to contemporary inflation rates, we fail to comprehend what the average annual inflation of

---

13   Hence, an upsurge in the trade in noble titles (everybody sought an *hidalguía*). Namely, "the noble status protects from prison for debts, secures several tax exemptions (e.g., on houses, horses, mules, and arms), and gives a freedom of traveling" (Borejsza 1937, 186).

14   "Earl J. Hamilton in his classic study *American Treasure and the Price Revolution in Spain* proved a clear interdependence between the inflow of bullion from America and price-rise. By the same token, he confirmed the assessment of several 16th-century Spanish economist, such as Azpilcueta. Later historians emphasized the relevant influence of other factors on the increase in prices, but they did not undermine Hamilton's basic thesis" (Miłkowski 2009, 143).

two percent, which produced a total increase of prices by five hundred percent over one hundred years, meant to people living in the 16th century. When compared with the late Middle Ages and their characteristic deflation, it was a veritable price revolution" (Miłkowski 2009, 143). As Europe's most expensive country with no labor force of its own (which is addressed below), Spain attracted foreigners with a promise of good wages, as a result of which domestic industry became unprofitable. Spanish underdevelopment was also bred by the "American money" in another way:

> Money was Spain's export product. Minted in America, the *real de a ocho* (a silver coin worth eight reales) was the first globally recognized international currency in the history of humanity (trade with Asian merchants was based on it). Because Spain was able to buy basically everything, the country stopped modernizing its own economy. Its internal development stalled, and a mechanism kicked in resembling one which was put in motion by Polish grain exports, which secured profit for today, but caused underdevelopment in the future.
> MIŁKOWSKI 2009, 144

Let us stress once again that neither silver nor gold ruined Spain. The mischief was done by a unique, contingent alignment of economic and cultural factors. There is a common consensus on this point. For example, Miłkowski concludes that "the supply of precious metals from America by no means had a purely negative impact on the Spanish economy. The crisis was caused by how the state used them" (144); and Lewandowski observes that

> the thoughtless squandering of American treasures is most dumbfounding. Between 1503 and 1560, 185 tons of gold and 16,000 tons of silver were brought from America. Given this, the state can be considered to have grown exceptionally rich. In fact, however, the king of Spain was a bankrupt. An economist suggested that Spaniards should get down to work and reduce imports, but it was too late. Philip II's secretary noted down: "Habit had the upper hand, and circumstances made Spain live beyond its means, without sufficient domestic production. Seemingly rich in all the treasures of America, Spain was systematically becoming poorer, and when it was eventually acknowledged as a fact, the country had neither means no desire to lift itself." Above all, the power of the empire was squandered over the one hundred and forty years of absurd warfare.
> LEWANDOWSKI 2005, 251

The reasons for the wars in which imperial Spain engaged are pithily summed up by Castillo:

> "Penury and false glory," the contemporaries of Philip II repeated in bitterness. Spain is wasting away, bleeding out to defend a chimera: the triumph of religion with which it identifies. Its armies fight absurd battles all over the place: in Flanders they fight the rebels; in Germany, Lutherans; in Italy, the French; at the English Channel, the heretic English; in South Africa, Berbers; in the Mediterranean, Turks. Why did Spaniards so doggedly fashion themselves into the defenders of the true faith? The reason was that Spain had to take up a desperate challenge: it mutilated itself to become Christian, and then it committed suicide to prove that it continued Christian.
> CASTILLO 1989, 62–63

The blame is first and foremost attributed to the "Spanish" values:

> The economic consequences of these policies [property confiscations replacing labor and taxes] were easily foreseeable: Spain slid into poverty from which it was never to rise again. In psychological terms, these ramifications would only be more serious: the values endorsed by the bourgeois, such as work, success, and progress, would be supplanted by typically aristocratic attitudes – contempt for manual labor, the cult of war treated as an industry, and caste pride in dynastic traditions. The poorest population groups were completely seduced by this myth. They may not have had enough food to go by, but they proudly repeated that they had been Christian for ages.
> CASTILLO, 56–57

Of course, pride was taken not only in the religious denomination but also in the fact of not laboring for one's livelihood and holding wealth in stoical disregard.[15] There were three ways in which money could be obtained honorably

---

15 Borejsza offers an illuminating example of such an attitude. It was described by Fray Juan de la Cerda, a well-known Spanish moralist of the 16th century: "The women of Seville like what is rare and costly rather than what is truly valuable. Cloth should come from Flanders, and ambergris from the most remote corners of the world to lend a pleasing scent to their gloves and leather doublets. Shoes must also be perfumed and shine, for gold should glitter in them, ribbons likewise … Everything must be new, fresh from the tailor, put on for a day and discarded the next …" (Borejsza 1937, 187).

and in compliance with the noble status: "*Iglesias, o mar, o casa real*: church revenues; the sea, that is, overseas plunder; and service at the royal court" (Borejsza 1937, 186). However, the poorest nobility, which was ironically portrayed in *The Ingenious Gentleman Don Quixote of La Mancha*, also shared the status similar to the king's, which was consistent with the proverbial description: *hidalgos como el Rey, dineros menos* (gentlemen like the king, except for the money). King Alphonso XIII (whose reign was terminated by the proclamation of the Second Republic in 1931) had such seventeenth-century aristocrats of the spirit in mind when saying that he ruled twenty-one million royals. Thus there were two causes of the crisis of Spain in the 17th century: one of them was financial (primarily inflation) and the other was cultural (therein wars of religion and the squandering of the wealth in a profligate lifestyle). It cannot be conclusively stated whether they actually disappeared for good when the end of the 17th-century crisis was announced.

5   The End of the Crisis?

It is an interesting question whether Spaniards realized that they were living in the age of crisis (that is, that the reality they inhabited was afflicted by something that was not "natural" to it, something that was not its "normal" state, that in other ages crisis was thankfully not experienced). It was after all so long-lasting that some people might not have known or remembered another Spain. Despite illiteracy and incomparably narrower access to information than we enjoy today, it seems that the awareness of "the crisis of the 17th century" and responses to it were quite similar to those we know today from mass media. Crisis was discussed as ubiquitously and fervently in the 17th century as it was a few years ago, when media and scholarship were seized by a real crisis mania (with many media experts claiming that crisis was an intersubjective media event). The Spanish crisis was also debated by an array of experts, and according to Miłkowski, the debate on and the proclamation of the "state of crisis" were fueled by the experience of difference and change:

> With the riches still flowing in from America, the contrast between the bygone prosperity of the country and a dismal decrease in the living standard of its inhabitants was so glaring that Spain was flooded by writings and treatises which tried to explain the reasons for this state of affairs and suggesting the ways (*arbitrios*) of overcoming the crisis to the monarchs. Their authors (*arbitristas*) were clerks, merchants, clergymen, and officers. The scale of the public debate on the condition of the state, the

economy, and politics was unprecedented in Europe at that time. Broadsides, pamphlets, satirical texts, and longer treatises had big print runs (considering the rate of literacy in Spain at that time), were widely read, and sparked common discussions. Eminent political personages (e.g., Count de Gondomar, an ambassador to England and an influential person at court) criticized the policies of the authorities, and common people (whose access to the king was easier than ours to political leaders today) publicly accused the king to his face that he did not do anything to save the country. The sense of Spain's demise was so prevalent that Philip IV himself and Olivares considered it indisputable.

> MIŁKOWSKI 2009, 170–171

I believe we can agree that while the primary impulse for the debate on the crisis indeed came from the experience of impoverishment, such a mindset cannot be attributed to the entire century. In this sense, the notion of "the 17th-century crisis" is rather a historical and philosophical construct, which is not reflected in real lives of individuals who did not know any better living conditions. Opinions are divided on whether the crisis magically ended with the onset of the 18th century (as the Bourbons ascended to power) or whether, on the contrary, Spain has ever shaken it off, which is evinced in the collapse witnessed by Generation'98. Historians favor the former option, whereby they cite quantifiable, concrete data. What they tend to be preoccupied with is rather to pinpoint as precisely as possible the moment marking the passage from the fall of Spain to its new growth.[16] To talk about permanent crisis in the life of a nation may be a sin against the logic of common sense, but this position is undoubtedly tenable (and promises interesting outcomes) if we adopt another, most generally speaking "philosophical" cognitive perspective.

Bibliography

Biały, Leszek. "Przedmowa [Preface]." In P. Calderón de la Barca. *Autos sacramentales*. Wroclaw, Warsaw, Cracow: Ossolineum, 1997.

Borejsza, Jerzy. "Na marginesie epoki Cervantesa." *Wiedza i Życie*, no. 3, 1937.

---

16 "Older historiographical studies located the economic revival of Spain in the 18th century. More recent research implies that the economic invigoration had already commenced under the reign of Charles II. Because the war for his succession caused considerable destruction in Spain, people failed to notice that before its outburst the Spanish economy had begun to grow more robust" (Miłkowski 2009, 170).

Castillo, Michel del. *Hiszpańskie czary*. Translated by D. Knysz-Tomaszewska Warsaw: Książka i Wiedza, 1989.

Domínguez Ortiz, Antonio. "Renesans i Oświecenie." In M. Tunon de Lara, J. Valdeón Baruque, A. Domínguez Ortiz. *Historia Hiszpanii*. Cracow: Universitas, 2007.

Fuentes, Carlos. "Cervantes, czyli krytyka sztuki czytania." *Literatura na Świecie*, vol. 109, no. 5, 1980.

Lewandowski, Edmund. *Pejzaż etniczny Europy*. Warszawa: Warszawskie Wydawnictwo Literackie Muza 2005.

Miłkowski, Tadeusz. *Historia Hiszpanii*. Wroclaw: Ossolineum, 2009.

Szmydtowa, Zofia. "Z wieku Cervantesa." In Z. Szmydtowa. *Studia i portrety*. Warsaw: Państwowy Instytut Wydawniczy, 1969.

Théophile, Gautier. *Wanderings in Spain*. Translated by Thomas Robert McQuoid. London: Ingram, Cooke, ad Co., 1853.

Unamuno, Miguel de. *The Tragic Sense of Life*. Translated by J.E. Crawford Flitch. SophiaOmni, 2014.

CHAPTER 8

Nation-Forming Processes in Latin America
A New Integration Model?

Tadeusz Paleczny

Any attempt to construct an account of how nation-building processes have unfolded in Latin America is fraught with controversies and theoretical difficulties. They invariably compel several questions of various generality and relevance. By organizing these questions, we may be able to formulate the problem more precisely and define the way to describe it and to explain the course of nation-forming processes in Latin America.

The questions that offer themselves in this context predominantly concern the character of integration processes which forge broader social systems of diverse racial, ethnic, regional, and religious components. For example, are these processes a continuation of European integration models, or do they represent a new cultural, political, and economic order? Did Europeans – in this case, specifically, the Iberians – exert a dominant influence on the formation of Latin American societies? In how far did the development of Latin American cultures follow a distinctive trajectory of its own? To what extent are we faced with a homogeneous culture and to what with a multiplicity of cultures? Can the community of religion, language, colonial tradition, its resultant values and shared customs be legitimately called a civilization? Do Latin American cultures boast their own unique spirituality and mentality expressed in mysticism, irrationalism, and pursuit of communality? How strong is the influence of racial amalgamation on the Latin American "variety" of integration processes, therein nation-making ones? What implications does it have for the position of Latin Americans of mixed racial origin, especially Mestizos? What role did the state play in the shaping of cultures and civilization in Latin America? Is "nation-state" an apt term in this context, or is it more apposite to talk of a civic society? Are Christianization and Europeanization indeed the most important processes in fashioning the identity of Latin Americans? Can the principles of the models of Westernization, globalization, or Americanization be meaningfully applied to Latin American cultures? Did the U.S. impose the concept of "dependent development" on Latin America? Is this concept enacted outside of the economy and the state, in the field nation-building processes.

Can the relatively highly socially integrated and acculturated civic societies of Latin America be depicted as nation-states or rather as nation-cultures?

By way of organizing these questions, as well as the unasked ones, I delineate the following analytical areas in this paper:

1. Can Latin American indigenous cultures represented by autochthonic peoples currently develop towards national societies? Or, rather, are prenational bonds dominant at present? Given their complexity, are Latin American societies transforming into communities of tolerably homogeneous national culture or, rather, of heterogeneous pluralistic civilization? What happens with local autochthonic communities and ethnic groups of migrants from Europe and Asia in nation-building processes? Are these cultures homogenized, do they disappear, are they reduced to a Brazilian-type identity or Mexican national identification, or do new bonds emerge in them, characteristic of culturally composite and pluralist societies? Are the pace and the degree of integration and nationalization the same for white Latin Americans and Latin Americans of color?

2. What mechanisms determined the course of integration processes in Latin American countries? Are any qualitatively different stages identifiable within these processes? Are Iberization and Christianization among the most important processes of Latin American cultural identity formation? What role did mestization, indigenism, pan-Indianism, and pan-Americanism play in Latin American nation-forming processes?

3. Do Latin American societies continue European integration models and reproduce the principles of European nation-building processes? Do they choose and develop their own model of cultural, civic, and civilizational bonds? To what extent are the principles behind Latin American assimilation processes original, distinct, and bound up with the nature of Latin American societies?

4. Are there nations in Latin America? If so, in what sense and to what extent are they nations? Is racial, ethnic, and regional diversity not a meaningful obstacle to forging national cultures out of complex, multi-cultural, highly heterogeneous, socially disintegrated, economically unstable, and structurally stratified civic societies? To what degree are Latin American ideologies and identities ethnocentric and nationalist? Is there a binary of, on the one hand, European monocentricsm of conservative political and cultural white minority elites and, on the other, polymorphism and pluralism of liberally-minded racially-mixed Latin Americans "of color"?

Demarcated by these four groups of questions, these analytical fields will help us organize the concepts and account of the nature and course of nation-making processes in Latin America: nation or civic society, culture or

TABLE 8.1   Analytical model of nation-making processes in Latin America

Culture	Civilization
Romantic model	Enlightenment model
Iberization	Integration
Christianization	Syncretism
Linguistic, religious and racial	Heterogenization, assimilation, acculturation
Homogenization	Amalgamation, Latinization
Nation	Civic society
Monocentrism	Polymorphism
Conservatism	Liberalism
Ethnocentrism	Pluralism

civilization, multiculturality and pluralism or monocentrism and homogenization, a conservative or liberal development model, Iberization and coerced assimilation or voluntary integration and acculturation, Christianization or religious syncretism, European, Western development path or domestic, Latin American one?

The actual nation-building processes in Latin America have unfolded in between these poles, involving both kinds of relationships, as well as combining and re-combining internal and external influences which stem from the cultural legacy of the indigenous populations of Latin America and from the cultures of settlers who colonized the continent.

Table 8.1 presents a general, simplified analytical model which I employ in my further argument to explain the causes, genesis, course, mechanisms, and consequences of nation-building processes in Latin America. Latin American societies have both developed upon European and American – Western – cultural standards and devised their own mechanisms of political, economic, and cultural integration.

1   The State and National Culture in Latin-American Tradition

The processes of social, cultural, and political integration of the peoples inhabiting both Americas were certainly impacted by two grand European traditions: the Enlightenment and Romanticism, which, though aligned in some respects, were largely divergent in terms of their tenets and implications for Latin American nation-making processes. The two grand traditions shared the idea that autochthonic peoples-cultures of both Americas found themselves beyond the mainstream of development and progress, consigned to the margin of phenomena and events dominated by European national culture. Champions of either theoretical tradition preached the hegemony of national European cultures in shaping social and cultural life in British, Spanish, Portuguese, French, and Dutch colonies.

Enlightenment thought held that the state surpassed tradition, language, religion, and culture as integrating and bond-forging factors. It insisted that social development found its fullest and supreme expression in the European nation-state, viewed as an organizational system of civic society. The nation was also conceptualized in terms of state-political integration as a community of citizens who were equal vis-à-vis each other and the sovereign government. Enlightenment theories only deemed cultural communities which had their own states to be nations. In order to exist and develop, a nation had to establish its own political organization. The Enlightenment concept of the primacy of the national bond developing within its own state was picked up by Hegel, whose Romantic framework "denied" non-European cultures the right to their own political-national subjectivity, framing them as historically belated and thus devoid of a specific national "spirit," which he considered to be a causative principle endowing primitive, savage, and barbarian peoples with a capacity to institute their own sovereign government. As Leopold Zea puts it, "Hegel differentiates two Americas through which the spirit realizes itself: one of them was conquered by Anglo-Saxon pioneering nations, and the other was seized by Iberian nations. Both of them must yet overcome what has remained of nature; they must liberate the spirit from the necessities that nature imposes on it" (Zea 1993, 37).

On this take, indigenous populations and tribal cultures, whose development lags behind that of European cultures and which are anchored "in nature" rather than in "culture," should be civilized by European cultures and absorbed – incorporated – by cultures of a "higher" degree. Following the same principles, the advocates of the rights of autochthonic Indians, such as Bartolomé de la Casas, laid the foundation for the Enlightenment principle of protecting individuals, but not necessarily cultural groups, which were destined either to be engrossed by European civilization and vanish or to be marginalized. Autochthonic cultures were supposed to be overthrown by Christianization and by the initially legally admissible racial and ethnic amalgamation.

The Romantic cultural model of national integration elevated the nation, conceived of as a cultural community, into the most important factor and site of social integration. Culture and in particular language, religion, and the belief in shared ethnogenesis, were supposed to determine the division of humanity into separate nations and ethnic groups. The state was regarded as a developmental stage in the rise of the nation; having fulfilled their integrative function, states could vanish (Znaniecki 1973). In "cultural" approaches, nations and ethnic groups embodied the most important kind of social integration, and states only represent large cultural communities capable of establishing civilizations as well. The diversity of ethnic, national, and racial groups led to the division of the world, in which tolerably homogeneous states played a dominant role. Nations which had a better political organization, greater military strength, and bigger populational, economic, and territorial potential exhibited a tendency toward expansion (Znaniecki 1973). As understood by the upholders of this theoretical position, nations were the largest communities arising from basically the same roots as tribal and ethnic group. National belonging is founded on birth and is a consequence of one's origin rather than an effect of choice. Individuals' identities are formed within a cultural group which is cemented with communal bonds and, importantly, ideological bonds, underpinned by the belief in the shared ethnogenesis, the endorsement of the same values, the use of the same language, and the worship of the same religion. The state caps a nation's cultural integration and sanctions its capacity for independent and sovereign being. In this sense, the nation is an autotelic and autonomous cultural group, the only one that has its own state institutions.

With its dominant principle of grounding cultural, therein national, bonds on the shared origin and biological legacy, Romantic tradition considered the primitive autochthonic cultures of both Americas to be incapable of transforming into nations. In the new realities, the social structure of the population of both Americas was theoretically envisaged as dichotomous. One pole was occupied by socially inferior, culturally deprecated, religiously and civilizationally backward "savages" envisioned as the conquered folk and slaves, while the other belonged to the dominant Christina "white masters," who represented more developed national cultures and European civilization. This model initially dominated the processes of social and cultural integration, permanently excluding indigenous peoples with their family-based and tribal cultures.

The rules of the colonial development model, which split the cultures of peoples inhabiting both Americas into the autochthonous and the European (the former backward, savage and barbarian, while the latter civilized and developed), had prevailed in socio-cultural development theoretically, at least until colonies gained independence and practically, in the sense of changes in the legal and political order, until the dichotomous slavery-based structure was dismantled. According to Zea, the European Christian project which justified the first waves of American expansion in the 16th century contributed to the emergence of Latin America's liberation project in the early 19th century. Thereby, the liberation project was an offshoot of another European project, which for its part represented the response of European modernity to the already outdated Christian project. This response was visible in the confrontation of Christianity and modernity. Modernity includes the European project which aims to command the entire world, at the same time denying the claim of Iberian imperialism to hegemony. This is the project of so-called Western Europe, launched by the nations of England, France, and the Netherlands in North America and some regions of the Antilles, whence it extends onto Iberian-ruled America. The project will be embodied in North-American Puritanism.

ZEA 1993, 22

The Enlightenment model, which promoted the establishment of independent states within the same Hispanophone, Catholic, Iberian cultural tradition, became attractive to the new republican political elites in Latin America. It conferred the status of nation-states on tribally, ethnically, racially, and linguistically divided populations. At the same time, the division criteria directly transferred from the Hegelian tradition were in force, as ethnic origin and membership in a cultural group determined one's position in the hierarchy of power, wealth, and prestige. Dimensions of socio-cultural stratification, regional and ethnic distinctions, and ideological and political divisions were developed and consolidated in this way over at least three centuries. Conservative and liberal concepts which either defended the hegemony of white Christian populations or appreciated the relevance of autochthonic tribal-racial groups were forged and refined as a result of debates on the extent to which members of non-European cultures could contribute to the establishment of a new social, political, legal, economic, and cultural order. Other conflicts and disputes around them were triggered by the presence of Africans, who had been brought to both Americas as slaves and stripped of the right to cultivate their cultural traditions. People of color had languages, religions, and values of national European cultures imposed on them, but this phenomenon was limited and constrained by social, religious, and political barriers.

Unfolding within colonial territorial, administrative, legal, and structural conditions, the initial stage of building integrated Latin-American societies ruled out – with minor exceptions – the full participation of indigenous Indian and African populations. The foundations of domestic cultures of future states were forged among the white colonial elites living within administrative units of Spanish, Portuguese, British, French, and Dutch colonies. With the ousting of the French (excepting Canada's Quebec and diasporic cultures of, for example, Acadians and Cajuns) and the Dutch (excepting small enclaves in the Caribbean and South America) from the two Americas, two models – the Anglo-Saxon and the Iberian (with its two varieties: Hispanic American and Lusitanian American in Brazil) – vied against each other in both Americas..

The cultural model had a far more limited field of application, because it impeded the integration of citizens of the new states coming from various racial, ethnic, national, linguistic, and religious backgrounds. Latin America became a site of the implementation of the Enlightenment principle which identified nation with civic society and erected the state into the most important nation-forming factor, as envisioned in Weber's sociological paradigm (1978). Enlightenment concepts fostered integration rules according to which all citizens of the state could belong to the same cultural and, at the same time, political space. People who did not use Spanish or Portuguese and did not practice Christian worship were relegated to the margin of national-civic societies. This was the case at least until the end of the 20th century. Currently, we are witnessing the rise of new concepts of Latin American society and civilization, of the cultural domination of a universalized and pluralist "cosmic race," and of multicultural, racially and ethnically mixed, and religiously syncretic new nations with hybrid, pluralist bonds and cultural identities (Campa 1999; Souto Maior 2003; Vasconcelos 1993).

In both Americas, the state has become the most important factor in the building of national and civilizational bonds. As in other multicultural societies of postcolonial and migrant lineage, in Latin America the state has promoted increasing territorial integration, linguistic homogenization, civic solidarity, and supra-racial and supra-regional bonds, leading to the formation and development of national identity. Civic societies in Latin America find themselves at different stages in the development of national bonds within culturally varied and racially, ethnically, and religiously mixed populations. Some of them, such as Argentina, Chile, Paraguay, and Brazil, approximate the concept of nation-state, while others, such as less racially and ethnically integrated Peru, Ecuador, and Columbia, maintain their territorial, political, economic, and cultural unity owing to state institutions.

2   Models of Nation-Forming Processes in Latin America

Both American continents have become an ideological "New World" and at the same time a tangible, cultural rather than geographical, area where ideas which stood no chance of realization in the "old" Europe could be elaborated and implemented on a large scale. Some of them, such as first attempt at creating conditions for the full integration and acculturation of Indians with European cultures – undertaken by Puritan Anglo-Saxon pioneers in British colonies in New England (Massachusetts, Rhode Island, New Hampshire), by Quakers in Pennsylvania, by Catalan and Aragon settlers in Spanish dominions, and by Lusitanians in Brazil – presupposed admitting indigenous Indian inhabitants of Americas to new cultural communities which were being built by the colonists. The model of racial and cultural integration which Bartolomé de las Cacas proposed, albeit in theory rather than in practice, proved more utopian than realistic. At the early stage of colonization, Spanish and Lusitanian conquistadores engaged in relationships with Indian women, allowing religiously and legally justified amalgamation. However, this was more a result of the situation in which the male colonizers found themselves than an effect of ethical principles, religious beliefs, or scientific concepts. As a consequence of this relatively long phase of paternalistic attitude to Indians, mestization began, the relevance of which has been increasing ever since. In Latin American nation-building processes, mestization has helped unite descendants of both European and autochthonic racial, ethnic, and national groups into one cultural – rather than solely socio-political – whole.

Nation-building processes in Europe were gathering momentum between the 16th and the 19th centuries. In this period, Latin America was a site of an encounter and clash of pre-writing primitive tribal cultures, which lived in cyclical, closed, non-linear time and inhabited a world dominated by magical practices, animist beliefs, and family-tribal patterns of social organization. European colonizers brought along not only a new technology which was unimaginable to Indians, but also different ideas and models of a new social and cultural order. These models were implemented without asking the consent of members of autochthonous cultures, without inviting them to participate, and without respecting their norms and values, except selectively adopted elements of the Indian legacy for the most part concerning plant cultivation. The transfer of European cultures to both Americas was basically one-directional for a long time. The dominant national cultures of European colonizers disregarded, marginalized, and suppressed the cultures of autochthonic peoples, replacing them with their own cultural and civilizational models in non-negotiable ways, which excluded dialogue and mutual integration. The basic elements of inculturation included religion, language, and state institutions, which used the system of education to impose European models of the internalization of cultural norms, to introduce Iberian legal and administrative regulations, and to drive out and destroy organizational systems of autochthonic cultures.

Only few of a multitude of diverse historical racial, ethnic, religious, linguistic, and regional groups which were transforming, in particular as a result of colonization and the culture clash in the era of great geographical discoveries, achieved the status of politically sovereign nation-states. Relative to other region of the world, nation-forming processes were fastest and most advanced in Western Europe, chiefly in Christian – particularly Protestant – Germanic, Gallic, Iberian, and Anglo-Saxon cultures. Most national civic societies, therein Spanish and Portuguese ones, which are based not only on cultural affiliations but also, if not primarily, on state-political bonds have long and complex historical geneses, frequently complicated ethnogeneses, and overlapping dimensions of the racial, ethnic, religious, and regional structures.

At one pole of the scale, there are nation-states of a relatively high cultural homogeneity, which are basically mono-ethnic, have one or at most two prevalent religious systems, use one language, and are politically unified. The nations of homogeneous ethnogenesis and uniform state solidarity are predominantly old nations with long histories, such as Jews, Italians, Germans, the French, Spaniards, Russians, and Poles. They are nation-cultures which enjoy political sovereignty guaranteed by their own states.

On the other pole of the complexity-and-heterogeneity scale, there are multicultural, postcolonial, and post-migration civic societies which are transforming into national communities of various types in the historical process. While in the case of nationally homogeneous states, culture – therein language, art, literature, and religion – has been a significant factor in nation-making processes which preceded state institutions, in case of multi-ethnic, complex civic societies, the state has been the most important agent in unifying the heterogeneous population substrate. This group of national civic societies or "new nations" (Gellner 2006; Lipset 1967; Kubiak 1975) includes nation-states of colonial or immigrational (or combined) origin, such as Brazil, Mexico, the U.S., Canada, Australia, Chile, Argentina, and other Latin-American countries. In the processes of historical development, the societies of respective countries have achieved differing degrees of social integration and cultural homogenization of the racially, ethnically (therein tribally and nationally), linguistically, regionally, and religiously composite human substrate. Owing to their relatively homogeneous racial and ethnic composition, some of these societies, e.g., Argentina, Uruguay, and Chile, have accomplished a relatively high level of cultural unity, which more resembles European nations than the multicultural civic societies of Peru or Bolivia. The most populous countries, Mexico and Brazil have developed their own models of national integration, which are largely based on the amalgamation-caused domination of the mixed-race population (Freyre 1951). The notion of "model" refers here to a set of ordered propositions about reality. The aim of the model is to organize and simplify phenomena and thereby to help explain and understand the core of the matter.

In looking for the most general patterns in the formation processes of nations which have their own states (Anderson 2006; Kubiak 1975; Smith 2003; Wiatr 1969, 250), sociology identifies the following models of nation-forging processes:

1. *The bourgeois-democratic model.* It is a classic developmental trajectory which was followed by European nations in their transition from feudalism to capitalism. The historical turning point of the process in the formation of bourgeois nation-states took place at the end of the 18th century, marked by a reorientation of political values caused by the French Revolution (1789), the American Declaration of Independence (1776), and Poland's Constitution of 3rd May (1791). The democratization of civic relationships, the liberalization of economic, political, and social bonds, the market economy, and individualism enhanced by the Protestant ethos of religious and moral values propelled the development of a new political doctrine of national civic states in which disproportions between estates were erased. This was the path of national and state development followed by societies of a relatively high cultural homogeneity and long-standing traditions of historical unity, such as France, England, Italy and, initially, Poland and Ireland as well. The independence-committed elite of Latin America derived its national and liberatory inspirations from this nation-making model. Republican ideologies espoused by the political elites overlapped with the idea of democracy in the first stage of Latin American nation-building processes. Nevertheless, the mechanisms of democratic development in Latin American countries practically failed to coincide with nation-forging processes in their first postcolonial phase. Racial, ethnical, and national divisions were very strongly correlated with social barriers, which resulted in the cultural and political exclusivism of the white Latin American elites. These elites enacted their own social and political agendas within specific models of political systems which, though evoking democratic and republican ideas, in fact promoted the autocratic, if not outright totalitarian, rule of narrow social groups dominated by the descendants of white colonizers. Today, Latin American civic societies are undergoing an accelerated democratization. This is due to at least two sets of reasons. One of them is connected with international relationships and with transformations in the position and role of Latin American countries in the structures of international organization. The processes of globalization, modernization, and cultural universalization make Latin American countries – particularly pluralist

and multicultural ones, such as Brazil and Mexico – succumb to internal pressures from media, legal and political campaigns (Stemplowski 1979). At the same time, the civil consciousness and the political subjectivity of Latin Americans from autochthonic and racially mixed backgrounds are increasing. Models of the democratization of civic societies in Latin America assume interesting forms, which nevertheless breed ideologies and doctrines of state nationalism, accompanied by a progressing cultural homogenization.

2. *The bourgeois-conservative model.* According to Jerzy Wiatr: "The bourgeois-conservative path to the formation of nations comes in two major varieties: through transformations of an existing feudal state or through the unification of fragmented feudal states into one political organism on the basis of which new national bonds are forged. This model of national development is vividly exemplified by the unification of Germany in the second half of the 19th century. The bourgeois-conservative trajectory of nation-formation has as a rule left several unsolved national issues" (Wiatr 1969, 263). The so-called Prussian path of the development of nations is based on a clear domination of one privileged socio-cultural group, a bourgeois class or stratum of unquestioned position in the structure of national-civic society. In a way, fascism was the culmination of such a rise of ideological doctrines and political structures of Italy and Germany. The choice of this developmental path resulted in cultural, political, and economic expansionism. The turn of the 19th century was marked by an exacerbation of conservative tendencies in Latin America, which was concomitant with advancing oligarchization and increasing socio-economic disproportions in most, if not in all, Latin American countries. The conservatism of the political elites was coupled with growing revolutionary leanings among the poorest social strata, which were chiefly comprised of autochthonous and racially-mixed populations. The increase in disproportions concerning not only the positioning in the hierarchy of prestige, wealth, and power, but also the preferred means of achieving ideologically determined national values led in Latin America to the rule of military and civil juntas, which thwarted nation-forming processes. The ruling elites of Latin American states simultaneously employed the national idea and implemented policies of racial and social exclusivism, which bred conflicts and fueled revolutionary moods. Such developments were particularly pronounced in Mexico and Middle America. However, basically no Latin America civic society was free from tensions and conflicts triggered by the policies of states dominated by the white political elites, which grounded their social status on the

models of Western economic doctrines. In the first half of the 20th century, the systems of republican Latin American countries took the form of conservatively oriented, autocratic, centralized governance of the white post-colonial elites, which based their power on the doctrine of defense against communism. The conservative governments of Latin American countries propped up their political agendas on international backing from Western countries, predominantly from the U.S. In the early 1960s, thus-oriented politics led to the notorious "Cuban crisis" and a global confrontation between capitalism and socialism. This crisis also had its internal, Latin-American dimension, as it aggravated tensions and conflicts between the pro-American political and economic elites and the radicalizing, leftist, pro-Marxists progressive circles of intellectuals and leaders of social liberation movements, who garnered the support of the masses. The latter group spawned leaders of new national and revolutionary movements, which weakened and overcame the tendencies of the conservative white political elites.

3. *The postcolonial model.* The postcolonial path of the formation of national civic societies is characteristic of countries and democracies established on the territories dominated by European or Asian (Japanese, Chinese) colonial influences, primarily in Africa, the South Pacific, and both Americas. The U.S., Canada, Brazil, Mexico, other countries of Latin America, and Australia followed the rules of the colonial model in the early stage of their nation-building processes. As a result of colonial dependence and military, economic, and cultural domination, the conquered autochthonic peoples had the laws of the dominant group – of Anglo-Saxon Protestants in North America and of Iberian (Spanish and Portuguese) Catholics in South America – imposed on them. If Latin America managed to cast off the political and cultural dominance of the Spaniards, the Portuguese, and the British, it is still economically dependent on Western countries. As experiences of the second half of the 20th century imply, Latin American countries are incapable of economic independence and are governed by the rules of the dependent model of economic development. This dependency results from the slowdown of technological, organizational, and economic development caused by colonialism. The U.S. wields a hegemonic role in economic and social transformations in Latin America. Theories of the globalization of Latin America through Americanization are advanced with an ever increasing frequency (Frank 1967; Galeano 1997; Haines 1989; Huntington 1997).

Iberian colonialism caused not only the suppression of the languages and cultures of the autochthonic peoples and their gradual decline, but also an almost exceptionless primacy of the religion, tradition, and values of the white colonizers and settlers. This tendency is incrementally changing as a result of indigenism and pan-Indianism as well as a growing role of intellectuals and politicians from outside genetically European racial and ethnic groups in nation-making processes. In the second half of the 20th century, Latin America entered the stage not only of accelerated national homogenization but also of cultural universalization in its Latin American iteration. The Latin American "model" of nation-forming processes is currently based on an almost universal racial amalgamation, religious and racial syncretism, and ethnic hybridization, coupled with an advanced linguistic, national, and civil homogenization.

Latin American countries implement the politics of integration with the world's political and economic system, all the while remaining organizationally, financially, and militarily dependent on highly developed countries. The formulation of the "dependent development" doctrine by the political and economic leaders of Mexico, Brazil, Chile, and Argentina represents one dimension of the neo-colonial dependency of Latin American countries, chiefly on the U.S. (Galeano 1997; Stemplowski 1996).

The decolonization of Africa was the most spectacular process. It was the establishment of states that initiated nation-forming processes in most countries of this continent, marked by ethnic, tribal, and religious fragmentation and lacking its own intellectual elites. State borders of most African, South-American, and Asian post-colonial republics were drawn along the division lines of the influences of the European colonial powers (Wiatr 1969, 269).

4. *The bourgeois-settler model.* This model of the augmentation of national and state unity is specific to countries of immigrational origin, which were built on the foundations of colonial administration. Civic societies of the U.S., Brazil, Mexico, other Latin American countries, Canada, and Australia were formed upon this pattern. The state provided the most powerful factor in the increased territorial, cultural, and national integration in these countries. What all the post-immigration nation-states have in common is that each of them boasts a strong homogeneous national (racial, religious) group which contributes an ensemble of fundamental cultural and ideological values to the new community, therein the shared language (English in the U.S., Spanish in Mexico, and Portuguese in Brazil), common religious system (Protestantism in the U.S., and Catholicism in Brazil and Mexico), and administration in which a relatively homogeneous social group prevails (White Anglo-Saxon Protestants in the U.S., and Lusitanians and Creoles in South America). As another

distinctive feature of this model, it involved a military conquest and a complete subjugation of the autochthonic population. In the U.S., Brazil, and Canada, Indian tribes were relegated to marginalized, subordinated, socially and culturally degraded ethnic and tribal enclaves. It was only in the closing decades of the 20th century that accelerated and robust indigenization commenced, crucially involving an increased participation of the autochthonous population in the social, political, economic, and cultural life of civic societies. Indigenization on the one hand entails an increasing cultural diversity of Latin American countries and on the other fosters the democratization of social life. Nevertheless, the autochthonous population not so much "melts into" Peruvian, Bolivian, or Mexican culture as rather generates its own, syncretic, and hybrid models of integration and types of cultural identity (Paleczny 2001; Posern-Zielinski 2005; Romano 1971). Biculturality, divided, dual or multiple identity, syncretic forms of religion, racially and ethnically mixed communities, all represent the dominant tendencies of transformations in nation-forming processes observable in Latin America in recent decades.

The bourgeois-settler model is based on the dominant cultural role of the white elites, which is bound up with their social and economic conservatism. At the initial stage, nation-making processes are limited to narrow groups of white settlers, who marginalize both the autochthonic populations and the descendants of African slaves. The development of the U.S. as a multi-ethic, racially complex, and religiously pluralistic civic society which is transforming into a nation in its own state has been thoroughly studied (Kubiak, 1975; Lipset, 1967). A similar scholarly attention has been devoted to Canada and Australia. The history of Latin-American nation-forging processes remains relatively underexamined in sociological research, at least in Poland (Łepkowski 1977–1983; Paleczny 2004; Urbanski 1978).

5. *The socialist model.* This model, which historically, albeit not exclusively, was implemented in East-Central Europe, originated in Russia in the aftermath of the October Revolution. In 1945–1989, it spread onto Poland and other countries of the so-called communist bloc. Although its consequences are still observable in the creation of conditions for the political and cultural integration (e.g., Belarus), it seems to be a dead end in nation-building processes. Despite concerted and repeated efforts, no "socialist East-German nation" or "Soviet nation" was crafted. Nevertheless, the model has indeed performed its integrating, nation-forming, and state-building role in several countries in Europe and other continents, e.g., in Vietnam, China, Cuba, and Libya. Some elements of the socialist

model have been taken over by social and ethnic liberation movements of the autochthonous populations in Latin America. They contributed to the radicalization of social, racial, and ethnic conflicts, which in extreme cases morphed into military revolutionary and terrorist movements, such as the Shining Path in Peru. Ernesto Che Guevara was one of the leading champions of this variety of nation-making processes, informed by the idea of and the faith in social justice. Elements of the socialist development path are foregrounded and manifested in ideologies of radical groupings, such as the Brazilian Landless Workers' Movement and Mexican guerilla leaders. Similarly to conflicts between the Brazilian oligarchy and poor population groups of color in Brazil, the social phenomenon of guerilla is characteristic of the transformation of racially and culturally dichotomous Mexican society into a national community. According to Urszula Drzewiecka, "at various moment in history, it [guerilla] accrued special characteristics, yet it has remained unchanged at its core, defying the state's mandate in order to empower various social groups to claim their rights. 20th-century guerilla in Mexico developed in two major directions: the armed rural movement and the urban movement, based among others on the ideology and the practical example of the Cuban Revolution. [...] Regrettably, Mexico's contemporary socio-political arena is not free from guerilla. For over twelve years, the EZLN, actively operating in Chiapas, has been fighting for the rights of Indians and rejecting the attempts to solve the conflict undertaken by consecutive governments. Enjoying the support of international public opinion, the Zapatistas constantly undermine the stability of Mexican democracy, because, as Professor Soledad Loaeza argues, 'the line between lawlessness and democracy is blurred in Mexico, which means that direct pressures are applied to enforce the realization of social demands'" (Drzewiecka 2008, 24).

Disproportions on social-position scales, especially in terms of property, wealth, affluence, power, and prestige have prompted disadvantaged strata to resort to the idea of socialist equality and justice. The ideas of "Latin American" socialism, which turned into aspirations of revolutionary-national armed movements, became a component of nation-forming processes not only in Mexico, Brazil, and Cuba, but also in Chile, Bolivia, Venezuela, Peru, Honduras, Nicaragua, and basically all Latin American countries.

As nations developed in their own distinct and varied ways, configurations of relationships among them differ from each other. Historically speaking, relations between nations depend on the kind and nature of processes that integrate them. Countries of colonial and migrant genesis were predominantly influenced by the culture and politics of their original national communities.

Following their own trajectories of development and civic integration in their own countries, the societies of the U.S., Mexico, Chile, and Brazil took over the values, languages, religions, norms, and ideologies of the home countries of colonizers and settlers. Transmission channels of people, ideas, technologies, and cultures have in fact been working till the present day. Political bonds characteristic of relations between Mexico and Spain or Brazil and Portugal are underpinned not so much by common economic and military interests as rather by the cultural legacy and natural connections specific to relations between the country of origin and the country of settlement, or between the colonizing population and the colonized one.

The development processes of civic societies and increasing national integration in Latin American countries have been dominated by the bourgeois-settler and postcolonial models. The basic characteristics of these overlapping models of nation-making processes in Latin America include:

1. The presence of a hegemonic,, dominant cultural group, which imposes language, religion, the most important cultural norms and values, and patterns of economic and social organization on autochthonous cultures. Across Latin America, these were chiefly patterns of Spanish and Portuguese culture at various stages of their historical development, excepting some regions under British, Dutch, or French domination. The South American cultural civilizational space is conceptually rendered in terms such as "Hispanic America" or "Latin America," which point to the cultural legacy and links between the native populations' traditions and the heritage of European colonizers and settlers. Suffice it to say that Latin American civilization is based on Spanish and Portuguese, on Catholic religion (with a growing influence of Anglo-Saxon Protestantism, mainly coming from the U.S), and on values and norms transferred from Europe and perpetuated by Creoles, Lusitanians, and other descendants of European colonizers and settlers.

2. The treatment of indigenous people as culturally inferior, socially subordinated, and economically dominated. Nation-forming processes were pervaded by the ideology o conquest and assimilationism, which entailed the absorption and inculturation of the autochthonic peoples. As one of prevalent strategies, indigenous populations were forced out from their home territories, pushed into cultural reserves, relegated to the margin of social life, deprived of political rights, displaced from areas to be industrialized and urbanized, spatially isolated, and racially segregated. However, as amalgamation and mestization were admissible, the elimination of autochthonous populations in Latin American countries never matched the degree and size of its counterpart in the U.S..

3. The domination of Christian values represented by the structures of the Roman Catholic Church. The clergy and religious organizations, in particular Catholic missions, played a prominent role in shaping the Latin American cultural identity. Religion became the most important channel through which European values were transmitted. Besides nationalization, cultural universalization, which bred a civilizational identity, and globalization, Christianization was and still is the central factor in social, political, and economic integration and in cultural homogenization.
4. Gradual admission of racially amalgamated groups of mixed populations (mainly Mestizos and, later, Mulattos) and syncretic, mixed, hybrid cultural groups (e.g., macumba followers, quimbanda believers, universalists, etc.) to social and cultural life (Bastide 1978; Brown 1986).
5. Increasing syncretism, polymorphism, and hybridity of the societies of Latin American countries. The most important, paramount role in shaping multicultural, pluralistic social structures and cultural identities is played by state institutions. State bonds and civic solidarity are the fundamental factor in nation-forming processes in which societies that belong to the same cultural area develop their distinctiveness. State bonds tie in with the sense of territoriality and the culturally objectivized and internalized identification with the homeland. The state identity, the bond with the ideological homeland, and the racial-ethnic structure unique to each civic society are the most important components of national bonds in Latin American countries, which unify the heterogeneous population substrate into a whole.
6. The pluralistic, complex character of civic societies and new kinds of Latin American nationalism. Still forming in nation-building processes, Latin American nations are by default heterogeneous and complex civic communities due to their varied ethnogeneses, historical processes of colonization and migration, the co-existence of autochthonous, African and European populations, and the involvement of numerous tribal groups side by side with white Iberian colonizers in the processes of social integration. As by sharing certain traditions, these communities have developed embryonic feelings of territorial, religious, and linguistic unity, they are now furnished with all necessary elements that constitute a nation.

Bibliography

Anderson, Benedict. *Imagined Communities: Reflections on the Origin and Spread of Nationalism*. London, New York: Verso, 2006.

Bastide, Roger. *African Religions of Brazil: Towards a Sociology of the Interpenetration of Civilizations*. Baltimore: Johns Hopkins University Press, 1978.

Brown, Diana. *Umbanda: Religion and Politics in Brazil*. Ann Arbor: UMI Research Press, 1986.

Campa de la, Roman. *Latin Americanism*. Minneapolis-London: University of Minnesota Press, 1999.

Drzewiecka, Urszula. "Guerrilla w Meksyku II poł. XX wieku/pocz. XXI wieku." *Kraje-Regiony*, vol. 60, no. 2, 2008, pp. 56–69.

Frank, André G. *Capitalism and Underdevelopment in Latin America*. New York: Monthly Review Press, 1967.

Freyre, Gilberto. *Brazil: An Interpretation*. New York: Alfred Knopf, 1951.

Galeano, Eduardo. *Open Veins of Latin America: Five Centuries of the Pillage of a Continent. 25th anniversary edition*. Translated by C. Belfrage. With a foreword by I. Allende. New York: Monthly Review Press, 1997.

Gellner, Ernest. *Nations and Nationalism. Second Edition*. Malden, Oxford, Victoria: Blackwell Publishing, 2006.

Haines, Gerald. *The Americanization of Brazil*. Denver: Scholarly Recourses, 1989.

Huntington, Samuel P. *The Clash of Civilization and the Remaking of World Order*. New York: Touchstone, 1997.

Kubiak, Hieronim. *Rodowód narodu amerykańskiego*. Cracow: Wydawnictwo Literackie, 1975.

Lipset, Seymour M. *The First New Nation. The United States in Historical and Comparative Perspective*. New York: Anchor Books Doubleday &Co., Inc. Garden City, 1967.

Łepkowski, Tadeusz (ed.). *Dzieje Ameryki Łacińskiej od schyłku epoki kolonialnej do czasów współczesnych*. Vols. I–III. Warszawa: Książka i Wiedza, 1977–1983.

Paleczny, Tadeusz (ed.). *Zbiorowości etniczne w Ameryce Łacińskiej: Odrębność czy asymilacja? Seria Polska a Świat Iberoamerykański*. Warsaw: Centrum Studiów Latynoamerykańskich UW, 2001.

Paleczny, Tadeusz. *Rasa, etniczność i religia w brazylijskim procesie narodowotwórczym. Wprowadzenie do badan latynoamerykańskich przemian społecznych*. Cracow: Towarzystwo Autorów i Wydawców Prac Naukowych UNIVERSITAS, 2004.

Posern-Zielinski, Aleksander. *Między indygenizmem a indianizmem. Indyjscy Indianie na drodze do etnorozwoju*. Poznan: Wydawnictwo Naukowe UAM, 2005.

Romano, Ruggiero. *Ameryka indiańska?*. Warsaw: PWN, 1971.

Smith, Anthony D. *Nationalism and Modernism. A critical survey of recent theories of nations and nationalism*. London and New York: Routledge, 2003.

Souto Maior, Luiz A. *O Brasil em um mundo em transição*. Editora Universidade de Brasília, 2003.

Stemplowski, Ryszard. "Modernizacja – teoria czy doktryna?." *Kwartalnik Historyczny*, vol. XXXVI, no 3, 1979, pp. 741–754.

Stemplowski, Ryszard. *Państwowy socjalizm w realnym kapitalizmie. Chile 1932 roku.* Warsaw: TRIO, 1996.

Urbanski, Edmund S. *Hispanic America and Its Civilizations.* Norman: University of Oklahoma Press, 1978.

Vasconcelos, José. *Rasa kosmiczna.* Warsaw: CESLA, 1993.

Weber, Max. *Economy and Society.* Edited by G. Roth and C. Wittich. Berkeley, Los Angeles, and London: University of California Press, 1978.

Wiatr, Jerzy. *Naród i państwo.* Warsaw: KiW, 1969.

Zea, Leopold. *Filozofia dziejów Ameryki.* Edited by J. Wojcieszak. Translated by J. Hintz. Warsaw: Centrum Studiów Latynoamerykańskich Uniwersytetu Warszawskiego, 1993.

Znaniecki, Florian. *Modern Nationalities. Sociological Study.* Westport: Greenwood Press, 1973.

PART 3

Contemporary Culture and Globalization

The last part of the volume is comprised of texts devoted to our contemporary global phenomena. Daniela Boćkowski's article addresses the response of the world of Islam and the entire Arab world to ubiquitous globalization. Adam Nobis explores the emergence of new kinds and models of money to conclude that locality should not be identified with a concrete place. The article contributed by Karolina Golinowska analyzes the relevance of contemporary global processes to cultural politics. Piotr J. Fereński discusses the political role of cities in the context of globalization. Authored by Rafał Nahirny, the closing article of this part looks into Doug Rickard's artistic project *A New American Picture*.

CHAPTER 9

From Córdoba to Tora Bora

Globalization in the World of Islam, the World of Islam vis-à-vis Globalization

Daniel Boćkowski

Globalization is a fact. There is hardly any place on earth where it does not affect everyday life. The world of Islam and, with it, the entire Arab world contemplate today how to proceed and carry on. While some people opt for adopting Western culture, even at the price of profound changes, others advocate forging an Islamic equivalent of Western culture. These strivings come in various forms and inevitably lead to disputes and clashes.

In the wake of worldwide terrorism, which is "perfectly" exemplified in the Sunni Al-Qaeda, the world is compelled to judge whether Al-Qaeda is an upshot of contemporary globalization processes, a product of fundamentalist Muslim forces which fights universal West-European and American-style globalization, or perhaps merely a terrorist organization targeting both the Western world and the West-supported governments of several Islamic countries in North Africa and the Arab Peninsula, which extreme fundamentalists regard as violating the Quran and collaborating with the Western "crusaders" in order to retain power. Extreme fundamentalist movements consider the rulers/presidents/dictators who do not directly implement the Quranic injunctions and prohibitions to be unholy apostates whose usurped power should be overthrown in compliance with the Quranic law. There are even more extreme voices insisting that the contemporary Islamic world, especially in the Middle East and the Arab Peninsula, has reverted to the era of *jahiliyyah*, that is, the times from before the revelations of the Prophet Muhammad (Muhammad Ibn 'Abd Allah), and consequently that a new *jihad* is necessary to restore the times of glory of the first four "righteous caliphs": Abu Bakr, Omar, Othman, and Ali,

The choice of the events in the history of Europe and the Islamic world which are evoked in the title of this paper is by no means random. Córdoba easily lends itself to serving as a symbol of Arab/Islamic-style globalization as the capital of an independent emirate established by Abd al-Rahman I, the last descendant of the Umayyads, who proclaimed Al-Andalus, the Moorish part of Spain, a caliphate independent of Baghdad in 929. Córdoba is also a symbol of the decline of the first stage of Islamic/Arab globalization. The fall of Córdoba in 1236 and the seizure of the city by Christian knights under the command of Ferdinand III of Castile mark the symbolic moment of the collapse of this idea (though its beginnings date back to the early 11th century, when the Almohads acceded to power in the city).

For its part, the cave complex of Tora Bora (Pashto: black dust), located in the proximity of the Kyber Pass in the White Mountains (*Safed Koh*) range, close to Jalalabad in South-Eastern Afghanistan, is a symbolic site of the first big clash of the U.S. troops with Usama ibn Ladin's Al-Qaeda in December 2001. It is also a symbol of a clash between the Western world and an entirely different vision of globalization, which can be described as a *worldwide caliphate* and which has arisen in response to globalization processes precipitated across the Islamic world by Western Europe and the U.S. It is a symbolic clash between the champions of establishing *dar al-islam* ("the house of Islam") in the land of *dar al-harb* ("the house of war"), which refers to the whole of the non-Muslim world. Finally, it is a clash between two visions of the future: globalization and *al-Kauniyya* (Mrozek-Dumanowska 2005, 13).

Interestingly, in the age of increasing migrations of Muslims to Europe, the notions of *dar al-islam* and *dar al-harb* are slowly changing their original meanings. Until recently, they practically indicated a rigorous split into two distinct areas, only one of which was proper for Muslims to dwell in. The Muslims who found themselves in the non-Muslim world were supposed to seek the possibly fastest return to "the house of Islam," as the world of infidels could contribute to their conscious or unconscious breach of the principles of their faith. Several Muslim scholars associate the major globalization-triggered risk with such a conflict of conscience afflicting Muslims in *dar al-harb*. The globalized Western world in and of itself is not a threat to the Muslim faith, but it is *dar al-kufr* ("the house of unbelief") and, as such, a factor whose appeal can possibly affect Muslims' decisions to stray from the rules of the Quran (Murden 2002, 123). This problem is perhaps most pithily grasped by Bryan Turner, who states that a real threat to Islam is posed not by Jesus, but by Madonna (1997, 15; Górak-Sosnowska 2007, 94).

Such perceptions of the West are quite widespread in the Islamic world. In the case of Muslims inhabiting South-Eastern Asia, the economic factor and temptations bound up with it are not viewed as a hazard. Countries such as Malesia and Indonesia successfully combine relatively high living standards ensured by the free flow of goods and services with the principles of faith.

One of the most recognized Muslim intellectuals, Switzerland-based Tariq Ramadan, insists that Islam is a European religion and believes that it is in the West that Muslim religious thought enjoys more favorable conditions of free development, because the liberty with which worship can be practiced in the West would be impossible in many Muslim countries, especially in North Africa and the Middle East. Given this, Ramadan calls for regarding the globalizing Western world as *dar al-shahada* ("the house of witnessing") or *alam al-shahada* ("the area, or world, of testimony") (2004, 77). This bears some affinity to the ideas that envision the mission of the Islamic world as filling the "void" which appeared in the globalized Western society when its communities abandoned God.

Ramadan also promotes the theory of "devout citizenship" in which the complete loyalty of Muslims towards the states and societies in which they live is combined with the full acceptance of Muslims' religious otherness. This partly overlaps with the notions touted by Omar Bakri Mohammed, the leader of the Islamist network of the most radical part of the UK's Pakistani community (Al-Muhajiroun), who claims that extreme European Islamic groupings and European governments have struck *Ahd al-Aman* ("the contract of security"), on the basis of which the former respect European laws and order as long as they are not persecuted as Muslims (Allam 2008, 43).

For several centuries, the Islamic world successfully competed with European culture and even surpassed it. Owing to the religion which skillfully linked various communities scattered between Spain and present-day Afghanistan, Pakistan and northern India (the Abbasid caliphate spread beyond Kabul, Kandahar, and Samarkand at the turn of the 8th century), Islam laid the foundation for the global (by the standards of the day) commercial, cultural, and scientific exchange earlier than Christianity did. Crusades marked the first confrontation of the Islamic world and the Christian world in *dar al-islam*. They also marked a turning point for Western Europe, which used the encounter with Islamic civilization and culture to consolidate its own position by adeptly absorbing the precious novelty that civilization could offer (science, culture, technology, philosophy, and distinctly superior urban culture and lifestyle). The Arab world did not learn any lesson from this clash, only perceiving what in their view was barbaric and backward Europe. It failed to realize that, like prior ancient empires, it had come to an end of its expansion, splitting into caliphates and yielding to the pressure of Asian tribes, in particular the Mongols, who – as the Vandals before them – symbolically sealed the first "global expansion" of Islam.

As soon as the development of Europe brought about a re-drawing of trade routes, shifting from land to sea, the incomes of the caliphates and consequently their significance rapidly decreased. The times of the Western world's domination commenced. Attempts to curb, if not to halt, it were made by the

Ottoman Empire, yet it was dealt a serious blow at Vienna; and when it tried to launch Western-style reforms, it ultimately collapsed.

North Africa, the Middle East, and South-Central Asia became territories of Europe's colonial expansion. WW1 and WW2 exacerbated the conflicts and frustrations of the world of Islam, particularly of African and Middle-Eastern countries. This triggered the establishment of first reformatory movements which were inspired by 19th-century Muslim intellectuals: Jamal ad-Din al-Afghani and Muhammad Abduh. This tendency is epitomized by the Society of Muslim Brothers (*al-Ikhwan al-Muslimin*), which was founded by Hassan al-Banna in Al-Ismailia (Egypt) in 1928. It was the first movement to oppose the constantly increasing influences of the (British-represented) Western world on Muslims' life and traditions. The Brotherhood's present-day motto is: "Allah is our objective; the Prophet is our leader; the Quran is our law; Jihad is our way; dying in the way of Allah our highest hope" (Hirsi Ali 2011). Al-Banna did not only oppose the growing influence of the West. At the same time, he believed that he was building an Enlightenment-underpinned movement which would peaceably garner enormous support in Muslim society and become a universal model of a truly Islamic state, one in which welfare would go hand in hand with the economy governed by Islamic laws (he strictly condemned *riba* – usury). Interestingly, Al-Banna ruled out any political pluralism, convinced as he was that his concept was enough to put an end to the already increasing economic and cultural pressure of Wester colonial powers.

The post-war period, in particular the times of decolonization and struggles over revenues from mining crude oil deposits, saw the rising hopes of the Islamic world that Western ideas, such as democracy, human rights, and elected governments coupled with Western technologies, would accelerate the development of societies, solve gnawing problems, and ensure equitable governance. All these hopes proved illusory. The technology was only used to excavate crude oil, the sales of which filled the treasuries of local sheiks, princes, or dictators, while they consolidated their positions with the tacit support of the U.S. and Europe, which turned a blind eye to the ruthless suppression of movements campaigning for democratic changes, therein of the pursuits of more or less moderate Islamic fundamentalists. As for Westernization, it entailed an uncritical absorption of technological and cultural novelties, as a result of which – orthodox believers worried – people were gradually drifting from faith, tradition, and culture.

As a response to these developments and because of an aggravating frustration at the Western world's failure to remedy problems while effectively "poisoning the wells of faith," the 1970s witnessed a renewal and revival of Islam.

This process expresses an escalating protest against globalism symbolized by ubiquitous American culture. It is a grand attempt at designing and implementing a universal, global, Islam-based project aimed, first, at effectively replacing the Western framework which is at odds with Muslim culture, and, second, at efficiently competing with pop-culture in the future. As Murden argues, it is the most comprehensive expression of protest on behalf of the Muslim population inhabiting Africa, Asia, the Middle East, and Europe (Murden 2002, 12–14). Mrozek-Dumanowska that the contemporary Islamic revival movement is the most powerful movement whose political and moral vision is completely divergent from the universal values ascribed to globalization in the Western politics (2005, 27). It is the universality of this movement that is supposed to help build an ideal Islamic state on a worldwide scale in a remote future, a state which, unlike Western projects, will be able to ensure lasting peace and prosperity for all the countries of our globe, not only for the highly developed ones of the global North. The "global" pursuits of the world of Islam are stabilized by being grounded on the Quran, which is viewed by many Muslim fundamentalists as the ideal model of universal, incontestable legislation coming directly from God.

The striving to build an ideal model of globalization, one pitted against and expected to replace Western projects, is not at odds with the continuing reliance of the technologies of the Western world. A range of Western economic, social, and even political solutions are employed in order to build something that could be called *pax islamica*. If we push aside the demands of extreme Islamic fundamentalists associated with Wahhabism-related movements, such as Al-Qaeda, we will realize that some of the visions of Islamic globalization are underpinned by ideas cultivated in European liberal democracies (Sulaymān Abū 1987).

Moderate Islamists are an alternative to extremist fundamentalist movements. Since, similarly to the latter, they are critical of the contemporary politics of the West and the U.S., especially in the Middle East, they win supporters among the Muslim community across the world and prevent sizeable groups of people engaging in militant activities. What makes for their strength in the struggle for Muslims' hearts is, at the same time, their weakness in contacts with the Western world. As Jerzy Zdanowski argues, overcoming distrust in relations with the West is vital to the future of moderate Islamism and, consequently, to a possible democratization of the Middle East in the age of universal globalization. Regrettably, the West is terribly afraid of any form of Islamism, even the moderate one, as no way has yet been found to dismantle the stereotyped perceptions of the Islamic world generated by the classic Western orientalists (Zdanowski 2005, 67).

The West refuses to acknowledge that many fundamentalist movements cultivate progressive ideas and that their goal is not to destroy the achievements of the global world order. Rather, they seek to achieve the same aims in accord with their own visions, on the basis of the Quran, and respecting the traditions and familiar principles, which make their world safe or at least safer than the culturally foreign and internally empty Western world devoid of God, who has held and continues to hold a very special place in the lives of Muslims.

Contesting the achievements of globalization, the contemporary extremist fundamentalist movements are characterized by pride in their past, the politicization of religion, and anti-Western attitudes (Danecki 2007, 488). Fundamentalists seek to constantly emphasize that most of the Western accomplishments are imitative of or derivative from the Islamic world. This concerns, for example, human rights, social insurance, and even democratic concepts. This is geared to enhancing pride in belonging to the civilization of Islam. The anti-European stance of fundamentalist movements is an offshoot of history, in particular of the colonial and post-colonial trauma. It is only reinforced by the attitude of Europe and the U.S. to the problems with which Arab countries are grappling (Palestine, conflict in Lebanon, civil war in Algeria, etc.). Extremist fundamentalist movements perceive globalization as another iteration of crusades, which is all the more dangerous as this time the enemy is not easily and unambiguously definable. Swords have been replaced by Coke, personal stereos, Barbie dolls, hamburgers, pop music, and American promiscuous lifestyle. Such an enemy is far more difficult to combat, because the struggle must be fought at the same time in individual souls of Muslims and at the global level. Islam is becoming a tool of politics, while politics is becoming a weapon of Islam. In a clash with globalization processes, fundamentalists as political activists strive to take over power in order to protect society against the loss of faith. Hence evocations of the foundations of faith and appeals for integralism.

To conclude this brief exploration of globalization in the Islamic world, we can usefully refer to one more characteristic figure. Yusuf al-Qaradawi – the host of popular programs broadcast by Al Jazeera and regarded by *The Foreign Policy* and *The Prospect* as an enlightened leader of the Muslim world and one of the world's most distinguished intellectuals – believes that globalization (in particular broad access to modern technology it offers) is a perfect tool for disseminating Islam. As such, it is a remedy to the problems of the contemporary world. In his insights, Al-Qaradawi draws on the ideas put forward by Mustafa as-Siba'i, a classic theorist of Muslim fundamentalism: "In our age, only the Muslim ummah can play this key role, becoming a standard-bearer of future civilization [...]. When we take in our hands the leadership of this long-awaited civilization, we will not escape into outer space and we will not deny the existence of God. We will not make our intercontinental rockets and missiles into a tool of menace against the nations of the world to pull them into the sphere of our influence. We will not transform the radio into an instrument for deceiving humanity and the cinema into a means of (demoralizing) people. We will not turn women into a tool for satiating our lust. We will not exploit and rob the nations of the world only to further civilizational progress; neither will we destroy their honor and wealth."[1] We are bound to find out which concept will ultimately prevail and what consequences it will have for Europe and the world soon enough.

Bibliography

Allam, Magdi. *Kamikadze made in Europe. Czy zachodowi uda się pokonać islamskich terrorystów?*. Cracow: Universitas, 2008.

Danecki, Janusz. *Podstawowe wiadomości o islamie*. Warsaw: Dialog, 2007.

Górak-Sosnowska, Katarzyna. *Świat arabski wobec globalizacji. Uwarunkowania gospodarcze, kulturowe i społeczne*. Warszawa: Difin, 2007.

Hirsi Ali, Ayaan. "The Quran Is Our Law; Jihad Is Our Way." *Wall Street Journal*. https://www.wsj.com/articles/SB10001424052748704132204576136590964621006. Accessed on October 24, 2011.

Mrozek-Dumanowska, Anna. *Między uniwersalizmem globalizacji a partykularyzmem kultur lokalnych*. In A. Mrozek-Dumanowska and J. Zdanowski. *Islam a globalizacja*. Warsaw: Wydawnictwo Naukowe ASKON, 2005.

Murden, Simon W. *Islam, the Middle East and the New Global Hegemony*. London: Lynne Rienner Publishers, 2002.

Ramadan, Tariq. *Western Muslims and the Future of Islam*. London: Oxford University Press, 2004.

Sulaymān, Abū, 'AbdulḤamīd'. *Towards an Islamic Theory of International Relations: New Direction for Islamic Methodology and Thought*. Herndon, Virginia: International Institute of Islamic Thought, 1987.

Turner, Bryan S. *Orientalism. Postmodernism & Globalism*. New York: Routledge, 1997.

Zdanowski, Jerzy. "Islam wobec wyzwań zacofania i rozwoju." In A. Mrozek-Dumanowska, J. Zdanowski. *Islam a globalizacja*.

---
1 Katarzyna Górak-Sosnowska, *Świat* ..., 119; citation trans. by Patrycja Poniatowska.

CHAPTER 10

Locality and Globality: Various Dimensions of Money

Adam Nobis

In his *From the Czech Silver Toler to the Global Dollar*, Petr Vorel follows Hess and Klose (1986) in observing that the 500th anniversary of the dollar was symbolically celebrated worldwide in 1986 (2010, 9). Elsewhere he explains that it was in 1486 that a mint in Tirolean Hall struck silver coins which weighed 10/88 of the Viennese *grzywna* of silver which was 15-lot fine. He informs that the Viennese *grzywna* was equivalent to 280.67 grams, and the fineness of 15 lots meant the ratio of 15 parts of silver to 16 parts of alloy. The coinage thus weighed 31.894 grams and contained 29.90 grams of pure silver (Vorel 2010, 66, 153). Vorel adds that the pieces bore the image and the name of their issuer: "SIGISMVNDVS ARCHIDVX AVSTRIE," that is, Siegmund the Archduke of Austria (2010, 17). Present-day Hall is a small town in the vicinity of Innsbruck. Still a prominent fixture of the town's skyline, the tall tower of the mint can be seen in a photo in Vorel's book (2010, 1 2013) or visited in person at the admission price of six euros, thereby learning that this is where the dollar and the thaler were born (Hall Mint Museum 2012). Following Vorel, let us add that the coins were an outcome of two years' worth of experimentation carried out at the mint, with repeated attempts to obtain a large silver coin, which was not an easy thing to accomplish in manual production. Round silver plates were placed between the upper and the lower seals, and then the former was struck with a hammer. With thicker silver plates, the impression of the lower-seal image was less clear. Eventually, however, a satisfying new coinage was obtained. The coin contained as much silver as to match the worth of the gold Rhenish gulden. Both were supposed to have the same purchasing power of sixty kreutzers, and be equal as currency despite their differences in size, weight, and metal (Vorel 2010, 17).

With guldens instead of dollars, our thoughts head to Rhineland rather than to America. Guldens were produced by the Rheinischer Münzverein (Rhine Minting Association), which was founded by the Duke of the Palatinate and the bishops of Cologne, Trier, and Mainz. Ian Blanchard explains that initially the gulden had the weight, fineness, and gold content "the same as the Florentine florin," but by a convention of 1419, "the nominal 24-carat Italian" was supplanted by "a 19 carat standard." The fineness of 19 carats means 19 parts of pure gold to 24 parts of alloy, while the fineness of 24 carats means pure gold. Reducing fineness entailed thus reducing the gold content of the Rhenish gulden as compared with the standard of the Florentine florin (Blanchard 2005, 1005; cf. Żabiński 1989, 36–7). Peter Spufford states that the convention of 1419 fixed the weight and the fineness of these rhineguldens at, respectively, 3.51 grams and 0.79, which meant about 2.77 gram of pure gold (2004, 408). Called guldiners, Tirolean silver coins contained as much silver as to be an equivalent of gold rhineguldens (373), which implies that the gold to silver worth ratio was then 2.77 to 29.90, i.e., about 1:10.8. Nevertheless, even if such an equivalence was actually the case, the coins and their values differed quite considerably. As Vorel concludes, the Hall-minted guldiners were probably struck in a limited quantity for the representational purposes of Siegmund himself. While their major aim was to generate an impression of their issuer's wealth and power, rather than serving as regular currency (Vorel 2010, 20), the rhinegulden, on the contrary, "was the most popular golden coin in fifteenth-century Central Europe" (Chilosi, Volckart 2009, 7). Lars Boerner and Oliver Volckart point to another significant aspect of the gulden and its value. The point is that the local markets of various Rhineland towns developed their own, local monetary systems. Those systems were based on silver coins of small weight and worth, which made them convenient in small local transactions, whereas gold guldens of a much higher value were fitting for long-range transactions and trade. The recognition and issuing of guldens in various towns served to integrate those disparate local monetary markets. As a result, it turned out that the "monetary diversity could be overcome by constituting a currency union" (Boerner, Volckart 2010, 5). As, with time, Rhenish guldens started to spread, they effectively promoted the integration of the monetary systems of German states. Although various local coinages and systems were used in those countries, the establishment of the gulden worth in the local currency made it possible to calculate value relations between various currencies. In this way, the dissemination of guldens contributed to the integration of local money markets, which, for its part, fostered a further development of long-distance trade. Transactions using the same gold gulden in various parts of Europe and its flows as coins or bonds became an important factor in trading exchanges.

How about jumping to America now? No, not yet. For now, our historical journey takes us to Florence, where the coin which the Rhenish gulden first imitated and then modified had originally appeared. In 1252, the minting of coinage which was referred to as *fiorino d'oro*, i.e., the gold florin commenced. Discussing the florin, Walter Scaife recounts: "According to Villani it was of pure gold, and weighed one-eighth of an ounce. [...] The Florentine ounce contained 576 grains [...]. The gold florin of Florence contain[ed] 72 grains" (1893, 167). In his account, Scaife draws on Giovanni Villani, a 14th-century Florentine merchant and diplomat who authored *Nuova Cronica*. Carlo Cipolla describes the Florentine mint's weighing system as based – "by a long-standing tradition" (1989, 139) – on the following units:

1 pound = 12 ounces = 288 denari = 6912 grains

1 ounce = 24 denari = 576 grains

1 denaro = 24 grains.

Cipola also provides the value of these units in the metric decimal system, i.e., in grams:

1 pound = 339.5420 grams

1 ounce = 28.295167 grams

1 denaro = 1.178965 grams

1 grain = 0.049123 grams.

The florin's weight of 72 grains converted into grams is 72 x 0.049123 grams = 3.536856 grams. When the gold florin began to be struck in Florence, its gold content was fixed so as to correspond to the value of 20 silver florins. Minted since 1237, the silver florin was worth 12 denari. John Munro explains that the gold florin "[t]hus [...] was worth [...] the pound or *lira* worth 20 shillings" (2008, 18). In this way, we obtain the following equivalence: 1 gold florin = 20 silver florins = 240 denari.

As Munro shows, one gold florin was worth one pound, and one silver florin was worth one shilling. What were those pounds and shillings? They were units of account used in money calculations. They are sometimes called money of account. The shilling was 12 denari, and the pound was 20 shillings or 240 denari. The mint in which those coins were struck has not survived till our times. Over one hundred years ago, Edgcumbe Staley wrote: "[I]n 1252 [...] a new Mint was erected at the Uffizi, where the present-day Post Office is situated" (1906, 566). Spufford cites Giovanni Villani's 14th-century description of the circumstances in which the new coin appeared: "I mercatani di Firenze per onore di commune, ordinaro col popolo e comune che si battesse moneta d'oro in Firenze" ("On behalf of the commune and in agreement with the people, the Florentine merchants ordered that a coin of gold be struck in Florence") (2004, 177; from *Cronica di Giovanni Villani*, Book VI, chapter 53). This report suggests that since its very inception, the coin and its worth were bound up with trade, and given its considerable value, that this was trade involving large-scale and long-raging transactions, which greatly differed from daily deals of local markets. However, if the value of this coinage was too big for ordinary local transactions, its worth was determined by local monetary units, both real and accounting ones: silver denari and silver florins, as well as by pounds and shillings of account. These units of account were nevertheless not of local character; they were used to count money in various countries throughout Europe.

Due to the Tuscan monetary conventions, Florentine denari had "identical fineness and weight" as those of Pisa, Lucca, Siena, and Volterra, weighing 0.25 grams in the first half of the 13th century (Spufford 2004, 402). They were an outcome of multiple modifications which reduced the silver content in the denaro, whose metrological standard was fixed in 794 by "an edict issued during the synod in Frankfurt am Main in which Charlemagne decided that new denars should be common currency" (Suchodolski 1982, 192). Weighing about 1.7 grams, the new denar was supposed to be heavier that the previously used old one. The new denar was calculated following the system already in place: "The silver solidus still had 12 denars, while 20 solidi added up to one pound" (207). The same calculation model was used in Florence, where the silver florin was a silver solidus equaling 12 denari, and the gold florin was a pound equaling 20 solidi or 240 denari. The reform launched in Frankfurt also involved the new pound which was an equivalent in weight of "fifteen Roman ounces (27.25 grams x 15 = 408.75 grams), i.e. the Roman pound enlarged by one fourth" (Suchodolski 1982, 209), that is, by three Roman ounces. Two hundred and forty new, bigger denars were to be made of one new, larger pound. If the new pound was a weigh unit of estimated 408 grams (240 x 1.7), the new denar was the only coinage to be minted in the quantity of 240 pieces from one pound-mass of silver. This Carolingian system also included money of account: solidi/shillings equal to twelve denars and pounds/liras equal to 240 denars. Convened to discuss the issues of faith, the synod was probably held at an already non-existing *domus regis* situated in the present-day Archäologischer Garten on the Cathedral Hill in Frankfurt, once called Frankonovurd or Vadum Francorum (Archäologischer Garten 2012). With the Carolingian solidi/shillings and pounds, we again revisit Florence, where they took a tangible shape as coins: silver and gold florins. If the Florentine gold florin of 1252 was the first pound of account from the Carolingian system presented in Frankfurt am Mein in 794, the Tirolean guldiner of 1486 was an equivalent in silver of this model, as modified in Rhineland in 1419. Besides, the silver florin of 1237 was, for its part, a Carolingian solidus of account in the monetary form.

Where do we go from here? How about taking a ride from Florence to Venice? On 31st October, 1284, the Venetian Council of Forty decided to issue new money. The relevant inscription in the registers of the Great Council reads: "There should be 67 of the new coin [...] per mark of gold, which is at least as good as that in the florin" (Stahl 2000, 31), with its original wording reading: "LXVII pro marcha auri tam bona et fina per aurum vel melior ut est florenus" (31). The formulation itself suggests that the new Venetian money was supposed to be a counterpart of the Florentine money. Like the florin, it was supposed to be of gold which the minting technique of the day regarded as pure. Its weigh and gold content were established as matching the florin's. However, it was to be a locally used Venetian coin. If, in Florence, eight florins were struck out of one Florentine ounce of gold, in Venice sixty-seven coins were minted from one Venetian mark. If the Florentine ounce equaled 1/12 of the Florentine pound (Kelly 1811, 420), the Venetian mark was divided into eight Venetian ounces and was itself a slightly modified (enlarged) mark of Cologne (Stahl 2000, 31). The Venetian mark consisted of 4608 grains, while the Florentine ounce consisted of 576 grains. If we divide 4608 Venetian grains by sixty-seven, we obtain about 68.8 grains going into the new Venetian coin, which would be called the ducat with time. If. we divide 576 Florentine grains by 8, we come up with the florin consisting of 72 grains. Alan Stahl states that "[i]t is explicit from the standards that the new coin was intended to be a response to the Florentine florin and to be its equal in value" (31), but he himself observes that, as the two cities established the value of their money by relying on their different local metrological units and systems, their respective coinages did not have identical weighs, gold contents, and values. The florin contained more Florentine grains than the ducat did Venetian grains. Despite that, "the ducat would then be about a half of a per cent heavier than the florin (3.545 grams compared with 3.53 grams)" (31), because the Venetian grain was heavier than the Florentine grain. If we wanted to depict the nature and value of the new Venetian ducat, we could say that, like the florin, it played an important role in distant trade, in which Venice participated as part of the transcontinental exchange network connecting remote regions of Europe, North Africa, and the Middle – and even the Far – East (Abu-Lughod 1991; Nobis 2011). At the same time, the ducat featured as a functionality in Venice's political rivalry against Florence and other cities of North Italy. Notably, the rivalry was simultaneously local, regional, and transcontinental. The *zecca,* i.e., the old building of the Venetian mint, is shown in Bernhard von Breydenbach's *Peregrinatio in Terram Sanctam* of 1486 (Stahl 2000, 283). It was situated at the Canale de San Marco, on the Piazzetta opposite the Palazzo Ducale, where the Biblioteca Marciana is located today.

If we set out from Tirol's Hall, we can head in several different directions. For one, we can visit the Swiss cities of Bern and Sitten, where money modeled on Siegmund's guldiners was issued, respectively, in 1493 and in 1498 (LHS-Numismatik 2010). Vorel asserts that, similarly to the Tirolean coinage, these coins were struck in small quantities and rather served representational functions (2010, 20). If we do not feel like venturing across the Alps, we can travel up north to the Ore Mountains (Czech: Krušné Hory; German: Erzgebirge) on the present-day Czech-German border. In one of the valleys of this mountain range, silver ores started to be mined and processed on the Schlick family's estate in 1516. Miners named the valley after Saint Joachim, thus calling it "Sanctus Joachims Thal." Starting in 1520, the regular striking of large silver coins based on the Saxon standard was launched on a big scale in the newly erected mint house (46). The standard was determined by the Leipzig Minting Ordinance (*Leipziger Münzordnung*), that is, an agreement of Saxon princes concluded in Leipzig in 1500, which stipulated that eight coins should be struck per one Erfurt mark of 15-lot silver. Vorel explains that this represented 29.3275 grams of alloy and 27.495 grams of pure silver, but adds that as the Jáchymov coins were 14-lot fine, they contained 27.291 grams of pure silver each, at the weight corresponding to the Leipzig standard (2009, 153). They were struck and sold in huge quantities at Leipzig's precious metal market, where they were called "St. Joachimsthaler Guldengroschen," after their place of origin. This rather longish phrase was soon abbreviated to "thaler" and has served as the name of the coins ever since (2010, 27). As the circulation of the coins expanded, this name took a variety of locally inflected vernacular forms: *daalder* in the Netherlands, *daler* in Denmark, *dalrar* in Sweden, and *talar* in Poland (Żabiński 1989). Vorel offers an important observation on the character and value of these Joachim thalers, which is relevant to our argument; specifically, he explains that for the most part, the first Jáchymov thalers were not directly used as currency, but they were sold further on as trading silver (2010, 29). Vorel adds that they were purchased as a raw material and used for manufacturing jewelry, tableware, and other coins. As such, their worth was not so much that of money, as rather of bars designating and containing a raw material of a high, monitored purity and quality.

How about a quick trip to the British Isles now? In Scotland, king James VI ordered the issuing of a large silver coin worth thirty shillings in 1567–1571. The coin came to be called the Sword Dollar because of an image imprinted on its obverse. When another coin was issued in 1578, it was referred to as the Double Merk or the Thistle Dollar as it bore a thistle head, the symbol of Scotland (Holmes 2006, 12; National Museums of Scotland 2010). The weight of the Sword Dollar was established at 472.5 troy grains – i.e., about 30.6 grams – by the Act of Privy Council of June 1567, while the weight of the Thistle Dollar was fixed at 344.5 troy grain – i.e., about 22.3 grams – by the Act of Scottish Parliament. (Cochran 1873, 389–90, 392). In England, "under the reign of Edward VI (1547–1553), the silver crown was struck for the first time. It was a five-shilling coin which was an equivalent of the continental thaler. It weighed one troy ounce and had standard fineness" (Żabiński 1989, 124; cf. Museum Victoria 2011). Notably, as was the case with other coins, although the crown was intended to match the thaler, its metrological parameters and worth were determined on the basis of the local, English systems and their units: it weight was fixed at one troy ounce, a unit used by London's Tower mint, which was one-twelfth of the troy pound and was itself divided into twenty pennyweights of 24 grains each; consequently, the ounce had 20 x 24 – that is 480 – grains (Żabiński 1989, 119). Besides, the standard Tower fineness was .925. The crown's worth was set in English shillings and continued so until 1971, when the UK adopted the metric currency system, which left no room for shillings and crowns. Nevertheless, the Tower of London, which once housed the mint, is still sturdily there, as impressive a sight at the Thames in the center of London as ever (Tower of London 2012).

Several years ago, William Sumner observed in his discussion of the beginnings of American money: "The history which interests us begins with the Ordinance of Medina del Campo of 1497" (1898, 607). Issued by the Catholic Kings, Ferdinand and Izabela, and dated to 13th June, the Ordinance proclaims: "WE order and command that in each of our mints, other silver coins be struck and be called Reales. These shall be sixty seven Reales to the Mark, and not less. The fineness shall be eleven *dineros* and four *grains*, and not less" (Muñoz 2010, 1). Sumner explains that the text refers to the Castilian mark, which "contained 4608 Spanish grains, 3550.16 troy grains, 230.0465 metric grams" (1898, 607). Set in *dineros* divisible into 24 *granos*, i.e., grains, the fineness of twelve *dineros* meant pure silver. Having calculated that the silver fineness of 11 *dineros* and 4 grains corresponded to .930.55, Sumner concludes: "The real was, therefore, 3.433 grams gross and 3.194 grams fine" (608). As can be seen, the weight of the real depended on the weight of the mark, if this weighing unit served to strike 67 reals. This was, of course, the legal standard of weigh, from which the weight of actual coins might well deviate. Manuel Carrera Stampa specifies that the mark was based on the mark standard in possession of "the Council of Castile (Torrents y Moner, 1885, 400*pass*)" (1949, 3). However, against what Sumner declares, this history did not start in 1497. Sumner himself admits that "'[t]he real was not a new denomination. There had been such a unit since 1369" (1898, 608). Spufford duly notes that reals were first issued by Pedro I (1350–69): "Standard unchanged to late fifteenth century; fineness 11 d. 4 gr. (0.93); wt. 3.48 grams" (2004, 405). Naturally, we can take notice of a minor difference in the weights of the real cited by various authors, but another thing of interest to us is the eight-reals piece. Sumner recounts:

> Under the law of 1497 pieces of 8 reals were coined. These, says Heiss, "are the first *pesos* which were coined in Spain. Their intrinsic value has continued to be almost the same until our time. They were known afterwards as *pesos, duros, duros fuertes, thalers, dollars,* and *piastres*, and

were destined to serve as universal money." The weight of such a piece of eight reals, by the law of its origin, was 550.2088 Spanish grains, 423.716 troy grains, or 27.468 metric grams, .930.55 fine. The pure contents would be 394.2889 troy grains. (1898, 609)

This meant about 25.5 grams. At that time, Medina del Campo in Old Castile was also famous for its fairs, which, as vividly described by Fernand Braudel, "three times a year occupied the long *Rua*, with its houses with wooden pillars, and the great *Plaza Mayor*, opposite the cathedral" (1992, 83). The fairs were primarily known for textile and money trading, meaning that they were sites of money exchange and loaning. The fact that this particular venue was selected to announce the ordinance on reals suggests that the coinage was introduced for commercial ends, including the fairs in Medina del Campo (Museum of the Fairs 2012). The ordinance regulated the striking of reals, their fractions, and multiples at seven mints, specifically in Toledo, Segovia, Seville, Burgos, Grenada, Cuenca, and La Coruña. Photographs of the old buildings of those mints are published by Glenn Murray Fantom (2012).

Ordenanças sobre la moneda de Plata y vellon, dadas por instruction, a royal decree issued in Madrid on 11th May 1535, fixed the rules for the organization of a new mint in the city of Mexico (Aiton, Wheleer 1931, 200). It made provisions for the production of one-, two-, and three-reals coins, as well as halves and quarters of the real, thereby stipulating that their weights and sizes should be in conformity with the laws of Spain (201). With further instructions provided by Antonio de Mendoza, the first Viceroy of New Spain, the new mint in the city of Mexico began striking coins in early 1536. They had an inscription reading "CAROLUS ET YOANA, REGES HISPANIE ET INDIARUM" on them (201). At Mendoza's request, a royal *cédula* was issued on 18th October 1537 to allow the production of eight-real coins (205), yet in all probability their minting only started under Philip II (215). Together with other real coins, pieces of eight were struck at various mints of the Spanish India (Spanish Cob Coins 2008), first in Mexico and subsequently in Santo Domingo, Lima, La Plata, Potosi, Panama, Cartagena, Bogota, Cusco, Guatemala, Santiago, and Popayan. They bore a characteristic image of two columns wrapped in a sash with an inscription that read "PLUS ULTRA" (Aiton, Wheleer 1931, 201). The columns represent the Pillars of Hercules, a name given by the ancients to the two promontories on either side of the Strait of Gibraltar. The inscription, in a gesture of contrariness and polemics, referenced the belief that the pillars marked the end of the ancient world. Two hemispheres of the Earth with outlines of the continents hovering over ocean waves were added between the columns on the pieces of eight which were minted under Philip V (Money Museum 2012). Kiriti

Chaudhuri emphasizes their wide circulation: "Silver coins bearing the arms of imperial Spain and the initials of mint-masters in Mexico and Peru were to be found in every major trading port from Alexandria, Basra, and Mocha to Manila and Canton. The real of eight became the accepted international currency" (1985, 97). Şevket Pamuk adds: "These coins became the globally recognized standards and means of exchange during the seventeenth century" (2000, 8). Dennis Flynn and Arturo Giráldez explain that they were global at least in the sense that after 1571 (when the maritime route between Mexico and Manila in the Philippines was inaugurated) they reached China alongside American silver, travelling from America in to opposite directions, i.e., across the Pacific and across the Atlantic, Europe, and the Indian Ocean (2006), thereby navigating around the globe. The old mint in Mexico City, where the coining of this money commenced, today houses the Museo Nacional de las Culturas and the headquarters of La Casa de Moneda de Mexico, i.e., the Mexican Mint (The Mexican Mint 2012), which strikes gold and silver coins and bars and offers them to customers from around the world, among others via the Internet. Instead of the Spanish imperial pieces of eight, the mint produces and sells other well-known coins with an impression of a winged angel of independence and an inscription reading "1 ONZA PLATA PURA," i.e., one ounce of pure silver, with the offer brochure specifying that this refers to the troy ounce. The nature and the value of this money are determined by their metal content, rather than by their role in the currency circulation, which was also the case with the first Jáchymov thalers, the difference being that the former tends to be thesaurized instead of re-forged into other money or objects.

Let us go back the pieces of eight minted in the Spain-ruled America and add that they also reached the English America, where they were both important currency and money of account. The colonists dubbed them Spanish dollars (Sandrock 2010, 2). They played an important role not only in the economic development and everyday life of the colonies of New England, but also in the process of their integration and increasing independence of the British Crown, which buttressed the formation of a new American state (Grubb 2010). In a report for the Congress drafted on 28th January 1791, i.e., after the declaration of independence was adopted, Alexander Hamilton defined the weight of Spanish thalers-dollars as 416 grains, i.e., about 26.96 grams. At the same time, he observed that their fineness varied between .88462 and .89904, which also entailed a varying quantity of pure silver content, ranging from 368 to 374 grains, that is, from about 23.845 to about 24.235 grams (Officer 1983, 581, Table 1). The second Congress convened for its first session (from 24th October 1791 to 8th May 1792) at the Congress Hall in Chestnut Street in Philadelphia. Erected in the years 1787–89, this was the building of the Court of the Philadelphia County, which can still be visited, including on an online tour – without even stirring from home anywhere on the planet. The tour offers an audio-commentary in seventeen languages, therein in Polish (The Constitutional Tour 2012). On 2nd April 1792, the U.S. Congress adopted "An Act establishing a Mint, and regulating the Coins of the United States" (An Act 1792), which founded a mint and authorized it to issue a new currency of the American state. Point 9 of the document established the names and features of the new money: eagles, dollars, and cents. Let us dwell on dollars for a while. The document stipulated the following: "each to be of the value of a Spanish milled dollar as the same is now current, and to contain three hundred and seventy-one grains and four sixteenth parts of grain pure." The standard for the new money was fixed as the average content of pure silver based on Hamilton's calculations in grains, specifically in tory grains.

Where shall we go now? The connections among events, standards, and coinages at any stop in our journey can send us in multiple directions in the semblance of an expanding rhizome. How about jumping from the Philadelphia of 1792 to a small town of Bretton Woods, New Hampshire, where a United Nations Monetary and Financial Conference was held in July 1944 to set the rules of the post-war international currency system, with the dollar as the major currency of reserves and transactions (Eichengreen 2008, 91–133)? Or shall we perhaps take a ride from Tirolean Hall to Vienna, where in the wake of Maria Teresa's death, thalers were still minted bearing the date 1780 and whence they arrived in Alexandria, Cairo, Algiers, Tunis, Tripoli, Aden, Mocca, Ethiopia, Sudan, Mozambique, Indonesia, and England? As a matter of fact, they are still struck today, and Kevin Rushby recounts seeing a man pay for a Kalashnikov and ammo in Maria Teresa thalers at a market in Thal, North Yemen (2006). Retracing the links among various money standards and values, our wanderings have already taken us to Hall in Tirol, towns of Rhineland, Florence, Frankfurt, Venice, Swiss cities, Jáchymov, London, Medina del Campo, La Ciudad de México, and Philadelphia. If eleven items on this list is not enough, we may travel from Frankfurt to Rome, where at the Templum Iunonis Monetae on the centrally located Capitol, the bronze-cast *as* was produced, weighing one libra and divided into twelve ounces (*unciae*). The exact weight of the *as* and the ounce, which was its one-twelfth, varied. If the as weighed about 323 grams, the ounce weighed about 27 grams (Scheidel 2010, 27). If we make this journey, we will end up with twelve elements adding up to a complete, perfect oneness, evocative of twelve lunar months making up one solar year. But in our case, this would not put an end to the sprawling of our network of interconnections, for we would be bound to realize, against a well-known saying, that from Rome our roads led to Greece and on to Asia Minor, Mesopotamia, and

... We will thus interrupt our peregrinations in the footsteps of links among events, money, and its standards appearing at various places and in different timeframes. The word-count for this paper has already been exceeded anyway. It is high time that we returned to our eponymous globality and locality.

Discussing locality, Ulf Hannerz observes that "[w] e are just giving up the idea that the local is autonomous, that it has an integrity of its own. It would have its significance, rather, as the arena in which a variety of influences come together, acted out perhaps in a unique combination" (1996, 27). Kajsa Ekholm-Friedman and Jonathan Friedman cite Hannerz and question his approach, stating that "the global only exists in its local effects. [...] the global is not a new place," "there is no global space floating above the local," and "[t]he global is always about interlocal relations, not about a supralocal organism" (2008, 12, 11, 9). Let us consider these two positions. On the one hand, locality is understood as an arena, or as a site, where multiple external influences converge and forge a particular local place. On this model, locality can be reduced to its exteriority and then, paradoxically, it turns out to be this very exteriority. We are thus faced with the question of what this exteriority actually is. Where do external influences come from, if other localities are also fashioned by them? If we are tempted to assume that locality is shaped by the global, the reservations advanced by the Friedmans prove extremely relevant: globality is not any extra-local place or a supra-local entity. The global only exists as a set of local effects in interlocal relations. On this take, interlocal interactions are reducible to locality, and interlocality – or globality – eventually turns out to be locality. Yet, a question immediately arises: What is this interlocality? Where is that "inter" to be found, and how does it exist? These questions pertain to the mode and place in which this "inter" is, i.e., to its ontic status and locus.

The bricks of ancient Harappan buildings in the Indus Valley are described as follows: "The predominant brick size was 11 by 5.5 by 2.75 inches, that is a ratio of 4:2:1" (Allchin, Allchin 1968, 242). Though different, their three dimensions – length, width, and height – of the bricks were interrelated and determined their shape. The two positions cited above identify locality with place. This prompts questions, doubts, problems, and two divergent solutions. Locality turns out to be exteriority and globality, or the other way round the external-and-global turns out to be the local. Instead of identifying locality with place and, consequently, locality with globality, would it not make more sense to recognize locality and globality as dimensions of places, of events which occur in them, and of relations between these places and events? In this paper, we have focused on very specific events concerning the standards of money and its worth. We have also explored connections between such developments at various places and times. These events and their interconnections are part of a broader and more complex process in which the contemporary global money and its value have been produced. I believe that the global and the local can be regarded as dimensions, first, of events occurring at particular places; second, of relations between them; and third, of the entire process of the formation of contemporary global money. By the way, these are not the only dimensions of these developments. At various points, this paper also indicates the relevance of other dimensions such as regionality and trans-continentality. The distinctiveness of these various dimensions is not as clear or obvious as is the case with the Harappa bricks. At the same time, their interdependences are far more complicated. Additionally, the rank and significance of these dimensions vary from event to event. In one event, a given dimension plays the key role, while being of secondary importance in another event. Nevertheless, as with the bricks, these various dimensions and relations among them determine the shape and the character of individual events and of their interconnections.

To draw the full circle, let us go back to 1486, when guldiners were minted in Hall. The authors who depict this event as the birth of the modern dollar highlight its global dimension. Of course, this is how we can describe it today in retrospect, but such an assessment was not possible back then, in 1486. At that time, other dimensions were of relevance to this event. I guess that the discovery of a silver deposit in Tirolean Schwaz and Siegmund's financial problems can be regarded as the local dimension. The transcontinental dimension of the event may be represented by the fact that Tirol is situated on an important trading route which cuts through the Alpine Passo del Brennero and connects countries north of the Alps with Venice, and via Venice, with the Orient. As for the interregional dimension, the reliance on the Rhenish standard is an important factor here. These events and their interconnections, as explored in this paper, are only part of a more comprehensive process in which today's global currency has evolved. This process and its components have other important – local, regional, interregional, and transcontinental – dimensions as well. The point is that various coinages and their values which have been part of this process have had their heterogeneous, specific, and various distinctive features, which were related to differing cultural practices in the contexts of varying compass. Charlemagne's pound was the money of account used to calculate denars produced by the mints of his state. The rhinegulden was money that integrated the local markets of Central Europe. The value of the florin was determined by the denaro as agreed upon by Tuscan cities. The Venetian ducat was used in large-scale, transcontinental trade, but it was also involved in regional political rivalry. The thaler of Jáchymov was initially just a bar of silver with a hallmark guaranteeing the quality and value of merchandise at the market in Leipzig; and the guldiner of Hall was a representational medal. The formation of the metrological standard of global American currency also involved a multiplicity of local standards, based on local systems and their units of account, weight, and worth, in which the smallest grains had specific local sizes, even if they were all defined as medium-sized barley grains from the mid-ear. To understand particular events and relations among them, we must study various dimensions and their local, interlocal, regional, interregional, continental, transcontinental, and global interconnections.

Acknowledgements

I would like to thank two people for their invaluable help in developing his paper. I am grateful to Professor Borys Paszkiewicz for bringing the studies of Petr Vorel to my attention and kindly lending his own copies to me. My thank-you also goes to Prof. Dr. Hab. Stanisław Rosik for educating me on the synod at Frankfurt am Mein.

Bibliography

Abu-Lughod, Janet L. *Before European Hegemony: The World System A.D. 1250–1350*. New York: Oxford University Press, 1991.

Aiton, Arthur S., and Benjamin W. Wheeler. "The First American Mint." *The Hispanic American Historical Review*, vol. 11, no. 2, 1931, pp. 198–215. http://www.jstor.org/stable/2506275. Accessed on July 4, 2011.

Allchin, Bridget, and Raymond Allchin. *The Birth of Indian Civilization: India and Pakistan before 500 B.C.* Baltimore: Penguin Books, 1968.

An act establishing a mint, and regulating the Coins of the United States. 1792. http://memory.loc.gov/cgi-bin/ampage?collId=llsl&fileName=001/llsl001.db&recNum=371. Accessed on September 3, 2010.

Archäologische Garten. 25 May 2012. http://www.frankfurt.de/sixcms/detail.php?id=3866&_ffmpar[_id_inhalt]=5011182. Accessed on September 3, 2010.

Blanchard, Ian. *Mining, Metallurgy and Minting in the Middle Ages, Vol. 3: Continuing Afro-European Supremacy, 1250–1450*. Stuttgart: Franz Steiner Verlag, 2005.

Boerner, Lars, and Oliver Vockart. "The Utility of a Common Coinage: Currency Unions and the Integration of Money Markets in Late Medieval Central Europe." *Working Papers*, no. 146, September 2010. http://eprints.lse.ac.uk/29409/1/WP146.pdf. Accessed on September 3, 2010.

Braudel, Fernand. *Civilization and Capitalism, 15th-18th century, Vol. II: The Wheels of Commerce*. Translated by S. Reynolds. Berkeley and Los Angeles: University of California Press, 1992.

Chaudhuri, Kirti N. *Trade and Civilisation in the Indian Ocean: An Economic History from the Rise of Islam to 1750*. Cambridge: Cambridge University Press, 1985.

Chilosi, David, and Oliver Volckart. "Money, States and Empire: Financial Integration Cycles and Institutional Integration Cycles and Institutional Change in Central Europe, 1400–1520." *Working Paper*, vol. 132, no. 9, 2009. London School of Economics, Department of Economic History. http://federation.ens.fr/ydepot/semin/texte0910/VOL2010MON.pdf. Accessed on September 28, 2010.

Cipolla, Carlo M. *Money in Sixteenth Century Florence*. Berkeley: University of California Press, 1989.

Cochran, Patrick, and Robert William. *Notes of some unpublished records of the coinages of James VI*. 1873. http://ads.ahds.ac.uk/catalogue/adsdata/PSAS_2002/pdf/vol_010/10_225_239.pdf. Accessed on September 13, 2010.

Eichengreen, Barry. *Globalizing Capital: A History of the International Monetary System*. Princeton: Princeton University Press, 2008.

Ekholm-Friedman, Kajsa, and Jonathan Friedman. *Historical Transformations: The Anthropology of Global Systems*. Lanham, Toronto, New York, Plymouth: Altamira Press, 2008.

Flynn, Dennis O., and Arturo Giráldez. "Globalization Began in 1571." In *Globalization and Global History*. Edited by Barry K. Gills, and William R. Thompson. London: Routledge, 2006.

Grubb, Farley. "Creating the U.S. Dollars Currency Union, 1748–1811." http://eh.net/XIII-Congress/cd/papers/39Grubb93.pdf. Accessed on September 28, 2010.

Hall Mint Museum. http://www.tyrol.tl/en/highlights/museums-and-exhibitions/hallmint-museum-and-mint-thtml. Accessed on May14, 2012.

Hanerz, Ulf. *Transnational Connections: Culture, People, Places*. London and New York: Routledge, 1996.

Heiss, Aloïss. *Descripcion General de las Monedas Hispano-cristianas desde la Invasion de los Arabes*. Madrid: R. N. Milagro, 1865.

Hess, Wolfgang, and Dietrich Klose. *Vom Taler zum Dollar 1486–1986*. München: Staatliche Münzasmmlung, 1986.

Holmes, Nicholas. *Scottish coins in the National Museums of Scotland, Edinburgh 1526–1603*. Oxford: Oxford University Press, 2006.

Kelly, Patrick. *The Universal Cambist and Commercial Instructor; Being a General Treatise on Exchange; Including the Monies, Coins, Weights, and Measures of All Trading Nations and Colonies; with an Account of their Banks, and Paper Currencies, Vol. I*. London: Lackington, Allen, And Co. lhs-Numismatik, 1811. http://www.medievalcoinage.com/earlydated/1490s.htm. Accessed on September 22, 2010.

Money Museum. "Real de a ocho." http://www.moneymuseum.com/moneymuseum/coins/periods/coin.jsp?lang=en&i=0&aid=6&gid=29&cid=137&pi=0&ps=10. Accessed on May 16, 2012.

Munro, John. "Money and Coinage in Late Medieval and Early Modern Europe." www.economics.utoronto.ca/munro5/MoneyLec.pdf. Accessed on June 26, 2008.

Muñoz, Miguel L. "A Coin Called Peso." http://www.chicagocoinclub.org/projects/PiN/ccp.html. Accessed on September 14, 2010.

Murray, Fantom, and Glenn Stephen. "Historic Spanish Mint Today." http://www.mcu.es/museos/docs/MC/ActasNumis/Historic_spanish_mints.pdf. Accessed on May 15, 2012.

Museum of the Fairs. http://www.museoferias.net/museum_of_the_fairs2.htm. Accessed on May 16, 2012.

Museum Victoria. "Crown, Edward VI, Reg. No: 345." http://museumvictoria.com.au/collections/items/54201/coin-crown-edward-vi-england-1551. Accessed on August 4, 2011.

National Museums of Scotland. http://nms.scran.ac.uk/database/record.php?usi=000-100-050-905-C. Accessed on September 15, 2010.

Nobis, Adam. "Ponte di Rialto. Most między." In *Nie tylko o pocztówkach. Szkice dedykowane Profesorowi Pawłowi Banasiowi*. Edited by S. Bednarek, and J. Jackowski, Warsaw: Korporacja Polonia, 2011.

Officer, Lawrence H. "Dollar-Sterling Mint parity and Exchange Rates, 1791–1834." *The Journal of Economic History*, vol. 43, no. 3, 1983, pp. 579–616.

Pamuk, Şevket. *A Monetary History of the Ottoman Empire*. Cambridge: Cambridge University Press, 2000.

Rushby, Kevin."A Fistful of Thalers." *The* Guardian. 14 January 2006. http://www.guardian.co.uk/books/2006/jan/14/featuresreviews.guardianreview23. Accessed on September 15, 2010.

Sandrock, John E. "Tobacco as a Medium of Exchange." http://www.thecurrencycollector.com/pdfs/Maryland_Colonial_and_Continental_Bank.pdf. Accessed on September 15, 2010.

Scaife, Walter. *Florentine Life during the Renaissance*. Baltimore: The Johns Hopkins Press, 1893.

Scheidel, Walter. "The monetary systems of the Han and Roman empires." *Princeton/Stanford Working Paper in Classics*. http://www.princeton.edu/~pswpc/pdfs/scheidel/020803.pdf. Accessed on September 18, 2010.

Spanish Cob Coins. "Reales." http://www.newworldtreasures.com/cobs.thml. Accessed on September 16, 2010.

Spufford, Peter, *Money and Its Use in Medieval Europe*. Cambridge: Cambridge University Press, 2004.

Stahl, Alan. *Zecca: The Mint of Venice in the Middle Ages*. New York: John Hopkins University Press, 2000.

Staley, Edgcumbe. *The Guilds of Florence*. London: Methuen & Co., 1906.

Stampa, Manuel Carrera. "The Evolution of Weights and Measures in New Spain." *The Hispanic American Historical Review*, vol. 29. no. 1, 1949, pp. 2–24.

Suchodolski, Stanisław. *Moneta i obrót pieniężny w Europie Zachodniej*. Wroclaw: Ossolineum, 1982.

Sumner, William G. "The Spanish Dollar and the Colonial Shilling." *The American Historical Review*, vol. 3, no. 4, 1898, pp. 607–19.

The Constitutional Tour. http://www.theconstitutional.com/selfguided/tour.php?lid=13. Accessed on May 16, 2012.

The Mexican Mint. http://www.free-bullion-investment-guide.com/mexican-bullion.html. Accessed on May 16, 2012.

Torrents y Monner, Antonio. *Tratado completo teórico y práctico de contabilidad mercantil, industrial y administrative*. Barcelona, 1885.

Tower of London. http://www.hrp.org.uk/TowerOfLondon/?gclid=CMLYvIGuh6IC FReZ2AodZ2fEVQ. Accessed on May 15, 2012.

Vorel, Petr. *Od srebrnego talara do światowego dolara. Narodziny talara i jego droga w europejskim i światowym obiegu pieniężnym XVI-XX wieku*. Toruń: Adam Marszałek, 2010.

Vorel, Petr. „From the Czech Silver Toler to the Global Dollar. The Birth of the Dollar and its Journey of Monetary Circulation in Europe and the World from the 16th to the 20th Century (East European Monographs)" New York: Columbia University Press, 2013.

Żabiński, Zbigniew. *Rozwój systemów pieniężnych w Europie Zachodniej i Północnej*. Wroclaw: Ossolineum, 1989.

CHAPTER 11

Global Paths of Cultural Institutions

Attendance, Participation, or Education

Karolina Golinowska

Directions of the development and strategies of cultural policy tend to be determined by temporary preferences or even particular vogues for certain models of culture-making and culture promotion. To say that this is so because culture itself and culture-related practices undergo transformations would be to state the obvious. Be it as it may, the concept of cultural attendance, whose meanings vary rather widely, appears to be the key aspect in the current transformations. How exactly cultural attendance is defined has implications for strategies of cultural policy. In very broad lines, the current understanding of cultural attendance shifts away from activities designed within narrowly circumscribed institutional spaces which guarantee involvement in high culture. This shift results, most generally speaking, from the dynamics of social processes and has been embraced by multiple research studies which reveal hazards associated with the dichotomous vision of culture, where high culture is glorified and low culture is deprecated. Such distinctions into high and low culture as tools of social hierarchization have been amply discussed by scholars, notably by the French sociologist Pierre Bourdieu in his celebrated *Distinction: A Social Critique of the Judgment of Taste.* Crucially, although Bourdieu's argument has invited an incisive critique (Schwarz 1997, 177–178), his studies unambiguously show that high culture has been ascribed to the ruling class. Of course, some of Bourdieu's insights have lost their relevance. Today, it would be quite unfeasible to discuss class society using the same concepts on which Bourdieu's analyses in *Distinction* relied. Profound socio-cultural changes have taken place since its first French edition was published in 1979. As globalization processes have intensified, voices have appeared claiming that social divisions run along slightly different trajectories now. Various social scientists have attempted to grasp these new hierarchies by means of different conceptual tools. For example, Richard Florida has announced the coming of the era of the creative class (Florida, 2002), and Zygmunt Bauman has portrayed the world as dominated by cosmopolitan elites (Bauman 2000, 13–14). Other scholars have observed that the traditionally defined working class (the proletariat) is being supplanted by the precariat, i.e., social groups of a low and uncertain occupational and financial status (Sowa 2010, 105–110). Without ruling in how far we are justified to rely on the notion of class society today, we cannot nevertheless fail to recognize that these social changes have considerably undercut the definition of high culture and altered the meaning of cultural attendance. Today, the belief is consolidating that culture and cultural practices should be democratized and universally accessible. Given this, cultural institutions are launching several initiatives framed as projects in artistic or cultural education. At the same time, we can witness a return to culturalist ideas which insist that culture-making practices far exceed the institutional space. In other words, cultural institutions are not the only stimulators or generators of cultural production and involvement. This was emphatically highlighted as early as in the 1990s by Henry Jenkins, who coined the term "participatory culture" (Jenkins, 2005, 46) to denote the space of cultural production and consumption. These changes, which eventually made Jenkins develop the notion of convergence culture, have irrevocably impacted the very form of efforts for designing trajectories of cultural activities. Given this, if we do not reductively regard culture-making practices as concerned exclusively with high culture, but instead follow Jenkins in exploring bottom-up initiatives and non-institutional spaces, we will have one more issue to consider. The globalization of art and culture has undermined the primacy of high culture, re-casting it as a tool of the domination of elites, i.e., of white Americans and Europeans. The incessant flow of multiple lifestyles, modes of living, and models of art-making triggered immense cultural chaos, which called for a new universalizing, coherence-restoring framework. As a result, the commonly used lexicon received an addition in the notions of global art and culture, which together with other "globally" perceived developments, formed a "global" reality.

This chapter aims to examine changes in the operation modes of cultural institutions affected by these social transformations, which make their imprint on the space of culture and cultural practices. The point is that as the notion of cultural attendance was redefined, these institutions found themselves compelled to adopt different modes of action. The specificity of processes in and through which the entrenched institutional operation model was modified only allowed incremental changes. To fully picture these transformations, we should also consider proliferating debates which were sparked by the problems faced by concrete institutions and resulted in the remodeling on the functioning paradigm of these institutions. This is vividly exemplified by the publication of *New Museology* (1989), a volume edited by Peter Vergo, whose contributors envision the museum as a living institution which is willing to take up various engagements and outreach activities, far beyond the organization of regular exhibitions. The palette of these activities should certainly be augmented with educational projects, which, for decades, have been a permanent and solid fixture in institutional programs as a response to globalization processes.

For a long time, it was commonly believed that the problem of cultural attendance could be solved by broadening access to institutions dedicated to the dissemination of the national heritage and contemporary cultural developments. The tendency to devise cultural policies primarily on the basis of the cultural infrastructure was also widespread in post-war Poland, resulting in a staggering increase in the number of cultural institutions. As a consequence, Poland now boasts twenty seven philharmonic halls, fourteen opera houses, and innumerable theaters, which are subsidized from the state budget. Paradoxically, thinking in terms of the accessibility of culture-offering institutions surfaced in a radically different context as well. This way of thinking, originating in the U.S., was addressed by Florida in his discussion of universal recipes for a global metropolis. According to Florida, over the last century, a belief prevailed in the U.S. that for a city to be cosmopolitan and have a truly urban panache, its traditional cultural institutions must offer varied artistic programs and be widely accessible (Florida 2002, 147–151). The fundamental ensemble of institutions contributing to the cosmopolitan image of the city included an art museum and the SOB triad, i.e., a symphonic orchestra, an opera and a ballet company. Of course, like most of the universalizing remedies to the maladies of cultural policy, such interventions proved ineffective. Florida attributes the decrease in the popularity of such institutions first and foremost to their low profitability rates, which prevented them from making their repertoires more attractive and varied as well as to the disinterest of young people who preferred other forms of cultural engagement. In my view, this would be associated with the dissolution of the hegemony of the high-culture paradigm, i.e., with the expansion of the field of cultural production. When examining corresponding developments in Poland, we should observe that the 1990s witnessed a profound re-appraisal of cultural practices. The traditional institutions offered an elitist and at the same time passive model of cultural attendance, which required quite substantial cultural and economic capital resources. As a result, a considerable majority of cultural institutions extended their practices by including educational projects which targeted various age groups and introduced a range of discounts and concessions to reduce admission fees. These endeavors are well illustrated by the considerable popularity of programs launched by the Polish Ministry of Culture and National Heritage, such as *Kultura dostępna* (*Accessible Culture*) and *Bilet za 250 groszy* (*A Ticket at 250 Grosz*),[1] the latter marking the celebrations of the 250th anniversary of Polish theater.

---

1 In Poland, 100 grosz equals one zloty; 250 grosz (i.e., 2.5 zloty) was less than an average price of a loaf of bread in 2015. (translator's note).

Another important issue concerning these cultural institutions involves their typical programs. Their cultural offer was supposed to familiarize audiences with globally recognized artists and artworks. These patterns and expectations are clearly revealed in analyses of visual art collections scattered across the world. The persistent recurrence of some names in them was and still is surprising. For example, works by Olafur Eliasson, a Danish-Icelandic artist born in 1967, are to be found in Poland (the collection of Grażyna Kulczyk), Turkey (the Istanbul Museum of Modern Art), and the U.S. (New York's MoMA and Guggenheim's Museum), to name but a few venues. Given this, these institutions can be posited to in a way co-produce a global narrative of artistic practice, which would be illuminated by a detailed analysis of their collections. Of course, there is a concomitant and gradually increasing tendency to make room for the local artists in such collections, which results in their growing diversification. Notably, the collection of Grażyna Kulczyk features Polish artists of the 20th century, and Istanbul Modern dedicates some of its space to an outline of the development of arts in Turkey, while MoMA and Guggenheim's display artists relevant to New York.

These patterns are even more clearly visible in international art festivals which, though ostensibly enjoying liberty without having to make decisions about the profile of any permanent collection, are eager to invite more or less the same artists. Although this tendency has been scathingly criticized in recent times within the debate on the art biennial as an institution, the same names still continue to reappear. For example, works by the British-German artist Tino Seghal were exhibited at the Biennale in Moscow and the Venice Biennale in 2005, at the Lyon Biennale in 2007, at the Gwangju Biennale in 2010, at the Gothenburg Biennale in 2011, at the Shanghai Biennale in 2012, and the Venice Biennale in 2013. As another example, works by the British artist Phil Collins were put on display at multiple exhibitions, including the Istanbul Biennale, the Tirana Biennale and the Sharjah Biennale in 2005, the Nordic Biennale in 2006, Palestine's Riwaq Biennale in 2009, the Berlin Biennale in 2010, the Singapore Biennale in 2011, and the Shanghai Biennale in 2012. Such examples can be multiplied, and the two cases only serve here to illustrate the global popularity of certain artists, which translates into the number of invitations to high-profile international artistic events. One paradox is that the intensification of globalization processes, which have undoubtedly affected cultural institutions, has put several constraints on the design of artistic programs. As a result, instead of illuminating alleged heterogeneity, institutions have become more eager to reproduce global trends, causing an enormous recurrence of some names. In this way, a global narrative of art has been and is still being produced, excluding peripheral zones and privileging artists from the most affluent countries as purportedly universal. Of course, such pursuits can be explained as an effort to educate the local audience about globally recognizable artists. At the same time, no biennial has ever been staged exclusively for the residents of the host city, serving rather as a perfectly fitting component of institutionally designed platforms of cultural tourism. In this sense, if we were to answer the eponymous question of a volume published a few years ago – *Is Art History Global?* – we should answer in the positive. Admittedly, the volume itself rather focused on scholarly parameters and the universal research methodology applicable to various cultural contexts (Elkins 2007, 5–21), but institutional approaches and exhibition practices are key factors in this regard. What art collections and biennials have been presenting over several last decades adds up to a very strong, homogenizing global narrative of the recent history of artistic practices.

Nevertheless, a homogeneous vision of global culture did not walk alone long. Since the 1990s, in a parallel development, the urgency of active attendance – or, more precisely, of participation – has been vocally advocated. The use of these two terms – attendance and participation – in this context begs an explanation. Although they seem synonymous, the different nuances of their meanings are not reducible to purely linguistic distinctions. Attendance is part of the older vocabulary of cultural policy. When taking part in culture, audiences attend various institutionally organized events, such as concerts, exhibitions, and performances. However, their attendance only entails a passive acquisition of cultural content, which, though obviously increasing their cultural capital, does not make them agents in the field of cultural production. Defined in such terms, the act of attendance corresponds to institutionalized forms of contact with high culture as described by Pierre Bourdieu. In contrast, following Jenkins, participation involves contributing to and co-producing culture, which means adopting an active and creative attitude. Understood in this way, participation is expressed in a variety of social spaces, in effectively utilizing modern communication technologies, and in dismissing the supremacy of institutions as generators of culture. In institutional settings, participation as envisioned by Jenkins is difficult to implement, since it contradicts the top-down delimited activity forms typical of institutional operations. The only way of applying the participatory paradigm to cultural institutions would be by suggesting a changed mode of functioning, where visitors are not only passive recipients of an artistic program, but also contribute to it by taking part in various educational or culture-promoting projects. Regarding strictly artistic pursuits, participation is above all associated with socially engaged art. Such relations between culture-making practices and the audience have invited numerous studies and inspired several world-famous publications. One of them was *Relational Aesthetics* by Nicolas Bourriaud, in which relational art was deemed a natural response to the human need of establishing bonds (Bourriaud 2002, 25, 29, 41). In Bourriaud's view, because the essence of relational art lies in the "space of encounter," it provokes unique situations which bear a social potential of channeling real human interactions. The observer's involvement, interactivity, and inimitability are thus the major characteristics of practices of socially engaged artists. Unlike cultural institutions, which are sites where people assemble, this kind of artistic practice only permits an individual experience of the situation, without imposing any fixed scenario. Activities undertaken in this sphere take multiple forms, unbounded by any artistic criteria.

The turn of the 20th century was thus marked by two contradictory movements. A homogeneous vision of global culture developed concurrently with the globally recognized socially-engaged art and the primacy of participation as defined by Bourriaud. The projects developed at that time bore various monikers, ranging from community arts, participatory arts, and experimental community projects to relational art and collaborative arts. Their major goal was to defy monolithic cultural institutions, which cherished the idea of the inaccessibility of high art, and to offer an alternative to the entrenched mainstream art world. Relational art laid the foundation for a global artistic movement which emphasized the local dimension, common life space, and community culture identical with practices of everydayness. Artists involved in participatory art, such as Artur Żmijewski, Jeremy Deller, Thomas Hirschhorn, and Oda Projesi came to be globally recognizable figures. Cultural institutions were eager to involve in efforts to bolster transnational fascination with such projects, both by organizing residency schemes or collaborative projects and by hosting exhibitions which documented the development of projects and their outcomes. Yet the fad for producing and globally exhibiting collaborations with people who were excluded from the global milieu only briefly excited enthusiasm. Community arts provoked a devastating criticism as a pursuit which breached various ethical and/or artistic standards. One of their most vocal critics was Claire Bishop, who pointed out the risks inherent in valorizing art through a worldview-colored lens (Bishop 2012, 19, 23). In socially engaged art, artistic intentions were the major theme of discussion, with the aesthetic form and the meanings of the accomplished artistic act left unconsidered. What only mattered was the sacrifice of the artist, who relinquished his/her own presence in order to let project participants speak on their own behalf. The final effect was produced by itself. The aimlessness and autonomy of art were ousted by overt commitment to social and political issues. As a result, the praise of humanism and political correctness triumphed. In other words, Bishop repudiated the fact that artistic pursuits were assessed in terms of implementing – or, for that matter, non-implementing – certain non-artistic values, such as the model of collaboration or an "incomplete" presentation of the community.

Other critiques focused on the problem of artists' authoritarianism and their unwillingness to perform the function of an activist or an educator. The point was that an artists invited the local community to join a project which aimed to produce its representation only on the strength of an institutional legitimation (Kwon 2002, 138–140). Having no requisite anthropological or ethnographic competences, artists faced the hazard of perpetuating authoritarian attitudes, abandoning the dialogic stance, and shutting off institutional criticism (Foster 1996, 173–174). At the same time, enjoying the status of social activists, artists gained the power to manipulate the spaces of cultural memory and to spawn alternative historical narratives. Artists spoke on behalf of a given community and thereby appropriated this community, so to speak, making its position in the symbolic and political sphere dependent on their representations (Kester 2004, 148–151). As a result, the activists bolstered their own ideological message and buttressed the power they exercised over communities. With the right to make pronouncements on behalf of the groups they represented, artists legitimized their moral, professional, and political positions and, at the same time, perpetuated the existing order, because, as Bishop aptly points out, all the projects eventually made it to galleries, which were visited by a narrow middle-class audience.

The criticism outlined above only highlights how complex the issue is. The idealizing assumptions underpinning the practices of socially engaged art did not preserve it from institutionalization. Given this, it would be misguidedly reductive to construe these activities merely as designed to disseminate knowledge about excluded communities. For one, the vogue for collaborative projects with local communities, in which the "local" and at the same time "authentic" dimensions of everyday life were brought into relief, was a response to the homogeneous vision of culture cultivated in the 1990s. In this way, an interesting fluctuation occurred, as the intensification of the local fueled the forging of global criteria of socially engaged art and the related institutional cultural policy. Spreading and gaining popularity worldwide, community art in fact perfectly maneuvered its way into the structures of the art world. It proposed a strictly participatory model founded on collaboration between an artist and a concrete community, but ultimately it bowed to high culture and traditional forms of cultural attendance. After all, the final outcome, i.e., a work that documented the project, was exhibited in enclosed sites of festivals and/or galleries, accessible to and visited by a small portion of the public. Therefore, we are left to inquire whether cultural institutions could offer other forms of participation than a somewhat disguised traditional cultural attendance.

To recapitulate, the dispersal of the high-culture paradigm entailed the necessity to re-model modes of cultural attendance and to adjust cultural policy to them. Associated with the ideals of high culture, attendance involved passivity and hierarchy in the reception of what was presented by designated cultural institutions. The appeal and application of this model were global, as similar infrastructural and institutional solutions were employed internationally. By practicing cultural attendance, audiences learned about globally recognizable artists and their works. For its part, participation was supposed to foreground the role of the individual and his/her environment in the generation of cultural content, to expose the non-institutional facet of culture, and to democratize access to culture. Defined by Jenkins, the idea of participation, which highlighted the multiplicity of forms of popular culture, could not be implemented within the institutional framework. Engendered by socially engaged art, the idea of participation aspired to explore local resources and to promote active involvement of various communities. Its practices served as the basis of a global artistic movement which came to be supported by institutional structures, without offering a possibility to abandon the traditional paradigm of cultural attendance. What implications does it have for cultural institutions? Does the institutional configuration always presuppose the domination of attendance and the impossibility of participation?

As Bishop insists, whenever art becomes a tool of education, it must be visible to people (Bishop 2012, 241). This triggers a series of abuses, which are epitomized in the criticized projects of relational art. The point is that education itself does not generate representative images, remaining in the shadow as a less spectacular activity whose regularity is stripped of a festival-like luster. This status is related to the fact that education has always been, for better or worse, an institutional domain. Thus a question arises in how far the existing cultural institutions would be able and/or willing to cast off paternalism, with which they are charged, and make their programs responsive to the needs of potential audiences as identified in studies which provide very concrete assessments. At the same time, we should inquire whether and why participation in culture should need any institutional anchoring in the first place. After all, there are informally structured communities which fare perfectly well without any institutional supervision. Nevertheless, cultural institutions should be expected to stimulate social interactions, as they are by definition less susceptible to market influences than the private sector is, and their operations go beyond the rigid restrictions of project work. To avoid sweeping generalizations, let us cite a specific example.

In her short study *Radical Museology* (2013), Bishop describes the profiles of three institutions which set out to redefine the relationship between education and cultural policy. The institutions she explored – the Van Abbemuseum in Eindhoven, the Metelkova City Alternative Culture Center in Ljubljana, and the Museo Nacional Centro de Arte Reina Sofia in Madrid – effected meaningful shifts in designing their culture-making practices. They elude any standard operational models of the art museum, offering artistic programs that provoke public debates on challenging issues which are often pushed deep down the social unconscious. Their exhibition activities form an institutional response to contemporary socio-political problems. These museums become sites of critical analysis of national traumas, as they challenge unreflectively accepted historical narratives (Bishop 2013, 27). The possibility of participation as related to the institutional context is predicated on the production of discourse informed by the analysis of current social problems, on the awareness of present issues and historical events, and on the reconstruction of identity narratives. Such pursuits can be embarked on if there are durable institutional foundations to support harmonious and long-lasting work and if a long-term strategy is designed for the operations of an institution. This is not a simple resumption of the traditionally conceived "work at grass-roots," implemented through educational workshops, discussions, and/or practical exercises. It also entails an attempt to breed an awareness that culture forms an indispensable element of public life and, as such, is closely interwoven with current socio-political issues, human relationships, and historical memory. It is still a widespread belief that cultural institutions are isolated entities which have little in common with what is going on outside their walls. This difficulty is partly revealed in the very way in which culture is popularly defined. According to the report on *Praktyki Kulturowe Polaków* (*Cultural Practices of Poles*), when asked what culture is, more than half of the respondents cited some forms of artistic practice (pop music, photography, dance), referenced cultivation and good manners (ability to converse with others, using appropriate forms of address), or identified culture with Polishness (morality and religion) (Krajewski 2014, 308–309). In this way, culture-making practices are divested of their political dimension, and turned into an ideologically neutral, innocuous, and thus inconsequential element.

The current surge in the popularity of institutionally launched projects in cultural education, global education, and culture promotion reveals the immense scale of change in devising cultural policies. Globally considered, cultural policy is to be eventually founded on locality, which manifests in rootedness in a particular geopolitical space, in shared micro-histories, and in common identity narratives. Rather than built on the model of an informed cosmopolitan dashingly frequenting cultural institutions and absorbing a globally recognized canon of artistic practice, civic awareness should be anchored in the local network of references and representations, which sustains profound relations with the closest environment, fuels creativity, and fosters people's self-awareness and consciousness of the shared historical memory. In Poland, this is vigorously represented by the newly opened POLIN Museum of the History of Polish Jews in Warsaw, which strongly aspires to critically scrutinize various components of the history of Poland.

This globally expanding vision of cultural policy, which powerfully emphasizes the exigency of participation, does not become embroiled in predicaments haunting other global trends. The previously touted idea of the global cosmopolitan presupposed a transnational human being, an individual without territorial and identitarian embedment. Inevitably accompanying thus-conceived cosmopolitism, elitism could be expressed in lower-situated classes through forging new social hierarchies which would fill the gap left by the narrative of global identity. This distinguishability at the individual level tended to become a new iteration of cultural extremism, driving violence-underpinned mechanisms of social exclusion or rejection. This is why it is so vital to launch long-term interventions to reduce the attractiveness of the ideas of national and cultural radicalism and, at the same time, foster a more self-reflective society. After all, at the end of the day, cultural policy should provide tools for building a society that consciously confronts the challenges of globalization rather than a collective of global citizens of the world.

Bibliography

Bishop, Claire. *Artificial Hells: Participatory Art and the Politics of Spectatorship*. London, New York: Verso, 2012.

Bishop, Claire. *Radical Museology or, What's "Contemporary" in Museums of Contemporary Art?*. London: Koenig Books, 2013.

Bourriaud, Nicolas. *Relational Aesthetics*. Dijon: Les presses du réel, 2002.

Elkins, James. "Art History as a Global Discipline." In *Is Art History Global?*. Edited by J. Elkins. New York, London: Routledge, 2007.

Bauman, Zygmunt. *Liquid Modernity*. Cambridge, UK, and Malden, MA: Polity Press, 2000.

Florida, Richard. *The Rise of the Creative Class and How It Is Transforming Work, Leisure, Community, and Everyday Life*. New York: Basic Books, 2002.

Foster, Hall. *The Return of the Real: The Avant-Garde at the End of the Century*. Cambridge, Massachusetts, London, England: Massachusetts Institute of Technology Press, 1996.

Jenkins, Henry. *Textual Poachers: Television Fans and Participatory Cultures*. New York, London: Routledge, 2005.

Kester, Grant. *Conversation Pieces: Community and Communication in Modern Art*. Berkeley, Los Angeles: University of California Press, 2004.

Krajewski, Marek. "Kompetencje kulturowe Polaków." In R. Drozdowski, B. Fatyga, M. Filiciak, M. Krajewski, and T. Szlendak, *Praktyki Kulturowe Polaków*. Toruń: Wydawnictwo Naukowe Uniwersytetu Mikołaja Kopernika, 2014.

Kwon, Miwon. *One Place after Another: Site-specific Art and Locational Identity*. Cambridge Massachusetts: The MIT Press, 2002.

Sowa, Jan; "Prekariat: proletariat epoki globalizacji." In *Robotnicy opuszczają miejsca pracy*. Edited by J. Sokołowska. Łódź: Muzeum Sztuki w Łodzi, 2010.

Schwarz, David. *Culture and Power*. Chicago: The University of Chicago Press, 1997.

CHAPTER 12

The Political Role of Cities: A Global Perspective

Piotr Jakub Fereński

> Man is by nature a political animal
> ARISTOTLE, 1999, 5

⁂

As we remember, Aristotle claimed in his *Politics* that "the state is a creation of nature" (ibid.). Since humans essentially lack self-sufficiency as individuals, they must live in a community. Whoever is self-sufficient does not belong to a state, and is, as such, either an animal or a god. All people who possess rational and moral faculties are characterized by a unique "instinct" to be part of a political community, with such communities as a rule being based on justice (or on attempts to establish what is just). It is on justice that any legal order must be grounded. A human being who defies such an order is denounced by Aristotle as "the most unholy and the most savage of animals" (ibid., 6). Further in his argument, Aristotle explains that human nature differs from animal nature, with the major disparity between the two lying in that humans enjoy the gift of speech. While multiple creatures have a voice in which they can express pain or joy, it is an exclusive capacity of humans to verbally convey what is useful or harmful, and fair or unfair, for only humans are capable of telling good from evil. The state is made of communities of such people – beings capable of recognizing justice.[1]

Consequently, the aim of all communities is to attain good. Aristotle argues that villages (assembling families) were the first political communities which then united to make up states, that is, larger and comprehensively self-sufficient organizations. Examining the critical survey of state systems outlined in Book II of *Politics*, we would be hard pressed to agree with multiple scholars and commentators who reductively interpret Greek debates on

---

1 In my argument, I pass over Aristotle's ideas about the social role of women and slaves, which are expressed at the very beginning of *Politics*.

democracy and governance as revolving around the Athenian model of city-state. Even Aristotle himself emphasizes further on in *Politics* that any reasoning on systems, power, citizens, and territories is greatly facilitated by the fact that *polis* is an ambiguous term which refers both to the city and to the state (ibid., 54–5). Rather than with a small, circumscribed area,[2] the meaning of the word was associated with the modes of governing a political community which unified citizens inhabiting not only cities but also neighboring village colonies. The form/organization of the system proves to matter more than its "urbanity" alone. Other relevant elements also include the language used by the community members and the hierarchy of values endorsed by them. We shall revisit Aristotle's political beliefs, especially those concerning the optimal political system, below; at this point, let us draw on Aristotle to examine the central thesis of Benjamin R. Barber's recent book *If Mayors Ruled the World* (2013). Striking a slightly triumphalist note, Barber asserts that the "city's epic history" has come the full circle, and in our globalized world, like at the civilizational and political dawn of our species, cities, which are natural (primordial) incubators of democracy, are again becoming democratic enclaves and democracy's greatest hope. The fundamental question posed by Barber, the author of a famed, if controversial, book on the clash of contemporary value systems (1995), is "Can cities save the world?" As early as in the first paragraph of his new volume, Barber announces that he is a firm believer in this possibility. Why is it so? The point is that Barber believes that, following the millennia of empires and monarchies, following the later political burdens produced by the invention of nation states, and, finally, following the exhaustion of thinking in regional terms, globalization is the only remaining recipe for democracy (2013, 3). We could add that this demise of national and regional projects, particularly regarding their promises of independence, freedom, and liberties, has significantly contributed to the rise of global phenomena and processes. Be it as it may, according to Barber, contemporary cities are sites where flows intrinsic to the worldwide network of (economic, political, technological, and other) interconnections are concentrated. His list of nodal urban hubs features, for example, New York Los Angeles, Denver, Bogota, Singapore, Seoul, Hamburg, Wroclaw, Gdansk, Rome, and Athens.[3] Nevertheless, these cities only serve Barber to explore the proper modes of governance forged and practiced by mayors. Currently, more than half of the world's population live in urbanized areas, and it is in this sense that cities turn out to be not only our civilizational

---

2 Greek. πόλις (plural: πόλεις *poleis*) originally denoted a "fortress" or a "fortified area."
3 Besides Barber's argument, *If Mayors Ruled the World* also includes interviews he and his team conducted with mayors of the enumerated cities.

and political cradle but also our destiny (future). "Urbanity may or may not be our nature," writes Barber, "but it is our history, and for better or worse, by chance or by design, it defines how we live, work, play, and associate" (ibid., 4). He frames urban space as a sphere of boundless creativity, innovation, community of interests, participation, citizenship, political pragmatism (instead of ideology), and consensual – i.e., peaceable – solutions. Since its very beginnings, modern democracy has struggled to reconcile participation, which is by default local, with power, which is inherently central. As nation states have failed in this challenge, now it can be more successfully tackled by a vast community (a point where Barber draws on John Dewey) uniting all people through collective actions and symbols clustered around social communication (ibid., 5). This is a vision of a civil society that consists of the residents of global cities who associate bottom-up (i.e., voluntarily) to collaborate over and across previous borders or divisions in their quest for the common good.

Although this goal can be construed as dovetailing with Aristotle's argument in *Politics*, to aver that the history of cities as bulwarks of democracy has drawn the full circle sounds somewhat misguided here. The problem is not exactly that the first political communities in Greece were composed of villages,[4] or that *polis* denoted both a city and a state, or even that the organizational form of the state system mattered more than the size of the area or of the population. The point is that in their efforts to establish what was good and just, the communities of old were supposed to be comprehensively self-sufficient and self-governing. Their democracy did not need grounding on any external entity; nor was it supposed to incubate/produce any external entity of this kind. As such, this democracy only depended on itself – or, more precisely speaking, on the will of its citizens – and this was what lay at its core. The "rule of cities," as called for by Barber, seems to be essentially different. Even though, as Barber assures, it would ensue from a grassroots movement rather than from pre-determined, top-down unifying directives legitimized by global laws and rules, Barber ultimately envisions not a Greek-like "inner" "urban" democracy, but rather a reproduction of the system or the order within the newly emergent global structures of knowledge, economy, and management.

Such great expectations associated with the role played, or soon to be played, by global metropolises are apparently shared by the American economist Edward Glaeser, whose *Triumph of the City* (2011) made it to the *New York Times*' list of bestsellers. Glaeser, Professor at Harvard University, dismisses

---

4 I assume that Barber has primarily ancient Greece in mind when he says that democracy was born in cities.

Rousseau's famous dictum that cities "are the abyss of the human species" as anachronic and argues that today's urban hubs are the healthiest, greenest, and most economically and culturally attractive places to live. According to Glaeser, the opportunities of collaboration which are offered by modern cities foster the historical glory of the human species:

> Because humans learn so much from other humans, we learn more when there are more people around. Urban density creates a constant flow of new information that comes from observing others' successes and failures. In a big city, people can choose peers who share their interest, just as Monet and Cézanne found each other in nineteenth-century Paris [...]. Cities make it easier to watch and listen and learn, [...] cities make us more human.
> GLAESER 2012, 247

In other words, the city enhances human powers and agency. Democracy, print, and mass production represent only a handful of plentiful inventions which we owe to urbanization (ibid., 250). Currently, global cities are characterized by staggering growth in nearly all spheres of life, which is fueled by global nodes – hubs promoting new ideas, producing knowledge, and implementing innovative solutions.

The insights proposed by Barber and Glaeser are not entirely novel, and they correspond to various positions developed within global studies, a discipline which, among other things, explores the role of cities in the contemporary world (Sassen, 2001; 2007; Hannerz, 1980) and examines issues involved in the management of Western metropolises. Barber's and Glaser's reasoning also resonates with the visions of ideal cities of the future, a movement represented by the publications of Richard Florida (2002) and Jan Gehl (2010). Generally speaking, they are part of a broader new-urbanist paradigm of ideas about global urban spaces.

Should we share the optimism of American political scientists and economists about the political and civilizational benefits of cities? Do cities really stand a chance of becoming genuine centers of power any time soon? What would the "rule of mayors" involve, and who would influence it most decisively? Let us revisit Aristotle's explorations of the state (keeping in mind that *polis* must not be reduced to the city). Admittedly, being in a community, mutual learning, cooperation, participation, concerted efforts for the improvement of the quality of life and the like, are all redolent of the pursuit to establish what is just, useful, and good. Yet, while they are redolent of it, they certainly do not always prove to be exactly that. Modern global cities are abundantly associated with a variety of doubts concerning fundamental questions, such as social, economic, and infrastructural development and, above all, thinking in terms of the common good. In modern cities, citizenship is intermingled with individualism, communality is coupled with particularisms, state power intersects with local self-government, globality clashes with locality, and materiality is intermingled with information. In the following, I will examine these issues and seek to answer the questions posed above.

Aristotle's political beliefs will serve us as a parallel introducing these concerns. We remember that Aristotle considered *politeia* (i.e., "true democracy") to be the best of all political systems. While his views of the general responsibilities of a political community and the role that citizens should play in it are basically irrefutable, the solutions he proposed within *politeia* sound quite disputable. The aim of the state is the happy life of people, and all other things are only a means to this end, as Aristotle repeatedly insists. The state is

> the union of families and villages in a perfect and self-sufficing life, by which we mean a happy and honourable life. Our conclusion, then, is that political society exists for the sake of noble actions, and not of mere companionship. Hence they who contribute most to such a society have a greater share in it than those who have the same or a greater freedom or nobility of birth but are inferior to them in political virtue; or than those who exceed them in wealth but are surpassed by them in virtue.
> ARISTOTLE, 1999, 64

What did it actually mean for the Athenian, though? Although he claimed that various systems could be good/suitable, depending on the type of community, he repudiated all the prior ones, i.e., monarchy, tyranny, aristocracy, oligarchy, and democracy, as defective in various degrees, if not downright pernicious. The only reasonable and responsible form of governance could exclusively be guaranteed, as he insisted, by a system based on a broad and influential middle estate, referred to as *politeia* (constitutional government). It is envisaged as negotiating between oligarchy, in which power is exercised by wealthy owners of property, and democracy, which means "the government of the many" (ibid., 61–62). *Politeia* would combined upsides of these two systems. The prevalence of the moderate, temperate, and rationally acting middle estate would constrain the excessive promptings of both the rich and the needy, thereby securing the stability and durability of the community. Derived from its sheer size, the strength of this estate would prevent divisions and, consequently social unrests, fighting, and bloodshed they implicated.

In what ways can this nearly two-thousand-and-five-hundred year-old recipe for freedom, balance, justice, good, and dignity be relevant to the current political situation? Where is the parallel? What does Aristotle's concept have in common with modern "civil societies" of global cities? Let us posit that although the leading role in the worldwide networks of capital and information interconnections, which boost the development of metropolises today, is played by huge international corporations, syndicates, and financial institutions (with their links to state actors), the economic and political benefits of the multidimensional expansion of urbanized areas are reaped first and foremost by the middle class. Admittedly, geography is a factor here, as at various places in the world middle-class members vary widely and sometimes are barely identifiable at all, yet it is the middle class that exerts a significant influence on the shape of urban spaces and the ways in which they are administered. What middle-class members rather universally share is a certain set of values. It stretches beyond the specifically defined public good (therein, an approach to solving social, infrastructural, environmental, and other problems) and beyond collective and individual interests and political pragmatism. Rather, it predominantly concerns attitudes, beliefs, and choices which are (axiotically) informed by self-development, mobility, communication, creativity, innovation, health, environmental investment, visual order, economic affluence, and cultural opulence. The lifestyle of the middle class undoubtedly contributes to sustaining the urban system of governance, as middle-class members hold positions in municipalities, offices, and city-affiliated companies, in education and research institutions, in development centers, organizations, and firms which operate/invest in a given area.

Given this, we should first ask to whom contemporary cities belong, or who constructs narratives about them. In conjunction with this, other queries offer themselves: What purposes or what needs are the daring future-visions produced for them supposed to serve? Do modern urban hubs really meet the conditions enabling their mayors and municipal officials to rule the world? Are globalization and the city one and the same thing? Are images of metropolises which arise from accounts similar to that offered by Glaeser indeed complete and holistic?

Indisputably, the city is a site where political struggles are concentrated. Urban interest groups incessantly pursue their own goals. This entails permanent mobility in which individual, social, local-governmental, commercial, and state actors endeavor to persuade various city-based communities to embrace their ideas, projects, solutions, demands, motions, and claims. Although they are often underpinned by agendas favoring very particular power relations and/or seeking material profits, it is characteristic of the democratic system that both disputes, tensions, and struggles as well as various forms of collaboration and participation are supposed to ultimately advance justice, utility, and the common good. No individual (and no isolated group, for that matter) is capable of single-handedly making changes within cities which could at the same time be reflected on the local, regional, or global scale. Whether mayors or urban activists are involved, political partners, supporters, and voters are indispensable one way or another. Collectives – groups of people – are needed to give momentum to any transformative action. Therefore, a broadly conceived community of interests is the first prerequisite of change, with multiple components of socio-cultural diversification, such as gender, age (generation), class membership, sexual orientation, education, work, and place of residence, locked in an interplay in it. The scale of political/social activity is another factor which determines the possibility and nature of changes. In the age of globalization, both municipal governors and members of urban movements can plan their actions/pursuits together with other actors who may be interested in their initiatives, even if they are spatially removed by thousands of kilometers. Today, success chances are improved not only by local cooperation but also by reliance on the global network of information flow. In both cases, the basis is provided by the tangible, material elements of reality, whose relevance we must not overlook, though we also must agree with Barber and Glaeser that the significance of cities and the transformations which can be launched in them are largely determined by global processes and phenomena (whether we talk of Bangalore or of Porto Alegre). The Polish architect and urbanist Krzysztof Nawratek, though openly skeptical about the optimistic appraisals preached by American researchers (at least by Glaeser) and himself calling for instigating urban revolutions, cannot deny that

> one of the reasons behind the thriving of contemporary cities is the fact that they are nodal points in the network of global "flows." These flows – of capital, of people, of ideas – form cities. Given this, cities exist in and through their instability, and should the "flow" be frozen, cities are bound to perish. In spite of this, contemporary cities use various methods to, in a sense, "contain" the flows. In doing so, they fall back on various measures and focus on various flows, from capital, to industry or trade, to people (Florida's "creative capital.") At the same time, they are (or at least should be) aware that such an activity is doomed to failure in a long run.
>
> NAWRATEK 2012, 18

This encapsulates an extremely interesting observation that even though the social class which invests in development, creativity, innovation, health, green environment, and culture stimulates the development of cities, aligning with the visions and current policies of their administrators, its mobility combined with the economic nomadism of global corporations (which transfer production and services where labor organization is more cost-effective) triggers insecurity about the future (of the metropolis).

Research has been attracted to contemporary cities and their links to global phenomena/processes not so much because of the demographic and economic data as such, but rather because of the belief that global urban hubs are the engine of cultural and civilizational development – generating new ideas, producing knowledge, stimulating artistic practices, and first of all boosting efforts for the improvement of the quality of life. This preoccupation entails scrutinizing transformations in value systems and exploring the strategies utilized to solve social problems (poverty, violence, drug abuse, weapons, etc.) and political problem (armed conflicts, terrorism, climate change, etc.). This being said, we cannot deny that "hard" data kindle the research imagination as well. Almost 250 million U.S. citizens inhabit as little as 3% of the country's total area, and anyway even greater densities of population can easily be found, for example in the Tokyo agglomeration, which is inhabited by thirty-six million Japanese (and foreigners). All people who are now living on our planet could find a place for themselves within the borders of Texas, and some of them would even own a "townhouse," as calculated by Glaeser in the Introduction to his *Triumph of the City*. Even though huge vistas of land are unused (unpeopled), the world is constantly shrinking. People are increasingly closer to each other as a result of new technological inventions, which afford unprecedented communication and transport opportunities.

As far as the economy and living standards are concerned, the quantitative data are "in sync" with "qualitative" statistics. For example, Glaeser shows how deeply – in his view – Mahatma Gandhi erred when insisting that India was not a few big cities but seven hundred thousand villages on which the development of the nation depended. Today, 10% of Indians live in huge urban agglomerations, but they produce 30% of the GNP. Actually, "[p]er capita incomes are almost four times higher in those countries where a majority of people live in cities than in those countries where a majority of people live in rural areas" (Glaeser 2012, 7). The world's top hundred largest agglomerations – or, as Nawratek puts it, "urbanized areas" (2008) – generate over 25% of GNP. Cities offer something else besides "knowledge," innovative solutions, better living conditions, and money, as Glaeser argues. Thereby, he discards the common notion that although modern metropolises generate immense opportunities for their residents, they also make city-dwellers unhappy. On the contrary, the more urbanized a country is, the happier its people are. The figures for happiness and unhappiness stand, respectively, at 30% and 17% in cities, while at

25% and 22% in rural areas (ibid.). Do these comparative data actually reveal something about cities and urban life for us?

Without a doubt, there are beneficiaries of the phenomena and processes characteristic of "urban globalization," as already mentioned. Nevertheless, the populations of contemporary metropolises do not consist exclusively of groups endowed with political, economic, and/or cultural agency or of actors predestined to take advantage of the economic prosperity at hand (with its related access to new technologies, knowledge, health, greenery, etc.). In the context of social stratification, such communities in fact represent privilege. In other words, for Florida's creative class to have its basic and secondary needs (consumption, cleanliness, security, transport, leisure, entertainment, sex, etc.) adequately met, someone has to put in considerable labor. It cannot be denied that marginalized or excluded groups are also there. With this, we return to basic questions, such as: Who has the voice (or the city as such)? Who organizes discourse as its self-appointed narrator? Whose images of the city do we see? Whose perspective do we adopt?

Another related issue is whether cities are indeed capable of taking power over from states. Barber asserts that typical features boasted by the residents of modern global metropolises, such as self-reliance, creativity, innovation, pragmatism, civic trust, collaboration, and participation, both found and guarantee democracy. Appointed by citizens in free elections, mayors, whether acting individually or in league, can more effectively cope with the most taxing problems/challenges of our times than states and international organizations, which are invariably ensnared in various ideological and economic conflicts. Or at least this is what Barber avers. His assertion certainly makes for a very promising vision of a new global order in which contemporary urbanity is appreciatingly recognized. However, Barber underestimates the fact that cities, in particular global ones, are also sites of constant tensions, rivalries, struggles, and – primarily perhaps – of huge contrasts, yawning gaps, and sharp social inequalities. Surprisingly, such concepts originated in American scholarship, while

> [c]ompared with Europe, the American state has been less ambitious in its ability to realize a good life for a majority of its citizens. But it remains the one political institution with the resources to tackle huge problems. It was neither cities nor individual states that made Social Security possible. Only the federal government could have guaranteed the civil rights denied to black people by slavery and segregation; indeed, rights in general are not so much protections against government as they are powers that only governments can enforce. No mayor could have pulled

> the country out of its recent financial crisis. Barber is surely correct that nation-states fail at some things. But they succeed rather well at others. His method of dealing with the successes, however, is to ignore them; Social Security, voting rights, and health insurance receive far less of his attention than bike lanes and community policing.
>
> WOLFE 2013

Groundbreaking communal projects, legal reforms, and social changes are a matter of political ideal promoted by supra-urban actors, such as parties, groupings, and huge social movements; they are passed by parliaments and implemented by governments (or transnational institutions/organizations). In this context, the vision of the rule of cities looks rather new-urbanist and middle-class, narrowed down to the horizon of values within which justice, utility, and the common good are mainly reduced to culture, aesthetic order, health, ecology, greenery, and their likes.

U.S. cities are deeply dependent on the (decisions of) central authorities, as Detroit vividly exemplifies. The adversities with which the world's once most rapidly developing urban hub is grappling today by no means result exclusively from the collapse of the car industry and the exodus of the population (in search of work). They are also a matter of party agendas and ideologies. While fifteen years ago, urban policy was at the center of attention of the Washington establishment and was treated as a priority, with mayors of metropolises being major players on the nationwide political stage, today the Democrats are turning their backs on cities, where they enjoy the greatest support, whereas the Republicans rekindle centuries-old conservative enmity towards urban zones (Nichols 2013, 27). The latter were greatly satisfied to watch the migration of people from metropolitan downtowns to the suburbs and smaller towns, a development already prophesized by Alvin Toffler in *The Third Wave* (1980). Anyway, urban development strategies including investments in infrastructure and economy failed as a dream recipe for growth on the American and, consequently, global markets. They were unable to prevent the economic meltdown, not to mention overcoming it. Cities were thus abandoned to fend off for themselves.[5]

---

5   The debt of Detroit is estimated at eighteen billion US dollars. As the city was unable to meet its financial obligations mainly vis-à-vis banks, it filed for bankruptcy with a view to obtaining debt relief and was found eligible for Chapter 9 bankruptcy. In order to have it granted, Detroit had to present a plan for adjustment of its debts and for restoring financial liquidity. Interestingly, the unemployment rate in Detroit stands at 18%, which is exceptionally high for the U.S., though not particularly big in global terms.

Another illuminating illustration of the financial dependence of cities on centrally made political decisions is provided by the capital of Germany. Unlike in Detroit and other U.S. cities, funding from the state budget is uninterruptedly flowing to municipal (private and public) institutions. With no industry to speak of, Berlin is one of the urban hubs which are supposed to be driven by the creative class (Nawratek 2012, 12). Europe's largest construction site, the metropolis attracts new residents not so much with new jobs as rather with a "pleasant atmosphere" of life. Innumerable cinemas, theaters, concert halls, museums, galleries, culture centers, cafes, restaurants, clubs, and discos make Berlin extremely appealing. The problem is, however, that the city has an enormous debt, and it would be utterly unable to carry on in its current shape were it not for the money from the federal government. Therefore, despite the inflow of global capital and people, Berlin is popularly described as *"arm, aber sexy"* (i.e., "poor, but sexy," as the SPD politician Klaus Wowereit put it in an interview for *Focus Money* ten years ago).

Still, Berlin is an exception, as perspectives for the development of most cities look rather different. The metropolises whose mayors Barber interviewed for his book depend on the global flow of money and people, innovative technologies, and primarily investments which produce new jobs.[6] Without international corporations, companies, and financial institutions, municipalities are unable to devise and sustain the image of cities promoting the middle-class – modern, affluent, creative, "cultivated," and green – lifestyle. The success of urban strategies is thus predominantly predicated on global capital, which is still subject to legal regulations introduced by nation states. The insights articulated by the Dutch-born American sociologist and economist Saskia Sassen in her interview for the Polish journal *Kultura Liberalna* are illuminating in this respect: Sassen explains that, as for the distinction between the national and the global, in her research she seek to show that global phenomena – institutions, processes, discursive practices, and abstract notions – go beyond nation states, but at the same time they derive from nation states and are limited by them. In this sense, globalization is something more than the increasing condensation of the network of interdependences and the establishment of institutions we refer to as global. Globalization also encompasses areas, processes, and actors at the national and sub-national level. Sassen observes that although there is no legal actor such as a global company, there are 370,000 companies which are known to act as if they were global, because they operate

---

[6] This is conducive to professional development and, through salaries, to maintaining expected living standards.

in many countries across the world, in the environments which consist of similar elements and, as such, help them do business in similar ways. Pondering what made such spaces possible, Sassen points out that they were generated by individual countries, which used means available to them – parliament bills, executive power decisions, court rulings – to achieve this aim, creating in this way a set of conditions which enable companies to function analogously across the world (Sassen 2012). Sassen emphasizes that while companies which are her examples are not constrained to one particular nation state, they are not entirely independent of nation states either. As a matter of fact, she claims that these companies would not be able to operate without states in the first place. In her 1998 book *Globalization and Its Discontents: Essays on the New Mobility of People and Money*, Sassen explains that if we deal with the problem of governance, many of the fundamental components of economic globalization do not contribute to supra-national structures at all, and the only guarantors of the "rights" of global capital are nation states (with the means which they have at their disposal to promote globalization, including, for example, deregulation tools). These issues are critical to the study of global cities and the emergent transnational urban system as potentially important areas of the implementation of governance mechanisms and responsibility in global economy (Sassen 2007, 183). Global studies scholars who believe that electronic space prevails in the world's economy and, consequently, that the role of nation states is decreasing apparently forget about the infrastructure and human resources, which are always physically anchored. Global processes and economic phenomena materialize in specific places. This is true even about the IT industry. Economic actors are located within a defined area (territory), in specific surroundings, and under defined legal conditions. They must engage in interactions and collaborate with other social actors. Both the city and the state are the site where these developments unfold.

One of Barber's interlocutors in *If Mayors Ruled the World* is Michael Bloomberg, the mayor of New York in 2002–2013, who tends to be called a technocrat. When running the administration of the biggest U.S. city, Bloomberg was also managing his own businesses. His property is estimated at 27 billion dollars. If in 2007, i.e., five years into his tenure as mayor, he was ranked 142nd on the list of the wealthiest Americans, by now he has climbed to number 13th. His take on the municipality as a corporation saw Bloomberg garner public repute as an equally good "city manager" as a businessman. A considerable majority of modern New Yorkers liked his policies: regulations, restrictions, prohibitions, and even taxes, which boosted the city's budget with substantial revenues. Eventually, New York became safe, healthy, green, environment-conscious, and innovative. However, the heads of American metropolises are not always able to keep expenditure in good balance. When leaving his position in 2011, Richard M. Daley, who had been elected mayor of Chicago, the U.S. third biggest city, as many as six times, left the public finances in disastrous disarray. The city which had been deemed a model of economic (and cultural) success for long decades, found itself facing the risk of bankruptcy.

What is the price of Aristotle's "beautiful life"? Can the municipal prohibitions, orders, guidelines, and recommendations, which are supported by social marketing, artistic campaigns, and grassroots projects[7] and aim to bring about permanent changes in attitudes to/beliefs about environmental protection, healthy lifestyle, and civic engagement, be construed not only as conveniences but also as a "timeless" quest for justice? Do these efforts come anywhere near grand projects of transformations which have been the domain of the state so far? Can the "management" of the global economy in the age of (alleged) domination of electronic space be taken over by a supranational urban system? Is the global parliament of cities a remedy for poverty, inequality, exclusion, hunger, epidemics, drug trafficking, terrorism, and natural disasters? Or is it perhaps the case that, to invert the title of a popular movie, for mayors "the world is just too much"?

Bibliography

Aristotle . *Politics*. Translated by Benjamin Jowett. Kitchener: Batoche Books, 1999.
Barber, Benjamin R. *If Mayors Ruled the World*. New Haven & London: Yale University Press, 2013.
Barber, Benjamin R. *Jihad vs. McWorld*, New York: Times Books, 1995.
Florida, Richard. *The Rise of the Creative Class and How It Is Transforming Work, Leisure, Community, and Everyday Life*. New York: Basic Books, 2002.
Glaeser, Edward. *Triumph of the City*, London: Penguin Books, 2012.
Gehl, Jan. *Cities for People*. Washington, Covelo, London: Island Press, 2010.

---

7 Today, various urban groups, both those which engage in efforts for broadly conceived social changes and those which are regarded as subcultures, embrace values, choices, and behaviors which approximate the preferences of the middle (or creative) class much closer than fifteen years ago. It can be said that their lifestyle not so much contests the new bourgeois orders as rather represents its "orthodox" version (in terms of nutrition, health, attitude to animals, cleanliness, the environment, clothes, aesthetic tastes, etc.). As such, they are not deprived of agency, but their attitudes and practices largely legitimize the existing social, political, and economic order.

Hannerz, Ulf. *Exploring the City: Inquiries toward an Urban Anthropology*. New York: Columbia University Press, 1980.

Nawratek, Krzysztof. *Dziury w całym. Wstęp do miejskich rewolucji*. Warsaw: Wydawnictwo Krytyki Politycznej, 2012.

Nawratek, Krzysztof. *Miasto jako idea polityczna*. Cracow: Ha!art, 2008.

Nichols, John. "Jak upadają miasta Ameryki." Translated by M. Madej. *Le Monde diplomatique*. Polish edition. Vol. 92, no. 10, 2013.

Sassen, Saskia. *The global city*. New York, London, Tokyo, Princeton: Princeton University Press, 2001.

Sassen, Saskia. *Globalizacja. Eseje o nowej mobilności ludzi i pieniędzy*. Cracow: Wydawnictwo Uniwersytetu Jagiellońskiego, 2007.

Sassen, Saskia. "*Globalna ulica, czyli demokracja bezsilnych*." Interview in *Kultura Liberalna*, vol. 163, no. 8, 2012.

Toffler, Alvin. *The Third Wave*. New York: William Morrow and Company, 1980.

Wolfe, Alan;"Book Review: Is the Nation-State Dying?" *The Chronicle of Higher Education*, September, no. 3, 2013.

CHAPTER 13

One Wrong Turn: Doug Rickard in the World of Google Street View

Rafał Nahirny

We all have been there, I guess.[1] To effectively lose out bearings, we must first fail to notice that we have gone up a wrong road. Our confusion is only incrementally growing. We hesitate more and more over every next turn. Up to that point, we have been engrossed in a conversation with our passenger or listening to the radio absent-mindedly. Suddenly, we seem not to know where we are and begin to carefully scrutinize the world around us: buildings, shop signboards, and street names. We are looking for any clues to help us establish the geographical location of where we have found ourselves. The surrounding space, which has so far been just a neutral backdrop for our musings or conversations, gradually makes us anxious. We start to notice waste littering the streets and long-unmown lawns overgrown with thick, tall grass and clumps of weeds. Suddenly, we discover that we are traversing an abandoned, forgotten, and slowly disintegrating world. By chance, inattention, or error, we have landed up somewhere at the margins of reality, in one of those neighborhoods or towns forgotten by the world, which are better not to be ventured into after dusk. We desperately want to find our way back as quickly as possible, but we are afraid to pull over and ask for help. One glimpse is enough to see that we are not from "here." We feel the prying gaze of the dwellers, who are eyeing us with curiosity.

Looking at Doug Rickard's photographs in the *New American Picture* series (2013), we have an impression that, while driving, we have incautiously taken a wrong turn and gone off our route to find ourselves in a space which is capable of inspiring such an anxiety in a lost traveler. Stray dogs are roaming at large in the streets, while playing kids, interested, turn their heads towards the camera. In front of buildings, scorched car wrecks are rusting away, with all parts of any value or use whatsoever prudently ripped out, leaving only a useless skeleton behind. At a house which resembles a plywood hut rather

---

1 This article was written as part of the University of Wrocław's developmental grant project for young researchers, *Artyści/eksploratorzy Świata Google Street View* (*Artists/explorers of the Google Street View World*), No 2301/M/IKUL/14.

than any human abode, a small plastic car is lying upside down. It is quite a stretch of the imagination to believe that this dirty space of dust, mud, and ash can be any child's playground. Admittedly, some dwellers of this world try to defy the inertia and desperately struggle to keep the place tidy and clean. However, there is no doubting that their efforts to stop the disintegration are doomed to failure. They are inexorably bound to run out of strength. The boarded-up doors and windows of many neighboring buildings eloquently speak to this inevitability. What happened with their lodgers? Did they give up? Did they abandon their homes without any sentiments, forgetting about them as a matter of course? Why was there no one else around to buy these houses and live in them? The churches in the world recorded by Rickard do not resemble those we know from our cities in the least. They have blended with the rows of regular secular architecture so thoroughly that they are hardly distinguishable from other buildings. Regrettably, there is no way to find out whether there is still any congregation to attend services in them, but nothing suggests that this is the case. A prayer house of the Seventh-Day Adventists looks like it was closed down a long time ago. Clearly, even the members of the mission have lost faith in the dwellers of this world and decided to leave it. Yet Christ, drawn on a steel roller blind protecting the front window of the house, is still waiting for new believers, his arms stretched out wide for them. That the times are hard can be seen from closed-down liquor stores, which are in operation until the very last moment as a rule. The population of this world is prevailingly Afro-American. Were it not for the title of the album, one could wonder whether one is perhaps looking at a reportage from a African township by a photographer concerned with the lot of the Third World's citizens. In fact, we are at the outskirts of Detroit and New Orleans, and what we see is a world branded by an economic crisis, recession, and a natural disaster.

We could end the description of Rickard's images at this point, were it not for one interesting fact. Even though the name and surname of the American photographer feature on the title page of the album, the photographs it contains were not taken by him. Or at least not only by him. The album is in fact a work of a strongly networked and dispersed authorship. Rickard's collection of photographs is an outcome of several hours he spent in the digital world of Google Street View, and its "author" is an explorer and an archivist rather than a photographer. Fascinated with a new reality constructed out of millions of photographs (most of which are not likely to ever be seen by anybody) by autonomous seeing machines and graphic algorithms, Rickard immersed himself in this world to devote nearly two years to searching for particularly interesting shots.

The works of artists who experiment with mechanical and "random" post-images (Zawojski 2012, 11) of the world of Google Street View, such as Rickard, Jon Rafman, Miskha Henner, and Michael Wolf, can be classified within the New Aesthetic movement. Art critics and artists use this term primarily to refer to phenomena which are specific to digital culture, e.g., glitches (digital noise with neither meaning nor sense, for example errors in computation processes while coding/decoding images [Menkman 2011]), photoshop disasters (distorted, unrealistic, and phantasmagoric bodies resulting from the digital processing of photos), images produced by CCTV and recorded by dashcams (car cameras), webcams (Internet cameras), drones, reconnaissance satellites, and facial recognition systems. The champions of the New Aesthetic, such as James Bridle (2011a, 2011b) and Joanne McNeil (2012), claim that we are now at a special moment in the history of art and visual culture. In the 1930s, Walter Benjamin pondered how the technical possibilities of mass reproduction of images affected the ways in which art was experienced. Today, we are witnessing another major shift which has been engendered by the rapid development of new communication technologies. We are facing not only the rupturing of links between an artwork on the one hand and time and space on the other, but also a digital overproduction of images and their mass networked cross-linking. Algorithms, locational media, computational systems, and vision machines incessantly generate, process, and multiply on the Internet millions of digital images, which are unbounded by any visual conventions and symbolic forms. Given this, Bridle and McNeil insist that objects which result from the operations of computational processes make it exigent for researchers not only to design a new theory, a new descriptive idiom, or new critical tools, but also to develop media competences in order to aptly grasp the new modes in which digital images exist.

1 American Dream 2.0

Googleplex, i.e., the famous headquarters of Google, is situated in Mountain View in Silicon Valley. In total, the complex is comprised of sixty-five tree-surrounded buildings. Designed in observance of open-space standards, its interior is worlds apart from boring corporation spaces, where employers, enclosed in their own boxes, are isolated from each other by makeshift partitions. Here, the space is dynamic, easily amenable to remodeling, and effortlessly adaptable to the challenges and demands of any project at hand. Everything is lively and colorful, as the interior of Googleplex was devised to promote open communication and thus to foster creativity and innovation

(Beahm 2014, 75). This is not the only reason why Googleplex seems to be a truly dream workplace. At any moment, Googlers are free not only to take stroll in the park surrounding the campus, but also play a volleyball match at a nearby court, use one of several cafés, help themselves to healthy snacks, do some workout at a gym, have a swim in the pool, or even go to a bowling alley. Other available options include yoga workshops, awareness training, and even napping for a while. This is the birthplace of the Google Street View project.

The public space of Silicon Valley is a totally different world from the one in Rickard's photographs. Silicon Valley is a smooth amalgamation of two architectonic and urbanist fantasies. First and foremost, it is an enactment of the American middle class's dream of affluent life in safe and picturesque suburbs. At the same time, the area is peppered with modernist office buildings which house companies such as Amazon, Facebook, eBay, Yahoo, Apple, and Adobe. Emblematic of the success of digital capitalism, the buildings are made of glass, concrete, and steel.[2] Unlike many modernist edifices, they were designed without any undue megalomania, rather in the spirit of sustainable development and harmony with nature. After all, one of the Google dogmas holds that "you can make money without doing evil." Hence, the buildings are surrounded by friendly parks and orange and peach groves, which have been cultivated in the nearby hills of long. First autonomous vehicles, equipped with autopilots and scanning the area in real time, drive along the streets of Palo Alto, San José, and Mountain View, while the sidewalks are trodden by hosts of early adopters (i.e., first users), who often talk to themselves while testing Google Glass, a technology of augmented reality. Sidewalk coffee shops buzz with discussions on technological start-ups, new models of smartwatches, fitness trackers, intelligent houses, and the Internet of things. This is a world of creative, innovative, and entrepreneurial people who believe in the power of glitches and the imperative of constant development. Stagnation is

---

2 Silicon Valley attracts world-famous architects. One of the last wishes of the dying Steve Jobs (who made his last public appearance at the launching of the mock-up of this project), "The Spaceship," i.e. Apple's new headquarters in Cupertino, was designed by Norman Foster, while Facebook's new campus – a huge open-space office in Menlo Park – is the work of Frank Gehry. Loath to fall behind in this race, Google commissioned the celebrated NBBJ to design the extension of the entire complex. In compliance with "green modernism," the Apple building will be circular and surrounded by trees. In the meantime, Gehry transformed the roofs of Facebook buildings into small parks, corresponding to the hills encircling Silicon Valley. After all, contact with nature improves the staff's moods and, as such, supports creativity and innovation.

a threat, as it can easily morph into inertia. Therefore, one must continually look for new solutions and repeatedly shake off the perilous feeling of calm and comfort. The ethics of creativity is tightly interwoven with digital capitalism. As a classic axiom of neoliberalism has it, rivalry on the market stimulates development and innovation.[3]

Established one by one in Silicon Valley, new start-ups speak to a deep belief that a team of young, ambitious, and passionate people can defy the unfavorable economic conjuncture and build an extraordinarily successful business. Despite the severe economic crisis and dirty war on terrorism, the dwellers of this world have not lost faith in the American Dream. A proper attitude (the "start-up mindset," [ibid., 73]) is enough to turn a tiny company set up at one's parent's garage into a staggering career. The faith in progress and in the possibility to build a better and fairer society does not seem to subside. The very fact that this world exists is the best exemplification of the robustness of the American Dream. The only thing is that it has become digitalized.[4]

---

3 Silicon Valley is thus waiting for its new temples of innovation and creativity. This mythical worlds already has a pantheon of its own, complete with ancestors (Nikola Tesla, Alan Turing, and Buckminster Fuller), heroes (Tim O'Reilly, Eric Schmidt, and Mark Zuckerberg) and saints (Steve Jobs), places of worship (HP garage at 367 Addison Avenue in Palo Alto), hallowed fetishes (Macintosh 128K), holy books (Everett M. Roger's *Diffusion of Innovations* [1962] and Clayton M. Christensen's *The Innovator's Dilemma* [1997]), and hagiographic narratives (David Fincher's *The Social Network* [2010], Caleb Melby's *The Zen of Steve Jobs* [2012], and Shawn Levy's *The Internship* [2013]). What it does not have yet is its own Roland Barthes, though perhaps the most deserving candidate for the status of the Silicon Valley myth-buster is found in Evgeny Morozov (to some extent such a critical role is also performed by the *Silicon Valley* sitcom).

4 When examined from close-up, the proclaimed culture of openness and tolerance toward sexual minorities (labeled Gayglers in official newspeak) and ethnic minorities (a Latino week is officially celebrated) proves to be founded on a latent caste system rather than being every employee's dream-come-true. Andrew Norman Wilson, the initiator of the Workers Leaving the Googleplex project (2009–2011), was scanning books for the Google Books projects. All people on the grounds of the complex must wear badges which define their status (interns have green badges, regular staff white badges, external workers red ones, and personnel of the Google Books project yellow ones). The badge color determines access to particular offices, as well as to cafés and restaurants. A huge group of the staff is thus excluded and cannot make use of various amenities and advantages offered by the culture of openness, innovation, and creativity, for they are reserved exclusively for the privileged creative class. Book-scanning workers, interns, and external contractors are just cheap labor force – the proletariat of digital capitalism. The world of Silicon Valley is in fact predominantly a world of white males, despite the official celebrations of the Martin Luther King day and attempts at overcoming the structural exclusion of women.

2 A Brave New World of Solutionism

Silicon-Valley designers and engineers propose effective and efficient solutions to a range of petty problems of our daily life. Multiple application and Internet services help us draft a shopping list, remind us where we parked the car, and keep us informed about the weather. Such tiny conveniences usefully assist us not only in daily chores but also in work matters. An array of applications enable us to effectively manage our time, fight procrastination, and handle multitasking efficiently.

Evgeny Morozov, the author of *To Save Everything Click Here* (2013), fears that in this way the ideology of Silicon Valley, which he calls solutionism, reduces complex social phenomena to technical problems. We can furnish our smartphones with applications which will help us, for example, make our child lose on weight, sort our waste, or combat global warming. This happens at the cost of curbing, if not entirely eliminating, dialogue and antagonism in public space, which are so central to democratic societies (Koczanowicz 2011). To the "will to improve" (Murray Li 2007), deliberation seems tedious, time-consuming, and consequently ineffective and inefficient. It is infinitely better to isolate a problem from the social context, narrow down our view, and focus on devising an effective, creative, and innovative solution.

The world of solutionism is a world in which everything should be *smart*. Consistently with the way of thinking specific to Silicon Valley, the Google Maps service has always been expected to be something more than just another map. The founders of this world were primarily guided by functional considerations. When Google Maps was launched (8th February, 2005), its point was not simply to make free maps available to users, but above all to supply tools supporting wise and smart decision-making. This is why Google will help us find the fastest route – "[...] we've designed Google Maps to simplify how to get from point A to point B" (Taylor 2005, n.p.) – and to find hotels in the vicinity: "Say you're looking for 'hotels near LAX.' With Google Maps you'll see nearby hotels [...]" (ibid., n.p.). We can also find out about opinions of other users, and make a right, that is smart, decision on this basis. Owing to Google Maps, we will not only avoid traffic jams (thereby reducing fuel consumption and adverse environmental effects), but also find a gas station offering petrol at the lowest price. In 2007, first street-level panoramic photos were introduced, with the new functionality aiming to supply users with more detailed information about routes and destinations.[5] For whatever it might seem, it was not

---

5 Algorithms and Google Maps API also assist us in solving more complicated problems, such as the so-called traveling salesman problem. Suppose that within a few days we must visit

an entirely novel solution. As early as in 1907–1910, Rand McNally published twenty-five *Photo-Auto Guides*, which besides the first roadmaps contained photographs with arrows pointing to proper turns at troublesome junctions.

In this way, the solutionist way of thinking imperceptibly, but radically, transforms photography. Once, we used photographs to capture and freeze time and to build a close relationship with the past. Within the Google Maps project, images are only functional if they are up to date. Subservient to fully objective utility, Street View images do not lie. They are supposed to bear testimony to presence and, as such, they must be fully synchronous (Higgitt, Wray 2014, 150). Thus, they are not yet another species of documentary photography.

3   Seeing Everything

Since its very foundation, Google has been guided by a very ambitious set of goals, including "to organize the world's information." Therefore it does not come as a surprise that one of the company's dogmas ("Google: Ten Things We Know to Be True") insists: "We see being great at something as a starting point, not an endpoint. We set ourselves goals we know we can't reach yet, because we know that by stretching to meet them we can get further than we expected." Hence, Googlers tirelessly aspire to achieve the impossible and never stop looking for new, apparently crazy challenges: to digitalize *the entire* achievement of humankind or to provide the Internet *everywhere* by means of drones or balloons. No wonder thus that Googlers wish to photograph *everything* so that we can go *anywhere*. The construction of the Street View world commenced from San Francisco, Las Vegas, Denver, Miami, and New York. With time, Google's solutionist gaze became nearly ubiquitous. Today, Google's cars, trucks, bicycles, and even snow scooters and camels reach the most remote recesses of the world, enabling us to visit the Antarctic, an Egyptian desert, and the coral reef.

However, it did not take long to realize that Google's vision machines see too much. Since its very onset, the Google Street View project has stirred a lot of controversy. Its opponents have argued that it can considerably encroach on our privacy. Admittedly, cars take photos of people in the public space, but not always in situations in which they would wish to be seen by others. As cameras are mounted on jibs, they capture objects and people over walls and fences whose height was calculated to block the curious sight of passers-by, but not of

---

several places scattered across the country and then return to where we started. The Google algorithm will help us choose the shortest and fastest way and in this way use less fuel and optimize our work. The problem is also known as the Chinese postman problem.

Google cars. Consequently, in 2007 Google set out to develop and implement an algorithm to detect and wipe-out faces of passers-by and number plates of the photographed cars.

Google Street View has proved another iteration of "photographic acquisition" (Sontag 2005, 121), which privileges the sense of sight. Despite the efforts undertaken by Google, the project ended up as a perfectly aligned component of the logic of post-panoptic society,[6] in which the difference between the surveilling and the surveilled – the Panopticon master and the prisoners – is effectively obliterated. We enter this reality through the windows of our Internet browsers. An individual using the service feels fully in control of reality. In conformity with the principles of perspective understood as a symbolic form, the user's eye is the central point of this world, as it can at will perform close-ups, approach any objects of its interest, and move away from them. Unlike people whom we pass while strolling, we are not prisoners of this world. We can leave this space whenever we like, can't we? In this way, Google Street View constructs a stable subject placed at the center of a systematically and consistently built reality.

The feeling of having things under control is reinforced by the reproduction of the experience of controlling public space and patrolling places at risk. We look at the world in Rickard's photographs from the vantage point of a vehicle driving along the streets. In a sense, this gaze overlaps with the gaze of power, specifically of police officers who patrol "unsavory" neighborhoods in their squad cars as a preventive measure. They do not only keep

order and peace in the public space. Their visibility emphatically shows that, consistently with the "broken windows" theory, the police are in full control in a given area.[7]

---

6   Our times are often referred to as the age of liquid surveillance. Such an appraisal is crucially underpinned by the belief that neoliberal post-democracies have developed their distinctive mechanisms for controlling and disciplining individuals. They are difficult to identify at first sight, because they do not in the least resemble control and surveillance practices of authoritarian and totalitarian regimes. We are lulled into a false sense of security by the belief that Michel Foucault's *Discipline and Punish* with its explication of panopticism gives us effective analytical tools to study and expose processes typical of disciplinary society. However, as the proponents of the liquid surveillance theory insist, we are faced today with multiple forms of surveillance and control which elude the previously developed critical tools, because they are founded on the seduction of individuals or on their self-surveillance, while surveillance by state institutions is not as oppressive as operations of Stasi, KGB, and NKVD.
7   The "zero tolerance" doctrine holds that the police are primarily a force that guarantees order and security in the public sphere. According to Loïc Wacquant, spaces such as those shown in Rickard's photographs are a site of processes typical of the penal state, in which the state abdicates its social roles (2009, 51–2), equal opportunity policies are abandoned, and poverty is subject to severe policing in the public space. This results in "an inflexible enforcement of

4 The Art of Surveillance

Why does Rickard seek to reproduce this panoptic gaze in his project? The American artist continues photography's revered tradition in which the photographer adopts the role of a distanced, or even hidden, observer of or peeper into often very intimate lives of other people. Brassaï traversed Parisian streets at night to photograph prostitutes. Kohei Yoshiyuki captured couples making sex in public parks and oglers staring at them. The perturbing experiments of Miroslav Tichý also expressively epitomize moments when photographers turn into intruders and voyeurs, and their activities become deeply ambivalent.[8]

Rickard used a similar strategy of putting the viewer in the position of a trespasser on the space of other people's private lives in his *Tom* (2014) as well. The anonymous photographer of found photography used by Rickard clearly did not bother much about composing the frames. Most of the pictures look as if they were made carelessly and in haste. The photographer primarily cared about capturing the characters. Practically all the images show young women. They are sleek and elegant. Many of them are wearing short skirts and tights. Several images taken with a telephoto lens are detailed close-ups of their

---

the law, particularly against such minor nuances as drunkenness, public urination, disturbing the peace, panhandling, [and] solicitation," as stressed by Wacquant (ibid., 15). In this way, poverty ceases to be a target of social welfare, being repositioned into an object of policing, surveillance, and control, with the (sub)proletariat bent "to the discipline of the new labor market" (ibid., 39). The police are increasingly aggressive towards the poor who commit petty misdemeanors in the public space, and racial profiling is strengthened, which may have been an important factors in the tragic deaths of Michael Brown in Ferguson and Eric Garner. Within this interpretive framework, Rickard's images can be construed as embodying a very particular form of panopticism which Wacquant labels social panopticism, in which the population of this world is constructed as a social problem, a pathology, or a subclass, rather than as people in need of the state's support. Most protagonists of Rickard's photographs are Afro-Americans wearing hoodies and cargo pants or baggy trousers, which is enough to make them suspects in the eyes of police officers.

8 In the times of liquid surveillance, this tradition acquires new meanings, and Rickard's photographs can be put on a par with other practices which probe the limits of our privacy, explore anxieties of a post-panoptic society, and interfere with surveillance processes. One of such ventures is *Coversnitch*, a surveillance-art project developed by Brian Haus and Kyle McDonald (2013). Haus and McDonald planted bugs at various public venues across New York, such as cafés, parks, and libraries. Recorded in this way, the conversations of unaware New Yorkers were then transcribed by cheap labor force – people doing micro-gigs for Amazon Turk, who are part of the proletariat of digital capitalism. Passages from the conversations were posted on the *Coversnitch* Tweeter profile. They mostly concerned very trivial matters, such as wondering whether superglue was indeed strong enough. However, some of the talkers addressed private issues related to work or even intimate relations, such as friendship or love.

thighs, calves, and feet. Sometimes, random passers-by are captured in the pictures. Some of the photos form sequences. We can see the observed women cross the street step by step, get into their cars, and drive away completely unaware that they are objects of the voyeuristic gaze. The style of clothes, car makes, and shop windows suggest that we are in the U.S. of the 1960s. Today, when we are controlled and surveyed by algorithms and ourselves leave irremovable digital traces everywhere, we are tempted to feel almost nostalgic for the times when surveillance was far more personal.

Where does the power of this strategy lie? What kind of aesthetic experience is produced in such cases? If Sontag states that "the camera [...] may [...] trespass" (Sontag 2005, 9), Google Street View represents such a trespassing insolence at its peak. Projects such as Arne Svenson's photographic series *The Neighbours* (2013) more often than not inspire ambivalent feelings. On the one hand, we are outraged. We wonder what right artists have to encroach, unsolicited, on our private and intimate lives. At the same time, a curiosity is bred in viewers. Artists provoke a reflection on the limits of privacy, simultaneously luring viewers into a trap. The point is that as artists take full responsibility for transgressing these limits, viewers can freely take delight in the possibility of intruding upon other people's lives with impunity. As such, viewers can suffer no remorse or guilt feelings about gazing at the pictures taken by photographers. Does it not reveal our hidden voyeuristic desires?

5   A Tender Gaze

In some respects, Ricard's photographs resemble Marcel Duchamp's *Fountain*. In both cases, we are faced with ready-made and mass-produced objects which are basically devoid of any aesthetic value. Both the porcelain urinal and the Street View images are completely subordinated to functionality. It is the artist's gesture that elevates them to the status of artworks. Given this, like Duchamp, Rickard confers an aura of a work of art on the digital image reproduced on our computer screens by embedding an everyday object in a new context, specifically by placing it in the art gallery space.

If aficionados of found photographs systematically rummage through basements and attics, and regularly forage at flea-markets and rural photography workshops, Rickard actively explores the world created by Google programmers. Art-making takes the form of searching and traversing the digital copy of reality. As a result, Rickard compiled over 15,000 carefully described and appropriately classified photographs. As a following step, the artist-explorer organized the found images in series, collections, and narratives. Given this, any exhibition or photography album developed in this way represents effects of creative interpretation.

However, before this moment comes, the artist must make another crucial artistic decision. The world of Google Street View is constructed of multiple panoramas stitched together by the computer, algorithms, and computation processes. Because of this construction, this world is, so to speak, devoid of any framing. Such framing is only provided by the interface components of our Internet browsers, by screen cases, and/or by tablet casings. Consequently, when crossing this world, we can freely look up and down, move closer or away. Of course, whenever we do this, the composition of the frame changes. Nothing is thus stable and fixed. All images projected on the screen are in this sense receptive to the user's activities and have a potential and temporary status. Contrary to typical photography, Google Street View images do not "make reality atomic" (Sontag 2005, 17). In this project, the world is continuous and the viewer always has an opportunity to see what lies outside the frame. A piece of this reality is only enframed by the artist-explorer who photographs the screen of his computer.

What effect is thus achieved by Rickard when he selects and composes his photographs? It is difficult to resist the impression that many of his pictures are redolent of Edward Hopper's paintings (particularly of the *Early Sunday Morning* of 1930). Their classical composition itself and their striving for balance and harmony make us feel that we are looking at a painting rather than at a photograph. This effect is paradoxically bolstered by the poor quality of the photos. In the era of digital, high-definition photography, viewers are accustomed to having all objects clearly and sharply delineated. Yet, visitors to a Rickard exhibition may wonder whether what they see are not a painter's works by any chance. Rickard very meticulously removes all graphic elements typical of the Google Street View interface from his pictures.

Like in Hopper, Rickard's photographs are subsumed in peace, sometimes pervaded by poignant melancholy, resignation, and sadness. Instead of interacting with the space around them, his protagonists are, so to speak, suspended and absent. That their minds frequently seem to wander far away. The wide angle sometimes makes viewers feel that the space engulfs people in the photos. Individuals captured by Rickard often sit and impassively look ahead, as if they were waiting for something. They are not in a hurry to get anywhere. If anybody is moving, they look as if they were rambling aimlessly, loitering sluggishly within strictly circumscribed limits. In a sense, all of them are imprisoned in this space and appear to be resigned to reality, having relinquished fantasies of the American dream.

Rickard snatches elements of the world of Google Street View from the solutionist narrative and inscribes them anew into the classical tale of art history. The pictures produced by vision machines become part of the history of American photography. They can almost be ranked in the proximity of the works of Dorothea Lange, Williama Christenberry, and Walker Evans, or discussed in terms of their resemblance to Paul Fusco's photographs in the RFK *Funeral Train* series (1968).

Thematically and compositionally, Rickard's photographs make one think above all of pictures by the Chilean-American photographers Camilo José Vergara. Vergara has systematically observed the de-urbanization of American suburbs since the mid-1970s. The famous album *The New American Ghetto* (1997) grew out of this project. Vergara very often uses wide-angle lenses in his work and frequently takes photos from the roof of his car to give them a more analytical touch. For this reason, many of his photographs uncannily resemble Google Street View images. As a matter of fact, the title of Rickard's album – *A New American Picture* – can be regarded as expressing his recognition of Vegara's years-long and extremely consistent work.

Rickard's project can also be viewed as another incarnation of "class tourism" (Sontag 2005, 44). Here is another artist photographer who ventures into the world of lower social strata. The camera helps him effectively distance himself from reality. Additionally, the Google Street View photographs were taken from the height of almost two meters. This is not a typical vantage point of common people, who usually look at the world from a slightly lower elevation. As a result, we do not feel part of the reality presented in the pictures. This perspective produces a distance from people captured in the images and makes the sense of the presence of the panoptic gaze more palpable. Yet Rickard's activities imbue this cold gaze with other qualities. The Google Street View photographs start to "breathe" (Bieńczyk 2010, 7), and we let them take us by surprise. One by one, previously unnoticed elements of reality reveal themselves to the viewer. As a consequence of this simple gesture by Rickard, the Google Street View photographs begin to affect us. A special bond is then born – an indefinite sense of affinity between the viewer and the figures captured by one of the eleven Dodeca 2360 lenses mounted on Street View vehicles. The impersonal, solutionist, and post-panoptic eye is ousted by a gaze which could be described as tender, but not sentimental. The artists successfully avoids paternalist humanitarianism and reminds us of the forgotten and marginalized spaces without exposing the onlooker to an emotional blackmail. Each photograph comes with detailed information about the location where it was taken. In this way, Rickard makes sure that all places retain their distinct identities, rather than melting into one, undifferentiated representation in viewers' minds. We can see a world on the verge of despair and look at its dwellers with a tenderness with which we would look at ourselves or at people wrestling with similar problems.

Bibliography

Beahm, George. *The Google Boys: Sergey Brin and Larry Page in Their Own Words*. Chicago: Agate Publishing, 2014.

Bieńczyk, Marek. "Medytacje migawkowe." In *Dno oka: Eseje o fotografii*. Edited by W. Nowicki. Wołowiec: Wydawnictwo Czarne, 2010.

Bridle, James. "Waving at the Machines. Web Directions." 2011a. http://www.webdirections.org/resources/james-bridle-waving-at-the-machines. Accessed on January 18, 2015.

Bridle, James. "The New Aesthetic." 2011b. http://new-aesthetic.tumblr.com. Accessed on January 15, 2015.

Higgott, Andrew, and Timothy Wray. *Camera Constructs: Photography, Architecture and the Modern City*. London, New York: Ashgate Publishing, Ltd, 2014.

Koczanowicz, Leszek. *Lęk nowoczesny*. Cracow: Universitas, 2011.

Menkman, Rosa. *The Glitch Moment(um)*. Amsterdam: Institute of Network Cultures, 2011.

McNeil, Joanne. "The New Aesthetic: Seeing Like Digital Devices." 2012. http://www.joannemcneil.com/new-aesthetic-at-sxsw. Accessed on January 15, 2015.

Morozov, Evgeny. *To Save Everything, Click Here: The Folly of Technological Solutionism*. New York: Public Affairs, 2014.

Murray Li, Tania. *The Will to Improve Governmentality, Development, and the Practice of Politics*. Duke University Press, 2007.

Rickard, Doug. *A New American Picture*. New York: Aperture, 2012.

Sontag, Susan. *On Photography*. Electronic edition. New York: Rosetta Books, 2005.

Taylor, Bert; "Mapping your way." Official Google Blog. 2005. http://googleblog.blogspot.com/2005/02/mapping-your-way.html. Accessed on January 18, 2015.

Wacquant, Loïc J. D. *Prisons of Poverty*. Minneapolis, MN, and London, UK: University of Minnesota Press, 2009.

Vergara, Camilo Jose. *The New American Ghetto*. New Brunswick, New Jersey: Rutgers University Press, 1995.

Zawojski, Piotr. *Sztuka obrazu i obrazowania w epoce nowych mediów*. Warsaw: Oficyna Naukowa, 2012.

Index

Abduh Muhammad   130
Abu-Lughod Janet L.   1, 137–138, 146
ACTA   14
ad-Din al-Afghani Jamal   130
Adam (from Bremen)   72, 74–75, 78
Adamson Lauren N.   52–54, 62
Africa   41–42, 47, 85, 96–99, 101, 116, 117, 127, 128–129, 130–131, 137–138
Agency   6, 164, 169
Aiton Arthur S.   141–142, 146
al-Banna Hasan   130
Alberti Rafael   95–96
Alcock Katherine J.   59, 62
Alighieri Dante   7–8
Allam Magdi   129, 133
Allchin Bridget   144–145, 146
Allchin Raymond   144–145, 146
Alphonso XIII   101–102
Ambrosius Aurelius   62
Anderson Benedict   114–119, 121
Appadurai Arjun   1, 5–6, 81–82, 87–89
Aristotle   82, 161–163, 165, 173
Armstrong David F.   48, 59, 61, 62
Aronoff Mark   62
Art   13, 94, 113–114, 150–151, 152–158, 159, 177, 184–185, 186
Asia   106, 116, 117, 128, 129, 130–131
Auger Emmanuel   59, 62
Australia   85, 113–114, 116, 117

Badyna Piotr   ix, 4–5, 46
Bakeman Robert   53–54, 62
Baldwin Dare A.   52–53, 62
Baraitser Michael   59, 62
Barbarian   72–76, 77, 109–110
Barbaruk Magdalena   ix, 4–5, 46
Barber Benjamin R.   1, 6, 161–164, 166–167, 169–170, 171–173
Bard Kim A.   53, 62
Baron-Cohen Simon   52–53, 62
Bastide Roger   121
Bauman Zygmunt   1, 150–151, 159
Beahm George   177–178, 187
Becher Tony   33–34
Beck Ulrich   1

Behne Tanya   56, 62
Benjamin Walter   177
Bering Jesse M.   52–53, 62
Bhabha Homi   42, 44
Biały Leszek   94–99, 103
Bieńczyk Marek   186–187
Bishop Claire   155–156, 157–158, 159
Black Jeremy   83–84, 89
Blackmore Susan   56, 62
Blanchard Ian   134–135, 146
Boćkowski Daniel   x, 6, 126
Bodamer Mark   53–54, 62
Boerner Lars   134–135, 146
Bohlman Philip   41, 44
Boleslaus II Wrymouth   76
Boli John   29, 36
Bonaparte   95–96
Borejsza Jerzy   99–100n13, 101–102, 101–102n15, 103
Bourdieu Pierre   40–41, 150–151, 154–155
Bourriaud Nicolas   154–156, 159
Bracha Krzysztof   76, 78
Braudel Fernand   141, 146
Bridle James   177, 187
Brown Diana   121
Bruner Jerome S.   52–53, 62
Bunuel Luis   95–96
Butterworth George   52–53, 62
Byrne Richard W.   53–54, 62

Calderón de la Barca Pedro   94–96, 103
Call Josep   49–50, 56, 62
Campa Roman de la   111, 121
Cann Rebecca L.   60–61, 62
Capitalism   40, 82, 114–115, 178–179, 179n4, 183–184n8
Carlsson Peter   59, 62
Carpenter Malinda   54, 56, 62
Cartmill Erica A.   53–54, 62
Casanova   95–96
Casas Bartolomé de la   108
Castells Manuel   1
Castillo Michel del   91–93, 92–93n4, 96–99, 98–99n9, 101, 103
Cernuda Luis   95–96

Cervantes Miguel de 93–96
Cellorigo Miguel 96–99
Charles II 91–93, 103n16
Chaudhuri Kirti N. 141–142, 146
Chilosi David 134–135, 146
Chomsky Noam 56–57, 62
Christenberry William 186
Christianity 75–76, 110, 129
Christianization 5–6, 72, 74–75, 105–106, 107t, 108, 121
Christians 73
Cities 6, 91–93, 137–139, 143–144, 145–146, 161–172, 173, 175–176
Civilization 2–3, 13, 15–16, 18–19, 43, 83–84, 91–93n2, 105–107, 107t, 108–109, 111, 120, 129, 132–133
Cochran Patrick 139–140, 146
Cold War 31–32
Colonization 43, 84, 111–112, 113, 121
Condillac Étienne B. 57, 62
Cook Jill 83–84, 89
Cooper Franklin S. 61, 62
Coppola Marie 58, 62
Corballis Michael C. 61, 62
Cosmopolitism 3–4, 22–23, 150–151, 152, 159
Creoles 95–96, 117, 120
Creolism 38–39, 42
Creolization 1, 42
Crisis 2–3, 5–6, 14, 82, 91–94, 95–98, 99, 100, 101, 102–103, 115, 161, 169–170, 179
Cultural crisis 94
Cultural memory 156
Cultural politics 6
Cultural studies 29–30, 33–34
Culture 1–3, 5–6, 7, 13, 14–15, 16, 17–18, 27t, 29, 35, 39, 40–42, 55, 62, 81–82, 87–88, 93–99, 105–109, 107t, 113–114, 117, 119–120, 127, 129, 130–131, 150–152, 154–159, 167–168, 170, 171, 177, 179n4
Culturology 3–4, 5–6, 32–34
Czech Franciszek x, 4–5, 12, 25–26, 35
Czerny Mirosława 30–31, 36

Danecki Janusz 132, 133
Darwin Charles 5–6, 48, 62, 82–85, 86–87, 89
Davidson Iain 52–53, 62
Decolonization 117, 130

Deller Jeremy 155–156
Democracy 114, 118, 130, 161–163, 163–164n4, 164, 165, 169–170
Dewey John 161–163
Diec Joachim 18–19
Diller Karl C. 59, 60–61, 62
Domínguez Ortiz Antonio 91–93, 94, 96–99, 98–99n7, 103
Don Quixote 97–98, 101–102
Donald Merlin 52–53, 55, 62
Drzewiecka Urszula 118, 121
Duchamp Marcel 184

Ebo 75–77, 78
Economic Crisis 2–3, 91–93, 94, 96, 97–98, 175–176, 179
Economy 1–3, 13, 26, 27t, 28, 29, 32–33, 35, 39–40, 94, 95–96, 100, 102–103, 105–106, 114, 130, 163, 168–169, 170, 171–172, 173
Edey Maitland A. 48, 62
Education 29, 56, 58, 83–84, 88–89, 112, 150–151, 157–159, 165–167
Eichengreen Barry 143–144, 146
Ekholm-Friedman Kajsa 144, 146
Eliasson Olafur 153
Elkins James 153–154, 159
Emancipation 1–2
Enard Wolfgang 60, 62
Erlmann Veit 40, 41–42, 44
Europe 3–4, 39–40, 41–42, 43, 47, 72, 80, 83–85, 86, 87–88, 91–94, 96, 102–103, 106, 110, 111–113, 118, 120, 127–128, 129–131, 132–133, 134–135, 136–138, 141–142, 145–146, 169–170
Evans Andrea 49, 62
Evans Walker 186
Everett Daniel 47, 62
Evolution xiii, 2–3, 4, 7–8, 12, 14, 47, 48, 49, 53, 54, 57, 58, 60–61, 86–88, 89, 95–96

Fereński Piotr Jakub x, 4–5, 126
Fernandez Juan 86–87
Filipowiak Władysław 72, 74–75, 78
Fisher Simon E. 59, 62
Fitch Tecumseh W. 56–57, 62
Florida Richard 150–151, 152, 159, 164, 173
Flynn Dennis O. 141–142, 146
Foster Hall 156, 159

INDEX	191

Fouts Roger S.   53–54, 62
Franco Fabia   52–53, 62
Frank André G.   116, 121
Fray Luis de Granada   94
Freyre Gilberto   113–114, 121
Friedman Jonathan   144, 146
Frisch Karl von   48
Frost Thomas   49–50
Fuentes Carlos   94–96, 103
Fusco Paul   186

Galeano Eduardo   116, 117, 121
García Lorca Federico   95–96
Gardner Allen R.   53–54, 62
Gautier Théophile   91–93n2, 103
Gehl Jan   164, 173
Gellner Ernest   113–114, 121
Generation'98   93–94, 95–96, 103
Geography   26, 28, 165–166
George Barbara L.   49, 62
Gergely György   56, 62
Giambrone Steve   52–53, 62
Giddens Anthony   1, 27t
Gilby Ian C.   50, 62
Giráldez Arturo   141–142, 146
Glaeser Edward   163–164, 166–167, 168–169, 173
Global culture   35, 39, 154–156
Global market   3–4
Global metropolises   3–4, 163–164, 169–170
Global phenomena   1, 2–3, 4–6, 14–15, 26, 161–163, 168, 171–172
Global processes   1–4, 6, 21, 23–24, 28, 41–42, 166–167, 171–172
Global society   1–2
Global studies   4–6, 23, 28–34, 35–36, 164, 171–172
Global village   1–2, 7–8, 27t, 38
Globality   1, 2–6, 23, 38–39, 81–82, 88–89, 143–145, 164–165
Globalization   1, 2–8, 13–19, 21–28, 25f, 27t, 29–30, 31, 34–35, 38–39, 41, 43, 77–78, 81–82, 93–94, 105–106, 114, 116, 121, 127–128, 130–131, 132–133, 150–152, 153, 161–163, 166–167, 169, 171–172
Globalization theory   23–25, 26–28
Gnitecki Janusz   30–31, 36
Goldblatt David Jonathan   23–24, 36

Goldin-Meadow Susan   52–53, 55, 62
Golinkoff Roberta M.   53, 62
Golinowska Karolina   xi, 4–5, 12
Góngora Luis de   95–96
Górak-Sosnowska Katarzyna   128, 133
Gould Stephen Jay   87, 89
Goya Francisco   95–96
Gräfenhain Maria   56, 62
Graham Fred K.   59, 62
Gray Asa   87
Gribbin John   82–83, 89
Grice Paul   50, 62
Grubb Farley   142–143, 146
Guilbault Jocelyne   42, 44
Guillén Mauro   21–23, 36
Gust Deborah A.   49, 62

Haarländer Stephanie   75–76, 78
Haines Gerald   116, 121
Hall Alfred Rupert   82, 89
Hamilton Earl J.   99–100, 99–100n14
Hannerz Ulf   1, 144, 164, 173
Hare Richard   15, 17–18, 19
Hauser Marc D.   47, 52–53, 56–57, 61, 62
Hegel Georg Wilhelm Friedrich   13, 108
Hegemony   1–2, 40, 106, 107–108, 110, 152
Heiss Aloïss   140–141, 146
Held David   23–24, 27t, 29, 35, 36
Henner Miskha   177
Henry John   82, 89
Henslow John S.   84–85
Herbord   75–77, 78
Herder Johann   7–8
Heritage   48, 120, 152
Hess Wolfgang   134, 146
Heterogeneity   26, 113–114, 153–154
Hewes Gordon W.   57–58, 62
Higgott Andrew   181, 187
High-culture   150–151, 152, 154–155, 156–157
Hirschhorn Thomas   155–156
Hirsi Ali Ayaan   130, 133
Holland Morris K.   57, 62
Holmes Nicholas   139–140, 146
Hopkins William D.   53–54, 62
Humboldt Alexander von   83–84
Huntington Samuel P.   116, 121
Hurst Jane A.   59, 62
Hybridization   1, 5–6, 116–117

Identity   4, 30–31, 42, 56, 96, 99, 105–106, 111, 117, 121, 158–159
Ideology   87–88, 118, 120, 161–163, 180
Inoue-Nakamura Noriko   53, 62
Iron Curtain   7–8

Jackendoff Ray   56–57, 62
James VI   139–140, 146
Jenkins Henry   150–151, 154–155, 157, 159
Jóhannesson Alexander   57, 62
Johanson Donald C.   48, 62
Julius Caesar   76
Jürgens Uwe   61, 62

Kant Immanuel   7–8, 17
Kegl Judy   58, 62
Kelly Patrick   137–138, 146
Kempny Marian   1
Kendon Adam   50–52, 62
Kester Grant   156, 159
King James   139–140
Klose Dietrich   134, 146
Knapp Sandra   83–84, 89
Kocur Mirosław   47, 50–51, 54–55, 62
Koczanowicz Leszek   180, 187
Koneczny Feliks   15–17, 18–19
Kopciuch Leszek   15, 17–18, 19
Kortlandt Adriaan   57–58, 62
Krajewski Marek   158, 159
Krause Mark A.   53–54, 62
Kruger Ann C.   49, 62
Kubiak Hieronim   113–119, 121
Kuhar Chris   53–54, 62
Kuhn Thomas   25–26
Kulczyk Grażyna   153
Kwon Miwon   156, 159

Lai Cecilia S. L.   59–60, 62
Lange Dorothea   186
Language   3–4, 5–6, 39, 47, 50–51, 52–53, 54, 55–56, 87, 105–106, 108–109, 112, 113–114, 117, 120, 161–163
Latin America   5–6, 105–107, 107t, 110, 111, 112, 114, 117, 118, 120
Leavens David A.   53–54, 62
Lechner Frank   29, 36
Leibniz Gottfried Wilhelm   18–19
Liberman Alvin M.   61

Liebal Katja   53–54, 62
Liebal Kristian   49, 62
Lieberman Daniel E.   49, 60, 62
Lieberman Philip   61, 62
Liégeois Frédérique   60, 62
Lipset Seymour M.   113–114, 118, 121
Liszkowski Ulf   56, 62
Literature   4, 5–6, 19, 29–30, 89, 93–96, 113–114
Loaeza Soledad   118
Locality   1, 3–4, 6, 14–15, 38–39, 143–145, 158–159, 164–165
Lope de Vega Félix   94, 95–96
Lorenz Konrad   48
Lu Min Min   60, 62
Lubaś Władysław   54, 62
Luhmann Niklas   40
Lysloff René T. A.   43, 44
Łepkowski Tadeusz   118, 121
Łuczak Robert   31, 36

Machado Antonio   95–96
Macrobius Theodosius   54–55, 62
Mägdefrau Karl   82–83, 89
Magee Judith   83–84, 89
Mahlapuu Margit   59, 62
Majbroda Katarzyna   14–15, 19
Makowski Jerzy   31, 36
Maps   41–42
Marx Karl   7–8, 39
Masataka Nobuo   52–53, 62
Matsuzawa Tetsuro   53, 62
Mcdonaldization   17–18
McGrew Anthony   23–24, 27t, 29, 35, 36
McLuhan Marshall   27t, 38
McNally Rand   180–181
McNeil Joanne   177, 187
Meir Irit   59, 62
Meltzoff Andrew N.   56, 62
Menkman Rosa   177, 187
Merton Robert   22–23, 36
Mestization   106, 111–112, 120
Mestizos   105–106, 121
Middle East   127, 128–129, 130–131
Middle-class   171–172
Migrations   2–4, 80, 81–82, 88–89, 128
Miłkowski Tadeusz   93–94, 96–97, 98–99nn. 8, 10–11, 99–100, 102–103, 103n16

INDEX

Minois Georges 86–87, 89
Mitani John 53, 62
Mittelman James 24–26, 36
Modernity 7–8, 81–82, 110
Modernization 4, 26, 27t, 114
Modzelewski Karol 74, 78
Moll Henrike 56, 62
Monaco Anthony P. 60, 62
Money 6, 98–100, 101–102, 134–135, 136–139,
    140–146, 168–169, 171–172, 178–179
Monson Ingrid 38–39, 40–41, 44
Moors 91–93n2, 92–93n4, 96
Morgan Lewis H. 53–54, 62
Morozov Evgeny 179n3, 180, 187
Morrisey Edward E. 60, 62
Moses Louis J. 52–53, 62
Mozart Wolfgang Amadeus 43
Mrozek-Dumanowska Anna 128, 130–131, 133
Muñoz Miguel L. 140–141, 146
Munro John 136–137
Murchison Roderick 87
Murden Simon W. 128, 130–131, 133
Murray Fantom 141, 146
Murray Li Tania 180, 187
Musicology 1, 4–5, 29, 38–39, 41, 42, 43
Muslim culture 130–131
Muslims 130, 131
Muszkalska Bożena xiii, 12

Nahirny Rafał xiii, 6, 12
Nations 7–8, 42, 72, 80, 91–93, 96, 106, 108–
    109, 110, 111, 113, 114, 119–120, 121, 132–133,
    143–144
Natural Sciences ix, 22–23, 46, 82–83, 87–88
Nawratek Krzysztof 166–167, 168–169,
    171, 173
Neptune 72, 74
Nichols John 170, 173
Nishida Toshisada 53, 62
Nobis Adam vii, 1–2, 6, 13, 19, 126, 146
Nowak Stefan 32–33, 36

Ortega y Gasset José 91–93, 95–96
Ossowski Stanisław 33, 36

Pacini Deborah H. 38, 41–42, 44
Paget Richard A. S. 57, 62
Paleczny Tadeusz 5–6, 46, 117

Pamuk Şevket 141–142, 146
Pankowicz Andrzej 33–34, 36
Paszkiewicz Borys 146
Petersohn Jürgen 75–76, 78
Pfeiffer John E. 60–61, 62
Philip II 100, 101, 141–142
Philip III 98–99
Philip IV 95–96, 98–99, 102–103
Philip V 141–142
Pika Simone S. 53, 62
Pinker Steven 56–57, 62
Plichta Paweł 33–34, 36
Polich Laura 58, 62
Pollick Amy S. 60–61, 62
Polo Marco 2–3
Posern-Zielinski Aleksander 117, 121
Poss Sarah R. 53, 62
Pratt Mary Louise 1
Premack David 50, 62
Projesi Oda 155–156

Quevedo Francisco de 95–96

Rae John 177
Rafman Jon 177
Ramadan Tariq 128–129, 133
Ramón y Cajal Santiago 94
Rębkowski Marian 75–76, 78
Religion xiv, 5–6, 29, 76–77, 86–87, 101–102,
    105–106, 108–109, 110, 112, 113–114,
    116–117, 119–120, 121, 128–129, 132, 158
Revolution 4, 14, 60–61, 82, 83, 95–96, 99–100,
    114, 115, 118, 166–167
Rickard Doug 6, 126, 175–176, 178–179, 182,
    182n7, 183–185, 186–187
Ritzer George 1, 17–18, 19, 27t
Robertson Roland 1, 21–23, 31–32, 36
Rokicki Jarosław 34, 36
Rolfe Leonard H. 52, 62
Romanes George J. 57, 62
Romano Ruggiero 117, 121
Rosik Stanisław 5–6, 46, 73, 74–75, 76, 77, 78
Ruiz de Alarcón Juan 94
Russo Claudia A. M. 54, 62

Sabater-Pi Jordi 53, 62
Saint John of the Cross 94
Saint Teresa of Avila 94

Saja Krzysztof   16–17
Sandler Wendy   59, 62
Sandrock John E.   142–143
Sassen Saskia   1, 164, 171–172, 173
Scaife Walter   135–136, 146
Scheidel Walter   143–144, 146
Scholte Jan A.   26, 27t, 28, 36
Schrago Carlos G.   54, 62
Schwarz David   150–151, 159
Security   x, 2–3, 14, 55, 167–168, 169–170, 182n6
Sedgwick Adam   87
Seghal Tino   153–154
Sherzer Joel   52, 62
Shu Weiguo   60, 62
Slobin Mark   39–41, 44
Smith Anthony D.   114–119, 121
Social Sciences   xii, 3–5, 12, 21, 22–24, 28, 29, 31–36
Social security   2–3, 169–170
Sontag Susan   182, 184, 185, 186–187
South America   83–85, 110–111, 115, 117, 120
Souto Maior Luiz A.   111, 121
Sowa Jan   150–151, 159
Spanish Golden Age   93–96
Spengler Oswald   146
Spufford Peter   134–135, 136–137
St. Otto   5–6, 75–77, 78
St. Paul   77
Stahl Alan   137–138, 146
Staley Edgcumbe   136–137, 146
Stampa Manuel Carrera   140–141, 146
Stemplowski Ryszard   114, 117, 121
Stoinski Tara S.   62
Stokoe William C.   58, 62
Strzelczyk Jerzy   75–76, 78
Studdert-Kennedy Michael   62
Suchodolski Stanisław   137, 146
Sulaymān Abū ʻAbdulḤamīd   131, 133
Sulloway Frank J.   83–84, 89
Sumner William G.   140–141, 146
Szmydtowa Zofia   91–93, 96–99, 103
Sztompka Piotr   21–23

Tallmadge John   83–84, 89
Taylor Bert   180–181, 187
Taylor Insup K.   57, 62
Taylor Martha M.   57, 62
Téllez Gabriel (Tirso de Molina)   94

Terrorism   x, 127, 168, 173, 179
The world system   1–2, 7–8
Thomson Keith   82–83, 89
Tichý Miroslav   183–184
Tinbergen Nikolaas   48, 62
Toffler Alvin   7–8, 170, 173
Tomasello Michael   49–51, 52–53, 55–56, 58, 62
Torrents y Monner Antonio   140–141, 146
Transformations   2–5, 6, 7–8, 21, 23–24, 29, 35, 82, 86–87, 95–96, 114, 115–116, 117, 118, 146, 150–152, 166–167, 168, 173
Travels   xi, 7–8, 21, 22f, 28, 42, 43, 82–84, 87, 89, 98–99n13, 138–139, 141–142, 143–144, 175–176, 180–181n5
Trowler Paul   33–34
Turner Bryan S.   128, 133
Turner Linda A.   53, 62
Tylor Edward B.   57, 62

Ueno Ari   53, 62
Unamuno Miguel de   91–93n1, 91–93n3, 95–96, 103
Universality   3–5, 12, 13, 14–16, 19, 130–131
Urbanski Edmund S.   118, 121
Užgiris Ina, C.   56, 62

Valle-Inclán Ramón   95–96
Values   2–3, 4, 7–8, 15–18, 21, 22f, 23–24, 27t, 75, 77, 95–96, 99, 101, 108–109, 110, 111–112, 114, 115, 117, 119–120, 121, 130–131, 134–135, 136–139, 140–143, 144–145, 156, 162, 165–166, 168, 170, 173n7, 175–176, 184
Vargha-Khadem Faraneh   60, 62
Vasconcelos José   111, 121
Veà Joaquim J.   55–56, 62
Velázquez Diego   94–96
Vergara Camilo Jose   178–179, 186
Vergo Peter   151–152
Versante Laura   51–52, 62
Vico Giambattista   7–8
Villani Giovanni   135–136, 146
Volckart Oliver   134–135, 146
Vorel Petr   134–135, 138–139, 146

Waal de Frans B. M.   50, 60–61, 62
Wacquant Loïc J. D.   182n7, 187
Wallace Alfred Russel   57, 83–84, 87, 89

INDEX

Wallerstein Immanuel 1
Waltz Kenneth 23–24, 26, 36
Warneken Felix 50, 62
Watkins Kate 59, 62
Webb David M. 62
Weber Max 111, 121
Welsch Wolfgang 1
Wertheimer Michael 57, 62
Western culture 1–2, 6, 113, 127, 128–129
Westernization 27*t*, 105–106, 130
Wheeler Benjamin, W. 146
White Michael 62, 83
Wiatr Jerzy 115, 121
Wilcox Sherman, E. 48, 59, 61, 62
William Robert 146
Wiszewski Przemysław vii, 78

Witkowski Grzegorz 78
Wolf Michael 177
Wolfe Alan 170, 174
Wray Timothy 181, 187
Wundt Wilhelm 57, 62

Yoshiyuki Kohei 183

Żabiński Zbigniew 134–135, 138–140, 146
Zawojski Piotr 177, 187
Zdanowski Jerzy 131, 133
Zea Leopold 108, 109–110, 121
Zhang Jianzhi 60, 62
Żmijewski Artur 155–156
Znaniecki Florian 108–109, 121
Zuberbühler, Klaus 50, 62